W9-BKP-312

WOODROW WILSON CENTER SERIES

Religion and twentieth-century American intellectual life

Religion and twentieth-century American intellectual life

Edited by
MICHAEL J. LACEY

WOODROW WILSON INTERNATIONAL CENTER
FOR SCHOLARS

AND

CAMBRIDGE UNIVERSITY PRESS
Cambridge
New York   Port Chester   Melbourne   Sydney

Published by the Press Syndicate of the University of Cambridge
The Pitt Building, Trumpington Street, Cambridge CB2 1RP
40 West 20th Street, New York, NY 10011, USA
10 Stamford Road, Oakleigh, Melbourne 3166, Australia

First published 1989
First paperback edition 1991

Printed in the United States of America

Library of Congress Cataloging-in-Publication Data
Religion and twentieth-century American intellectual life / edited by
Michael J. Lacey.
p.   cm. – (Woodrow Wilson Center series)
Essays from a conference held in 1986 at the Woodrow Wilson
International Center for Scholars in Washington, D.C.
Includes bibliographies and index.
ISBN 0-521-37560-6 (Cambridge University Press)
1. United States – Religion – 1901–1945 – Congresses.   2. United
States – Religions – 1945 – Congresses.   3. United States –
Religion – 19th century – Congresses.   4. Religious thought – United
States – Congresses.   5. United States – Intellectual life – 20th
century – Congresses.   I. Lacey, Michael James.   II. Woodrow Wilson
International Center for Scholars.   III. Series.
BL2525.R4625   1989
200′.973 – dc19
89–962
CIP

British Library Cataloging in Publication applied for

ISBN 0-521-37560-6 hardback
ISBN 0-521-40775-3 paperback

WOODROW WILSON INTERNATIONAL CENTER FOR SCHOLARS

BOARD OF TRUSTEES

The Center is the "living memorial" of the United States of America to the nation's twenty-eighth president, Woodrow Wilson.

The U.S. Congress established the Woodrow Wilson Center in 1968 as an international institute for advanced study, "symbolizing and strengthening the fruitful relationship between the world of learning and the world of public affairs." The Center opened in 1970 under its own presidentially appointed board of directors.

Each year the Woodrow Wilson Center holds open international competitions to select approximately fifty residential fellows to conduct advanced research, write books, and contribute to seminars, conferences, and discussions with other scholars, public officials, journalists, and business and labor leaders.

Research at the Woodrow Wilson Center ranges across the entire spectrum of the humanities and social sciences. Staff and fellows employ comparative, multidisciplinary approaches. The process of discovery that operates at the Woodrow Wilson Center frequently illuminates new understanding of the world in which we live, an expanded awareness of history, choices, and future consequences.

Results of the Center's research activity are disseminated internationally through the book-publishing programs of the Wilson Center Press, of Cambridge University Press's Woodrow Wilson Center Series, and of other co-publishers as appropriate; and through *The Wilson Quarterly*, a scholarly journal published four times a year. Additional dissemination in the United States includes monthly *Meeting Reports*, providing summaries of formal seminars and conferences, and Radio DIALOGUE, a weekly FM series of half-hour programs.

In all its activities the Woodrow Wilson Center is a nonprofit, nonpartisan organization, supported financially by annual appropriations from the U.S. Congress, and by the contributions of foundations, corporations, and individuals. The Center seeks diversity of scholarly enterprise and points of view. Conclusions or opinions expressed in Center publications and programs are those of the authors and speakers and do not necessarily reflect the views of the Center staff, fellows, trustees, advisory groups, or any individuals or organizations that provide financial support to the Center.

Contents

Acknowledgments

Thanks are due to all the contributors whose patient cooperation made possible the completion of this volume. The editor wishes particularly to thank James H. Billington, former Director of the Wilson Center and present Librarian of Congress, for his advice and support, together with those who served as members of the planning committee for the development of this project: Richard W. Fox, Bruce Kuklick, and John L. Thomas. A special word of gratitude is in order for Robert Peyton and his colleagues at the Exxon Education Foundation, without whose encouragement and support the undertaking would not have been feasible.

Introduction: The academic revolution and American religious thought

MICHAEL J. LACEY

The essays in this volume are drawn from a conference on religion and American intellectual life held in 1986 at the Woodrow Wilson International Center for Scholars in Washington, D.C. The purpose of the gathering was to explore the status of religious thought—and thought *about* religion—in the cultural history of the United States over the past century. Although most historians acknowledge the importance of certain religious ideas in the belief systems that dominated American culture in the seventeenth and eighteenth centuries, the history of American religious thought since the nineteenth century's scientific and scholarly revolutions and the rise of the modern university reveals a more complicated and ambiguous role in American culture.

Major patterns of response

The revolutions begun in the nineteenth century have not ended, even as we near the twenty-first century mark. The new hermeneutics, the intricate methodologies of the "higher criticism," and continual refinements in knowledge of evolution agitate thought about the nature, grounds, and functions of belief.

Three broad patterns of response to these historical confrontations can be discerned: the fundamentalist response, which resisted the inroads of the new thinking and developed a new emphasis on literal understanding of the Bible; the modernist response, which embraced the spirit of critical inquiry without abandoning religious commitments and sought to construct its theological interpretations along evolutionary, developmental lines; and the naturalist response, which challenged both these conservative and liberal forms of theism at their very core. Each response

1

is part of a complex tradition of thought, internally varied and marked by the strains of ongoing disputation. The naturalist response was the important newcomer, historically speaking, within the culture of the best-educated American elites. The naturalists could, and on occasion did, appreciate the social and psychological functions of religious belief, but they did so on grounds not likely to ease the minds of their traditionalist or modernist contemporaries. As John Herman Randall, one of its ablest historians and expositors explained, naturalism is an epistemology, growing out of the premises and assumptions of scientific method, that "finds itself in thoroughgoing opposition to all forms of thought which assert the existence of a supernatural or transcendental realm of being and which make knowledge of that realm of fundamental importance to human living."[1] This position, of course, has important implications for the character and quality of theological inquiry in the academy.

Until the last third of the nineteenth century, the life of the mind in the United States was largely dominated by the concerns and controversies, innovations and accommodations, of the Protestant clergy. The academic revolution and the rise of the modern, research-oriented university, however, changed all that. With its secular and pluralistic conventions, its specialized hierarchies, and its precise and principled segregation of fields of learning, the emerging university system broke up this cultural situation and supplanted its style of leadership, gradually crowding its spokesmen toward the background and into the interstices of what was becoming the institutional powerhouse of modern thought in all its varieties, both pure and applied. The difficult question of what happened, in the course of these institutional developments, to traditions of theological reflection and their place within the general culture figures in a number of the papers in this volume.

Certainly the naturalists, given their philosophical family ties to the natural and social sciences, felt especially at home in the new university environment. Theological modernists of one sort or another seem always to have been present on campus, but most have not been especially visible or influential there. The seminaries and divinity schools at Harvard, Yale, Princeton, Chicago, and Stanford, Union Theological Seminary in New York, and many other places have provided an institutional setting for religious and theological inquiry, but, as Van Harvey points out in his essay, their specialized and segregated place within the wider university

[1] John H. Randall, Jr., "The Nature of Naturalism," in *Naturalism and the Human Spirit*, ed. Yervant Krikorian (New York: Columbia University Press, 1944), p. 358.

community has worked to render their undertakings marginal to the deeper currents of intellectual life in the United States.

The university proved to be an inhospitable environment for traditionalist evangelicals. Despite its high birth and Princeton lineage, conservative evangelical scholarship in the period between 1920 and 1950 entered a kind of dark ages. As George Marsden points out in his contribution, secularist and positivist assumptions were in the ascendant during this period: in addition, the new voices of Jewish scholars and scientists, with no interest, understandably enough, in reviving the vestiges of Christian civilization, began to be heard in the affairs of the academy and the burgeoning new learning. And so traditionalist energies turned elsewhere. One result was the Bible Institute movement, which spawned practical training centers focusing only on the scriptures.

The naturalist ethos and secularization

Thus a naturalist ethos became dominant in the nation's principal universities. By the 1930s, as Bruce Kuklick observes in his paper on John Dewey, the great seminal figure in the systematic elaboration of naturalism, high religious thought had gone out of fashion among the educated middle class, and politics became the field in which questions of ultimate commitment were to be confronted. A naturalist reading of the historical development of the American mind itself flourished in the new university environment. In that interpretation, the Puritans, with their complex, Calvinist theological inheritance, stood at the far end. At the near end—and, as they claimed, at the growing end—were the scientific and philosophical naturalists, with their lines of affiliation extending outward to colleagues in the university. In between were a series of liberation movements, given purchase by an ever firmer grasp of methods of analysis and an ever more precise rigor in their application. As Henry May reports on his encounter with the naturalist perspective in the 1930s, it was a progressive, democratic outlook on history, based in part on a set of assumptions of Enlightenment vintage, "lodged in the unconscious where assumptions are hardest to dislodge," that while reason and democracy were advancing, religion was necessarily in decline.

Many deduced from this view that although religious thought and sentiment may have been important elements in the experience of people in the past and might even continue to be so for those furthest removed by class, denomination, or education from any sustained experience with the canons of the new inquiry, it was of no genuine importance for the elites most visibly engaged in building up contemporary cultures through their work in the arts, sciences, and humanities. As Henry May succinctly put it, this was so because religion was "known to be dependent on a series of dogmas and legends that no serious intellectual could entertain."

Although a naturalist outlook remains the predominant one in the nation's research universities, its application to American intellectual history over the past century is less satisfactory than it was once thought to be, and concern on that point prompted The Wilson Center's conference. For all its strengths, there were some obvious shortcomings in this particular naturalist perspective, rooted mainly in the premises regarding secularization on which it was based. First, there was the evident high quality of certain branches of contemporary thought on religion. Whereas the assumption of continuing secularization seemed to predict that these traditions of inquiry were destined for enfeeblement in the modern period, it is now apparent that the twentieth century is a great age of theological reflection, comparable in depth and scope to the nineteenth century. Some "serious intellectuals," in other words, have in fact entertained dogmas and legends to good effect, as is demonstrated in the careers of Karl Barth, Paul Tillich, Rudolph Bultmann, Bernard Lonergan, Karl Rahner, Yves Congar, Martin Buber, Abraham Heschel, and others, not to mention Reinhold and Richard Niebuhr, who figure so frequently in the essays that follow.

It was becoming clear, also, that simply as an empirical matter we knew a good deal less than we ought to know about the religious ideas and beliefs of modern academic intellectuals, if the evidence for a naturalist reading of intellectual history were to be properly weighed. It is now evident that some among the founding fathers of the modern American academic ethos held more complicated views on religion than a naturalist account would allow. A great many who played important roles in working out the origins of the modern consciousness were in fact theists and "supernaturalists" of a sort, rather different from their successors, among them Charles S. Peirce, William James, Josiah Royce, Henry Carter Adams, Albion Small, Charles Horton Cooley, and other builders of modern traditions of research in philosophy and the social sciences. On the contemporary scene there are a number of influential scholars whose positions are difficult to classify in old-fashioned, naturalist terms, among them Robert Bellah, Peter Berger, and Henry May.

In addition to these considerations, there was the desire to supplement and offset to some degree the concentration of the media and the attentive portions of the scholarly community on relations between religious belief and mass political behavior, the principal cases in recent years being the stirrings within Roman Catholicism in the United States and the new burst of activism shown by the conservative evangelical community. The widespread assumption that the main role played by religious belief in American culture has to do with its bearing on mass political behavior points to an important set of relationships and has a well-established framework of analysis behind it. But it calls attention away from the questions of modern religious thought and the problems of relating them to the experience of the country's cultural elites over the past century. Thus the focus of these papers.

Recognizing these flaws in a secularization view of the past century and yet being aware of the philosophical power of the naturalist outlook that encompassed and accompanied it, we suspected that some new ground might be opened up by questioning the sufficiency of categories themselves and concentrating not on secular thought alone, or on "religious" thought as an alternative to it, but rather on the incessant interactions between these two poles. The interplay itself has a history, and is deeply rooted in the dynamics of thought that arose during the American Enlightenment on the relations between science and religion. For reasons of space we have not been able to explore these early roots, but the continuing flow and interplay of reciprocal influence for the modern era figures in a number of the papers in this volume.

The conference participants were drawn primarily from two sectors of the academic community that have had relatively little to do with one another in the past. On the one hand were the cultural and intellectual historians in university departments of history and American studies, who are preoccupied with the problems of relating ideas and beliefs to the broader patterns of social change over time. On the other hand were the theologians, church historians, and philosophers of religion from the seminaries, divinity schools, and those curious academic hybrids, the departments of religious studies.

So far as denominational connections were evident, and by convention it is thought hardly pertinent to inquire into this aspect of biography when dealing with intellectual historians, the participants were drawn primarily from the principal Protestant churches. The situation of the Catholic and Jewish communities was not dealt with in the program, nor was there any attempt to consider the situation of religious thought in the black churches or in the churches of other minorities. These are, of course, regrettable omissions, and in arranging the event we understood that the pluralism and diversity of the American experience as a whole were hardly captured by the limited focus we chose to adopt. Our intentions were of a more modest and exploratory nature, and we hope that people familiar with the ongoing discussion of the role of religious ideas in American life will find that the framework selected provides at least a plausible starting point for an undertaking of this kind.

Outlooks in tension

To establish a context for the conference's scholarly presentations, and for the reader of this volume as well, there were two introductory addresses, representing both sectors of the academy from which participants were drawn. In the essays that follow, they now appear as the first and last chapters, respectively. Coming from the tradition of university history and fully aware of the gulf that divides its practitioners from the scholarly work under way within the divinity schools, Henry May writes autobiographically of the problems entailed in the treatment of religious ideas as elements within what were thought to be the broader conventions of intellectual history at Berkeley. As an example of what he called the "vitalizing argument" between secular and religious outlooks on American history, he discussed the importance for his own scholarly work of the writings of Reinhold and Richard Niebuhr, both of whom were influential in loosening the grip of the secular, progressive synthesis in which he had been trained.

David Tracy addressed the conference as a theologian, and in his remarks, which appear as an afterword to the volume, he took up the special problems, both conceptual and institutional, that beset the theological enterprise in the contemporary United States, and speculated upon changes that might improve the situation. Unlike scholars in other fields, theologians need to keep constantly in mind the bearing of their work on three distinct publics, each with different problems, interests, capacities, and limitations for understanding trends in religious thought: the academy, the church, and the general public in all its pluralistic exfoliation. Suggesting that theology ought to be viewed not as a specialized and denominationally oriented inquiry but rather as one of the liberal arts, Tracy presented a case for moving theology out of the restrictive confines of the divinity schools and into a new place in the faculties of arts and sciences. Citing the widespread phenomenon in the 1950s and 1960s of "atheists for Niebuhr" as an example of cultural encounter occurring across deep-seated boundaries of philosophical outlook that might offer a valuable lesson on how to deal with the divisive realities of cultural pluralism, Tracy suggested an approach to theology as a liberal art based on the interpretive treatment of the classics of the various traditions. He argued for the understanding of culture itself as a "conversation" in which theology has its proper place.

Historical contexts

The essays that are collected in this volume take up various aspects of the historical response in traditionalist, modernist, and naturalist circles to the challenge brought by the new scientific and scholarly ways of thinking. George Marsden concisely reviews the relationship between science and religion in nineteenth-century America and analyzes the principal subsequent reactions within the community of conservative evangelicalism to the implications of scientific naturalism. He also discusses the "mini-renaissance" that has occurred within the world of conservative evangelicalism since 1950, and describes the main features of its institutional and intellectual context.

By way of contrast, David Hollinger offers a portrait not of religious thinkers coping with the challenge of scientific method to established belief, but rather of a group of scientific intellectuals taking the language of religious experience and appropriating it to express—and indeed to exalt—the ethical aspects of scientific inquiry, in which the quest for objectivity, so central to the scientific pursuit, entails the transcendence of undisciplined, subjective impulses. While steering clear of the philosophical or theological status of what he calls "the intellectual gospel," to suggest its parallels with the reform-oriented social gospel movement within liberal Protestantism in the same period, which was adapting for its own uses the influence then pouring in from the surrounding scientific culture, Hollinger draws attention to the religiosity of the ethic and the prevalence of the idealistic construction of science that it represented. His account supplements the more familiar ones that highlight the conceptual challenges of science to Christianity. In concentrating on one aspect of the moral challenge of scientific method to Christian doctrine, Hollinger depicts a widespread form of naturalist piety in late-nineteenth-century America, comparable in many ways to the tradition of British agnosticism that was then so important in informing contemporary culture. The existence and earnestness of the type of outlook Hollinger examines make it easier to appreciate the relatively smooth and sudden rise of naturalism to hegemonic status within the university, and to sympathize with Marsden's evangelicals, who, like most of the modernists, did not appreciate the scope of the challenge of naturalism until it was fully established at the center of things.

William King offers a new reading—and an important clarification of older readings—of one of the principal episodes in Protestant modernism in America: the theological status, conceptual character, and historical influence of the social gospel movement. As King points out, the most accessible views of the social gospel are based on stereotypes inherited from adversaries of the movement: from religious conservatives who saw it as theologically shallow, destined for a brief career as a minor way-station on the road to naturalism, or from the naturalists, who saw it as a tepid and selective expression of loyalty to tradition, and a tradition that was essentially prescientific and philosophically anemic in any case.

King sees the social gospel not as the last gasp of theological liberalism but as evidence for the continuing importance (throughout the first third of this century) of theological reflection for intellectuals in Protestant circles, and as a major source of influence on contemporary religious thought. From this new perspective, the social gospel is not displaced by neoorthodoxy, as earlier accounts have held, but rather gives birth to neoorthodoxy as a form of self-critical liberalism. Although engaged in the same quest for a new, personalist position on experience that preoccupied other movements of thought in its day, King's social gospel is theologically sophisticated—aware amid all the confusions over immanence and transcendence that the basic issue remained the reality of God. Thus the movement appears to have been not so much a reaction to European neoorthodoxy as an indigenous development, a response to the naturalists with their functional and psychological understandings of religion.

Dewey and the Niebuhrs

Other essays in this book deal with the continuing cultural influence of both naturalism and Protestant liberalism by examining biographically the principal recent exemplars of each viewpoint—John Dewey on the one hand and the Niebuhr brothers on the other. Dewey's is the paradigmatic case and embodiment of the kind of secularization that the traditionalists predicted and the modernists feared. His career represents the dogged pursuit and systematic elaboration of the intellectual gospel that Hollinger has identified. In his treatment of Dewey, Bruce Kuklick examines the theological origins of Dewey's instrumentalism in the world of late-nineteenth-century New England Congregationalism; identifies the shift that so many intellectuals would undergo from theology to philosophy; describes the abandonment of religious language and its replacement by a new, scientific vocabulary; and discusses how the resulting philosophical naturalism became a common cultural assumption associated with pragmatic liberalism in the American political tradition.

In his essay on two of the leading adversaries of Dewey's instrumentalism, Richard Fox develops a case study of the continued potency of liberal Protestantism by examining the contrasting but compatible and convergent ideas on religion and society held by Reinhold and Richard Niebuhr. In so doing he confirms the basic thrust of William King's treatment of the social gospel as a theological incubator for a new style of critical religious thought. In the positions staked out by Fox and King, the familiar distinctions among the social gospel, theological liberalism, and neoorthodoxy are collapsed, with the continuities in thought and value among them emphasized instead.

The rest of the essays in this volume deal in historical terms with the university, religious thought, and thought *about* religion. Noting that there are no Niebuhrs or Tillichs on the academic scene at the moment, Van Harvey discusses what he considers the intellectual marginality of contemporary academic theology in America by examining its peculiar institutional setting. Rather than attributing the neglect of religious thought to the blanket term *secularization,* as is often done, Harvey suggests it is more useful to think in terms of some combination of the mistaken course of professionalization, which normally conceived theology as if it were merely a minister's arcanum, and to specialization and role change resulting from the rise of other disciplines, all of which were added to the original and intractable conceptual challenges to theological reflection presented in the nineteenth century.

Murray Murphey's essay breaks new ground and opens up for scholarly appraisal the course and content of the scientific treatment of religion as an object of study over the past century. Concentrating on the disciplines of anthropology, psychology, and sociology, Murphey outlines the principal achievements, influences, turning points, and shortcomings of work in each area. His analysis makes clear the enduring importance of the nineteenth-century encounter with scientific theories of evolution, and details its continuing effects in the evolutionary thematics that extend downward through time in the writings of Talcott Parsons, Anthony F. C. Wallace, Robert Bellah, and Clifford Geertz. In isolating and laying out for study this aspect of the naturalist heritage that has developed in the traditions of social scientific inquiry, Murphey makes an important contribution to our understanding of religion in the history of American thought.

Suggestions for further inquiry

This volume, then, is the work of many people, and given the diversity of experience, interest, and viewpoint represented by the authors whose work is included within it, perhaps it will come as no surprise to the reader that no firm consensus emerges about the current status of religious thought as an element in the culture of American elites. There are, however, a few points of convergence, or perhaps tacit agreement, on lines of inquiry that might repay further investigation.

In thinking about belief and the requirements for useful descriptions of it, there are, of course, deep problems of method and the meaning of terms and relationships to be encountered. As Murphey suggests at the close of his paper, perceived difficulties in the tradition of the scientific study of religion have less to do with problems of empirical data, as conventionally understood, than with inadequacies in the underlying philosophical premises regarding the scope and limits of the empirical itself as a category of experience. A more sophisticated and robust understanding of the empirical is clearly in order. And if studies in the scientific tradition are to get beyond the current impasse, the circularities of merely functional and psychological explanations also might be addressed by dealing more directly with sensitive matters of doctrine, the role of ideas in systems of belief, and the grounds for particular ideas.

Another point has to do with the institutional context within which matters of belief are discussed and appraised. Perhaps the reluctance to focus on questions of doctrine—whether modernist, naturalist, or traditionalist—is encouraged by the institutional arrangements that have become established in the American university. Although it is admittedly difficult to imagine circumstances different from those that now prevail, there was a suggestion at the conference that it may be appropriate in the future to consider more carefully the consequences of isolating and segregating the theological enterprise within the university. Such a practice, although considered natural enough and indeed inevitable to most American observers (and clearly rooted in sensitivities regarding the proper institutional treatment of belief that underpins the cultural pluralism of the university) is not considered so natural an arrangement elsewhere; for example, in Germany and England, where theological inquiry is accorded a more central place in university life, and so plays a more prominent role in public thought generally.

Finally many of the participants implied that an appraisal of the naturalist tradition in all its branches is long overdue, and that to move understanding ahead, it ought to be open to premises other than those of the naturalists themselves. The epistemological assumptions of the entire Enlightenment tradition have in recent decades come under increasing criticism from many points of view in both Europe and the United States. Perhaps the dialectic of religious thought and naturalism in American culture could be further clarified by reexamining the ways in which that dialectic was shaped during the American Enlightenment, modified subsequently by the work of the principal figures in the turn-of-the-century "golden age" of American philosophy, and altered once again under the influence of theorists who emigrated from Europe to the United States in the twentieth century.

1

Religion and American intellectual history, 1945–1985: reflections on an uneasy relationship

HENRY F. MAY

In dealing with this subject, I find that I cannot avoid an autobiographical mode. My excuse for this is that my own teaching experience is probably much like other people's and is therefore representative. The truth is, though, that because I have been working hard on an autobiography, my internal computer is set in the autobiographical mode, and I cannot seem to find the key that would shift it to another.

In the late 1930s, when I was in graduate school, the progressive interpretation of American history had the allegiance of nearly everybody I knew. Part of the progressive ideology was the assumption that religion was and must be declining. Democracy and progress were closely associated with the liberation of mankind from superstition. Religion was dependent on a series of dogmas and legends that no serious intellectual could entertain. This set of views, proclaimed with passion in the late eighteenth century and gathering strength through the first half of the nineteenth, had often been challenged. Yet for many these assumptions were deeply taken for granted, lodged in the unconscious where assumptions are hardest to dislodge.

So strong, in fact, was this progressive and secular view of history that Auschwitz and Hiroshima only damaged, rather than destroyed, it. In the years after World War II the disillusion of most American intellectuals with the Soviet Union, the self-proclaimed heartland of progress and bastion of secularity, did rather more damage. Yet the progressive view of history succumbed only very slowly. For many American intellectuals in the complacent 1950s, disillusion with foreign ideologies rather reinforced their belief in the rise of American civilization.

In 1947 I got a job at Scripps College, where I inherited a course called "American Social and Political Ideas." Five years later, in 1952, I was invited to join the history department at the University of California at Berkeley, with the specific assignment of introducing a brand-new course in American intellectual history.

To me, no assignment could have been more gratifying and challenging than this, and for the rest of the 1950s I spent most of my time developing and improving this course. (In Berkeley, the fifties lasted until the fall of 1964.) This was, for many reasons, a time of high academic morale, and nowhere more so than at Berkeley.

I had worked at Harvard with Arthur M. Schlesinger, Jr. I liked and respected Professor Schlesinger but wanted to break sharply with his way of teaching U.S. social and intellectual history together. If one had to move rapidly between a short summary of Emerson or Thoreau and a description of the effects of the invention of the detachable collar, it seemed to me that critical examination of either kind of phenomenon was impossible. I tried, therefore, to organize a course in which the foreground was clearly and exclusively ideas, the background society. The way I constructed this course was to choose a set of sources for the students to read and for me to discuss with them. I had already learned at Scripps how quickly intellectual history could pall if undergraduates read many monographs. Sources were the subject itself: the style, tone, and passion were as important as what was said.

I am afraid my choice of source assignments was a bit arbitrary, and it was greatly affected by what was available in the bookstores then—right at the beginning of the paperback revolution. Of course I started with the New England Puritans. This choice was not only congenial, it was inevitable. I had, after all, learned about the Puritans from Perry Miller, who had discovered—some critics have almost said invented—them. Equally obviously, it was necessary to spend some time with the great political intellectuals of the Enlightenment. A little later, I clearly had to deal with the Transcendentalists, proclaimed—once again by Perry Miller—the patron saints of all American intellectual rebels. After that, things got more complicated, but one could hardly leave out the pragmatic philosophers, so often said by themselves and others to be quintessentially American. Beyond these it seemed right to pay my respects to recent American literature and social science.

These were all the ideas of respectable intellectuals. But I had my own democratic allegiances, and I knew that there were large numbers of people in the country who were interesting and articulate and yet not concerned full-time with the ideas of Edwards or Emerson or James. So the course had to find a place for another range of topics, for the less systematic ideas of Jacksonian Democrats, southern nationalists, and abolitionists, and later those of Populists, progressives, socialists, isolationists, one-worlders.

There is no doubt that I was combining apples and oranges with not a few pears. Every now and then a bright graduate student who was auditing the course would politely suggest that it was an epistemological jungle. I suspected that this might be right, but for a while it did not bother me greatly. The excitement of creating the course was too heady. Not all undergraduates liked it; some decided it was not for them about halfway through my—or really, Perry Miller's—treatment of the tension between Arminianism and antinomianism. But those who stayed often were enthusiastic. After all, in their reading they were coming into direct contact with some pretty exciting people. A solid handful of excellent graduate students found topics for research in my course and seminars. Their close and intense reexaminations of many important topics gradually refined and improved my lectures.

Intellectual history was not, of course, accepted by all members of the history department. Some of my senior colleagues occasionally made slighting remarks about the difficulty of nailing jelly to the wall. But nobody was persecuted; there was just enough disapproval to give teachers and students working in American intellectual history the feeling of being a daring minority. Intellectual history was just enough out to be in, and by the end of the 1950s it was unquestionably in.

From time to time a student would ask me why we were spending so much time on *religion*. It was easy to argue that this topic had been all-important in the seventeenth century. After that, because the question had not been settled by Perry Miller, my answers became more complicated. I had, however, begun to encounter Paul Tillich, who seemed to define religion to mean—almost—anything that was really important to anybody.

Far more important to me (as to many in these years) was Tillich's colleague Reinhold Niebuhr. *The Irony of American History* was published in 1952, the year I arrived in Berkeley. Here was a godsend for the end of my course in intellectual history. Here was an unquestionably serious thinker to balance Jonathan Edwards near the beginning. He was talking about the whole range of American culture and about the most

pressing problems of the moment: war, peace, the bomb, relations with
the Soviet Union. Moreover, the view he was expressing was the one
toward which I, like many of my colleagues, had been slowly moving—
a point of view balanced between the old radicalism and the new, somewhat reluctant patriotism. Above all, Niebuhr seemed to be looking at
these matters as nearly as possible *sub specie aeternitatis*. He was telling
us we could not make the right political decisions if our starting point
was political. Going through the *Irony* year after year and reading Niebuhr's other works, I was brought to the question, if politics is not primary, what is? (I was temperamentally unable to answer "nothing.")

This was at least part of the transition from an interest in religious
history to an interest in religion itself. These were the years of the much-
discussed revival of interest in religion. The churches around the campus
were filling up and so were their treasuries. If on the campus we dismissed most of the public religiosity of the Eisenhower era, there were
still the intellectual theologians. Tillich's visit to Berkeley in this period
was a public triumph. In an overflow meeting in the gym he proclaimed
that the war between science and religion was over: they were simply not
talking about the same subject. Another visitor was Billy Graham, who
spoke in the Greek Theater. The first part of his talk was a convincing
and well-informed discussion of the despair of modern culture. This far,
the large crowd went with him. When he started talking about where one
could turn for help in this situation, he probably lost most of his audience.

There were, of course, many people who opposed the revival and
probably many more who knew nothing about it. Only a few joined
churches. The group of academics most typical of the period were those
characterized with great acuteness by Sydney Ahlstrom as "curious about
religion."[1] I belonged in this category. In my teaching in the 1950s I
made use of Richard Niebuhr's two books on American religion. In one
of these, *The Social Sources of Denominationalism* (1929), Niebuhr had
applied to American religion a straight Weberian social science analysis.
In the second, *The Kingdom of God in America* (1937), he had somewhat repudiated his earlier approach. A person who wants to understand
religious history, he then told us, must concern himself not just with
social causes and results of religious movements but with the actual intellectual and, still more, the emotional content of faith: not just with the

[1] Ahlstrom, "Theology and the Present-Day Religious Revival," *Annals of the American Academy of Political and Social Science*, CCCXXXII (November 1960): 27.

sociological banks, but with the living stream that flowed between them. In the 1950s, newly "interested in religion," I found this metaphor extremely powerful. It asked us to treat religion in just the way I was trying to treat all the ideas I talked about in my class.

Outside the universities, sometimes, as at Berkeley, almost across the street, were the seminaries. In this period of revival some seminary historians were feeling their oats and calling for a church history entirely free of secular influence. This meant a sharp separation from university historians. A few excellent scholars were able to transcend this division. From the seminary side Sidney Mead was a biting critic of complacency. Among university historians, Sidney Ahlstrom, William Hutchison, and Timothy Smith were for different reasons acceptable on both sides of this particular divide.

It was against this background that I wrote, and after some years of thought and revision, submitted to *The American Historical Review* an essay on "The Recovery of American Religious History." In this essay I talked about a coming together of various tendencies in social history, literary history, and intellectual history under the twin influences of religious revival and theological renewal. The result was, I said, a restoration of the historic and vitalizing American argument between religious and secular interpretations of the American past.

This article was, I think, a satisfactory statement of the way things looked to me then. The only trouble was that it was published in 1964, exactly when all the conditions I had talked about in the article were coming to an abrupt and dramatic end. Both religious revival and theological renewal suddenly slowed down. Neoorthodoxy in general and Reinhold Niebuhr in particular underwent harsh attack. Niebuhr was rejected by the excited optimists of the early 1960s as a merchant of gloom. For a very brief period his teachings seemed to be replaced by the cosmic optimism of Harvey Cox, who pinned his religious hopes on, of all things, the American city. Later, in the less euphoric late 1960s, Niebuhr was attacked as a cold warrior. The churches, dwindling somewhat in numbers and funds, became embroiled, sometimes heroically, in the civil rights movement and later in the opposition to the Vietnam War.

Sweating out the 1960s at any major American campus was an experience never to be forgotten. Not only did we live through brief periods of the actual breakdown of social order, but, more important, the *intellectual* order of the 1950s was shattered beyond repair. Detachment became cop-out, intellectuality elitism, tolerance repressive in Herbert Marcuse's phrase. The more we tried to understand and analyze the movement of the young, the more it changed its form in our grasp. I remember once I was threatened with disruption of my class unless I would allow some political announcements to be made at the beginning of it. "Do you think," I was asked, "that American intellectual history, of all irrelevant subjects, is more important than justice for the Third World?" Reduced to intellectual rock-bottom, I answered, "Right here, in 151 Dwinelle Hall at three o'clock, it is." That time I got away with it, and the class went on.

In the 1960s, although the popular revival came to an end, the intellectual interest in religion did not. In my class I found it very easy to explain what antinomianism was—it was all around us. Once I was concluding a lecture on Transcendentalism and remarked that the movement really could not have lasted; it had no program but a change of heart. A student told me that this was typical academic blindness; ideas just like those I had been discussing were all around us on the campus. Robert Bellah, who moved in 1967 from what he called "the magisterial certainty of Harvard" to the "wide-open chaos of Berkeley" because he found the latter more congenial, was one of the first to present the contemporary student movement, with approval, as a religious revival.[2] The more I thought about this the more completely persuasive I found it. Like the many religious revivals of the American past, the movement was unpredictable; like the spirit, it blew where it would. Like the other revivals, it was, at its height, impossible to resist or control; like them, it was soon over, leaving different kinds of effects on different people.

Meantime the historians who had come to maturity in the 1950s were attacked from quite another quarter. Professor John Higham, a rigorous moralist who was anything but an ally of the young rebels, seemed in part to echo their criticisms in a series of powerful and influential essays on what he called consensus history. According to Higham, historians reacting against the progressive synthesis had produced "a bland history, in which conflict was muted, in which the classic issues of social justice were underplayed, in which the elements of spontaneity, effervescence, and violence in American life got little sympathy or attention."[3] Higham's picture was largely accurate and his criticism was taken to heart; it was part of the period's shaking of academic complacency. On behalf

---

[2] Bellah, *Beyond Belief* (New York: Harper and Row, 1970), xvii–xviii.
[3] Higham, "Beyond Consensus: The Historian as Moral Critic," speech at American Historical Association, 1960, reprinted in *The American Historical Review* in April 1962 and in *Writing American History* (Bloomington: Indiana University Press, 1970); quotation p. 146.

of those criticized as consensus historians, I would like to make only two points. First, it is one thing to say that in American history—as opposed to, for instance, French or Russian history—consensus has prevailed; it is quite another to say that this makes the United States superior. Second, the historians who had in the age of Niebuhr abandoned the tradition of Charles A. Beard and Vernon L. Parrington, with its clear dichotomies between progressive and conservative, had done so reluctantly, as they gradually found this progressive synthesis unworkable.

One minor—to some of us not so minor—effect of the major upheaval of the 1960s was to make intellectual history unfashionable. This loss of prestige continued in the 1970s with the many triumphs of the new social history. Using a whole battery of exciting new techniques, the new social historians were finding ways to learn about people in the past things they had never known about themselves. Ideas consciously held and articulated became correspondingly less interesting. This was no doubt a perfectly legitimate, although not an inevitable, choice. The other part of the attack was less convincing—the argument that an interest in intellectual history was somehow elitist, a view that seemed to imply that ordinary people do not have ideas, opinions, or ideologies.

The prestigious new social historians were, however, intensely interested in the history of religion, with certain strict provisos. It must be popular religion, preferably heretical, antiestablishment religion. What was interesting was not developed theologies or successful institutions, but rather the practices, however strange and painful, of the Cathari, the shepherds of the Pyrenees, or the decidedly eccentric cosmology of an Italian miller victimized by the Inquisition, or the cults and sorceries practiced by anonymous villagers.

Part of the reason for these particular negative and positive choices was that this new social history spread from Paris. In continental Europe, and especially in France, attitudes toward religion are often inseparably connected with political loyalties going all the way back to the great Revolution. On one side are the Republic—the Enlightenment, democracy, and, for many, socialism. Against these are ranged the church and the other forces of reaction. The power of this traditional division was made clear to me at a series of international conferences I attended. At a meeting on the Enlightenment held at Yale in 1975, a brave French professor, Georges Gusdorf, questioned the dominant organization of French eighteenth-century religious history. This tends to move from the anticlericalism of the Enlightenment toward a widening and deepening rejection of religion culminating in the official revolutionary de-Christianization prompted by Robespierre. Gusdorf suggested that the story was really a lot more complicated than that, that the conventional French view ignored large groups of passionately religious people. This produced two hours of impassioned oratory in which Gusdorf was accused of treason to the memory of the *lumières*.

For another meeting, in Poland, I was asked to give a paper on the Enlightenment in America. In passing, I made the point, to me obvious, that evangelical Protestantism was the usual religion of the people, whereas religious liberalism was usually associated with the upper middle class. I found that some people in my European audience found this statement not so much wrong as incomprehensible. Religion was associated with authority; the people were revolting against authority and therefore against religion. Whether or not this is a tenable synthesis of modern European religious history, it will certainly not work for the United States. We have learned a great deal from recent European historians; there are some lessons we should reject.

In addition to the challenge from European and American social history, intellectual historians were strongly affected by American social scientists, and religious historians were especially influenced by anthropologists and sociologists of religion. Among the latter were some committed Christians like Peter Berger and Robert Bellah, whose prestige helped to widen the choices available. Berger in particular told us that culture was in part constitutive of social reality, which gave useful ammunition against social historians who strongly implied the opposite. Unquestionably the most influential figure, however, was Clifford Geertz—literate, elegant, catholic in sympathies, empathetic but supremely detached. To Geertz, religion was an all-important set of symbols, indispensable for giving meaning and legitimacy to a culture.

In political science, brilliant students of the history of political theory—Quentin Skinner, John Dunn, John Pocock—were talking about the history of speech, of discourse, of changing paradigms. All this seemed to legitimate some kinds of intellectual history.

Many of these tendencies appeared in the 1977 Wingspread conference on American intellectual history.[4] There an extremely talented group of young intellectual historians showed themselves on the defensive toward

---

[4] Many of the papers given at this conference are reprinted in *New Directions in American Intellectual History*, edited by John Higham and Paul K. Conkin (Baltimore, Johns Hopkins University Press, 1979).

the new social history and profoundly appreciative of legitimation by social and political scientists. The devotion and intelligence of this group of young scholars seemed to me to make their sometimes defensive and apologetic tone highly inappropriate.

The much-discussed decline of intellectual history in this period was not a decline in the quality of the books written or the courses taught. It was a decline in professional prestige and esteem, and this was reflected, concretely and damagingly, in changes in curriculum and the loss of job opportunities. I would like at this point to state my respect and admiration for the many young historians then entering the field, who insisted on doing the kind of history they believed in, often at truly heroic cost.

On the other hand, religious history continued to gain in this period in vitality, diversity, and excellence, although it was not the religious history of Perry Miller and his followers or of the traditional church historians.

Let me finally (and briefly) consider how things are now with these two topics, in the mid-1980s. First, intellectual history has recovered some of its lost prestige. One can see this in the most concrete terms: there are a few more positions advertised. Perhaps this partial recovery is related to the widespread, or at least much-articulated, concern for the humanities in general. People may have realized that although there is an excellent case for exposing students to other cultures, there is no good reason to keep them ignorant of their own. There is no liberation in not having read Jonathan Edwards, Ralph Waldo Emerson, and William James.

To some degree, I think, intellectual history has been educated by its vicissitudes. There is less tendency to separate it from social history—the separation was always temporary and tactical and may have been unwise. There are fewer books tracing the influence of one book on another. There is less tendency to talk about the Puritan mind, the southern mind, the American mind, citing only the few most accessible sources.

Second, I think American *religious* history may be better and more esteemed than ever before. There is some recognition that it combines intellectual history, social history, and the anthropological study of rituals and symbols. Among general American historians, some topics in religion have reached center stage. Puritanism remains there, and the discussion of it is still likely to center on where Perry Miller was wrong. This is the greatest compliment a later period can pay to a great historian. (When I was in graduate school, all historiographical discussion began with the question where Frederick Jackson Turner was wrong.) Moving forward into the nineteenth century, revivalism is almost as much a standard topic as Puritanism. Few historians of antislavery, whatever their ideological preferences, would now leave out the massive influence of evangelical Protestantism.

When one gets to later periods, recognition of the importance of religious history is more sporadic. At a recent meeting one of the very best intellectual historians in the country announced, a little in the tone of a person who has had a special revelation and can't quite believe it, that in dealing with late-nineteenth-century social reform one really must take social Christianity seriously.

How about religion itself? I was very surprised to see a recent survey cited in the *New York Review of Books* saying that 64 percent of all faculty members consider themselves "deeply" or "moderately" religious, and 48 percent attend worship services once a month or more. This must include denominational colleges; it certainly would not describe the institutions I know well.

In a recent committee meeting in Berkeley an eminent biochemist told me that he did not see how any research dealing with religion could be significant or interesting. I think that this forthright and robust sort of statement has become much rarer than it used to be. Certainly among historians it is now generally regarded as crude to be rude in talking about religion. It is still much easier to be respectful when talking about times past. The idea that science, somehow in alliance with broadening democracy, has made religion impossible dies very hard. In discussing the present, there is a tendency among academics to fear fundamentalism, and sometimes to identify all religion with evangelical Protestantism and, equally incorrectly, all evangelical Protestantism with the political Far Right. In a recent review David Davis, a historian I admire, characterized the present as "a time when American culture is ominously divided between fundamentalists and secular humanists."[5] That seems to be what fundamentalists themselves think. Most of the sound and fury does indeed come from these two camps, but there are still millions of Americans and even quite a few academic intellectuals who belong in neither of them.

And now I come to the last and most personal part of my talk. I would like to suggest a few planks in a platform on which historians dealing with American religion might be able to come together.

First, nobody questions openly, and I think few question privately,

[5] *New York Review of Books*, 7 February 1986, 7.

that ordinary standards of scholarly accuracy must apply to sacred subjects. This has always been necessary in a country that does not agree on what is sacred. If there are any exceptions to this rule—and there should not be—they probably apply to subjects that are sacred to the civil religion rather than to the religions of the churches.

Second, the idea is long dead that one needs to belong to a certain persuasion to write well about it. This was first courageously demonstrated in 1958 by Robert Cross, a Protestant who wrote one of the best books on the history of American Catholicism. It is easy to think of a Catholic doing excellent work on Mormonism, an Episcopalian dealing sympathetically with Boston Unitarianism, a Mormon writing with insight about New England Calvinism. It is impossible to say how many of the best books in religious history are written by agnostics; many of them, I suspect.

But that is not quite all I want to say. My third plank is clearly more controversial. To write excellent religious history, I believe, one must have something like religious sensibility or imagination. Obviously, one does not have to be a believer. It is possible to write well about something one totally disbelieves, fears, or hates. But it is really not possible to write excellent history about something one dismisses, however tacitly, as unimportant. Somehow one's definition of reality must be broad enough to include the religious stream as well as the social and intellectual banks between which it flows.

2

Evangelicals and the scientific culture: an overview

GEORGE M. MARSDEN

One science or two?

In 1902, Princeton Theological Seminary's Benjamin B. Warfield, who was supposed to be writing an introduction to a volume on apologetics by Francis R. Beattie, a fellow American Presbyterian, made a few perfunctory remarks about Beattie and then quite gratuitously turned to a critique of another conservative Reformed theologian, Dr. Abraham Kuyper of the Netherlands. Warfield, a hard-hitting and sometimes brilliant polemicist in a day of increasingly polite theology, had by this time established his reputation, for better or worse, as the John L. Sullivan of the theological world. He was always ready to spar, even with a close theological ally such as Kuyper. Kuyper was a truly remarkable figure. In addition to being a first-rate theologian, he was a newspaper editor, the founder of a university, the organizer of a denomination, and ultimately prime minister of the Netherlands.

Despite his admiration for Kuyper, Warfield found the Dutch theologian's view of science (and hence his view of Christian apologetics) "a standing matter of surprise." Kuyper denied that there was one unified science for the human race. Rather, he argued that because there are "two kinds of people," regenerate and unregenerate, there are "two kinds of sciences." The differences in the two sciences, of course, would not show up in simple technical analyses, such as measuring, weighing, or the like; but insofar as any science was a *theoretical* discipline, Christians and non-Christians would reach some conclusions that were different in important ways. Each would be equally scientific, but they would be working from differing starting points and frameworks of assumptions.

So, said Kuyper, Christian and non-Christian scientific thinkers were not working on different parts of the same building, but on different buildings. Each "will of course claim for himself the high and noble name of science, and withhold it from the other." Kuyper, who anticipated some of the insights of Thomas Kuhn (although working from a much different philosophical base) was thus one of the early challengers to the dream that had dominated so much of modern Western thought—that the human race would eventually discover one body of objective scientific truth.[1]

To B. B. Warfield, Kuyper's view was sheer nonsense. Warfield was a man of his age at least to the extent of believing that science was an objective, unified, and cumulative enterprise of the entire race. "The human spirit," he said, "attains this science . . . by slow accretions, won through many partial and erroneous constructions." In response to Kuyper, he maintained that "men of all sorts and of all grades work side by side at the common task, and the common edifice grows under their hands into ever fuller and truer outlines."[2] Warfield differed from most of his contemporaries not in this classic view of science, but rather in his resistance to the recent trend to limit the meaning of "science" to the natural sciences and the new imitative social sciences. For Warfield and his colleagues at Princeton, theology was still the queen of the sciences and its truths could be discovered once and for all on the same foundational epistemological principles as the truths of Newtonian physics had been established.

Building on such assumptions, Warfield's confidence in demonstrating rationally the truths of Christianity knew no bounds. "It is not true," he insisted "that he [the Christian] cannot soundly prove his position. It is not true that the Christian view of the world is subjective merely, and is incapable of validation in the forum of pure reason." Indeed, "All minds are of the same essential structure; and the less illuminated will not be able permanently to resist or gainsay the determination of the more illuminated." The reason of the regenerate, in fact, "shall ultimately conquer to itself the whole race." With such a prospect for total apologetic victory, Kuyper's insistence that science or rationality for the regenerate and

---

[1] Abraham Kuyper, *Principles of Sacred Theology,* translated by J. Hendrik DeVries (Grand Rapids, Mich.: Baker Book House, 1980 [1898]), 150–59.

[2] Warfield, Introduction to Francis R. Beattie's *Apologetics: or the Rational Vindication of Christianity* (Richmond, Va., 1903), *Selected Shorter Writings of Benjamin B. Warfield,* vol. II, edited by John E. Meeter (Nutley, N.J.: Presbyterian and Reformed Publishing Co., 1973), 101–02. These same remarks appeared about the same time in a review of *De Zekerheid des Geloofs* by Herman Bavinck in the *Princeton Theological Review,* January 1903, quoted in Warfield, *Shorter Writings,* II, 106–23.

for the unregenerate operated in differing frameworks seemed to Warfield to border on cowardice. As long as science was the common task of all people, said Warfield, "it is the better science that ever in the end wins the victory. . . . How shall it win its victory, however, if it declines the conflict?"[3]

In retrospect, this rhetoric seems of the ilk that might have sent Custer to the Little Bighorn. The Princetonians were fighting overwhelming odds but going down with their guns blazing. To them, however, it might not have been obvious how hopeless their position was. Only in 1902, for instance, had Warfield's good friend, theologian Francis L. Patton, retired as president of no less an academic center than Princeton University. Patton held the same views as Warfield on the simultaneous triumph of Calvinism and science. "Believing in Calvinism," Patton had proclaimed, "we believe that if Christendom shall have one unanimous faith, it will be the Calvinistic faith."[4] Patton was, however, virtually the last of a kind, the last clergyman president of a major American university. During his presidency, nonetheless, he had helped create the very scientifically specialized structures of the modern university that were making his own views such an anomaly. He and the other Princeton theologians remained confident that any structures that would help promote true science would in the long run promote true religion. So, far from seeing themselves as making a heroic last stand, they were confident that the forces of science, by which they were surrounded, were on their side.

The historical problem stated

As they would have been the first to tell you, the strict Calvinist theologians at Princeton did not represent all of American evangelicalism. *Evangelicalism,* as I am using it here, refers to that broad movement, found especially in British and American Protestantism, that insisted that "the sole authority in religion is the Bible and the sole means of salvation is a life-transforming experience wrought by the Holy Spirit through faith in Jesus Christ."[5] Although the Princetonians were unhappy with many

---

[3] Ibid., 103.
[4] Patton, *Speech . . . at the Annual Dinner of the Princeton Club in New York,* March 15, 1888 (New York 1888), 5, quoted in Laurence R. Veysey, *The Emergence of the American University* (Chicago: University of Chicago Press, 1965), 52.
[5] Grant Wacker, *Augustus H. Strong and the Dilemma of Historical Consciousness* (Macon, Ga.: Mercer University Press, 1985), 17. This is as economical and careful a definition as I have seen.

of the emphases of this broader evangelicalism, they nonetheless were allied with it and eventually became the intellectually most influential group in the conservative, or Bible-believing, evangelicalism that survived and now flourishes in the twentieth century. In fact, the Princetonians have been more influential in twentieth-century evangelicalism than they were among their nineteenth-century contemporaries. The intellectual traits of this elite, then, although not exactly typical, represent unusually well-articulated tendencies that have resonated with the assumptions of an important segment of popular (white) evangelicalism, especially as it faced the secularizing threats of the twentieth century.

Why were the Princetonians and so many of their twentieth-century conservative, evangelical, intellectual dependents so committed in principle to a scientifically based culture even while the scientifically based culture of the twentieth century was undermining belief in the very truths of the Bible they held most dear? I do not pretend to answer this question in its entirety, because it has many dimensions—theological, philosophical, psychological, sociological, institutional, and so forth. What I attempt to do in this paper is to present a historical overview of the relationships between American evangelicalism and modern scientific culture, so that we can better understand the Princetonian and twentieth-century evangelical stance in terms of the tradition that nourished it.

Evangelicalism and the American Enlightenment

The crucial dimension of this American tradition becomes apparent if we ask what was centrally different about the cultural experiences that lay behind the outlooks of our two turn-of-the-century Calvinists, Abraham Kuyper and B. B. Warfield. Some similarities are immediately evident. Each of their nations had a predominantly Calvinist religious heritage. Each had been an early leader in tolerance and religious pluralism. Each had been much influenced by the Enlightenment and reshaped politically in the age of revolution.

The big difference, however, was in the Calvinists' relationship to the Enlightenment and revolution.[6] In Holland the Enlightenment had been associated largely with the secularism that had been on the rise since the seventeenth century. The Dutch revolution of the 1790s was widely regarded, at least by many Dutch Calvinists, as an outgrowth of the French

[6] This idea was, I think, first suggested to me by Mark Noll.

Revolution and hence of "infidelity." During the first half of the nineteenth century, a pietist revival in the Netherlands paralleled the Second Great Awakening in the United States. The Dutch version of the revival eventually took the form of a "neo-Calvinist" resurgence. By the 1870s Abraham Kuyper had become the leader of this formidable neo-Calvinist movement. For the next four decades he infused it with a vision of reforming all culture under Calvinist leadership. Kuyper eventually became an effective political leader because he recognized, in good Dutch fashion, that competing world views had their rights. But he often spoke of an "Antithesis" between a Calvinist world view and contemporary world views controlled by the "humanism" and "materialism" growing out of the Enlightenment.[7] His Calvinist political party was called the "Anti-Revolutionary" party.

In the United States, it made a world of difference that Calvinists and their evangelical allies had been on the side of the American Revolution. This fact is crucial to understanding their view of the Enlightenment and their subsequent view of science. It is true that for a time after the French Revolution, some Calvinist leaders in the United States, most notably Yale President Timothy Dwight, raised an antirevolutionary flag in the name of Christianity versus Enlightenment "infidelity." Vestiges of this Dwightean viewpoint persisted throughout the next century (indeed, they survive today), so that many American evangelicals have spoken of "the Enlightenment" as synonymous with "rationalism" and "skepticism." This usage should not, however, lead us away from the true picture. Insofar as the Enlightenment represented an attitude toward rationality and scientific thinking, American evangelicals have been in many respects its champions, even while repudiating certain other tendencies in the eighteenth-century outlook.

Our understanding of this ambivalent, but essentially positive, relationship to Enlightenment thought is clarified, if we remember, as Henry May has taught us, that the Enlightenment in the United States had several manifestations. According to May, we can divide the European Enlightenment ideas that influenced the United States into four categories: First is the early Moderate Enlightenment associated with Newton and Locke—the ideals of order, balance, and religious compromise. Second is the Skeptical Enlightenment, represented best by Voltaire and Hume. Third is the Revolutionary Enlightenment—the search for a new heaven

---

[7] James D. Bratt, *Dutch Calvinism in Modern America: A History of a Conservative Subculture* (Grand Rapids, Mich.: W. B. Eerdmans, 1984), 21, cf. 3–33.

on Earth—that grew out of the thought of Rousseau. And fourth is the Didactic Enlightenment, stemming from Scottish Common Sense thought, which opposed skepticism and revolution but rescued the essentials of the earlier eighteenth-century commitments to science, rationality, order, and the Christian tradition.

Of these four types of the Enlightenment, only the first and the fourth had major lasting influence in the United States. The American Revolution was managed primarily by proponents of the Moderate Enlightenment, such as Adams and Madison. More radical revolutionary ideas, such as those of Paine and Jefferson, were significant for a time, but were discredited in many influential circles when they became associated with the French Revolution and Paine's skepticism. Neither radical revolution nor Enlightenment skepticism took deep root in American culture. Instead, the Didactic Enlightenment of Scotland provided the basis for a synthesis.[8] According to the principles of Scottish philosophy, it appeared that the three great strands in American thought—modern empirical scientific ideals, the self-evident principles of the American Revolution, and evangelical Christianity—could be reconciled, or, rather, remain reconciled. Thus the Scottish Enlightenment had a remarkable afterlife in the United States, dominating American academic thought for the first six or seven decades of the nineteenth century.

In contrast to the situation in Europe, then, not only did an important component of the classic Enlightenment outlook survive, it was closely allied with biblically conservative evangelicalism. What lived was not any explicit commitment to the "Enlightenment" as such, but rather a dedication to the general philosophical basis that had undergirded the empirically based rationality so confidently proclaimed by most eighteenth-century thinkers. Thus, as many authors have observed, among the great heroes of the faith for evangelical intellectuals during the first half of the nineteenth century were Isaac Newton and Francis Bacon. Theodore Dwight Bozeman, in fact, documents the "beatification of Bacon," notably among those who were most theologically conservative.[9] This "beatification of Bacon" coincided with the Second Great Awakening. It helped provide for it a popular epistemology (as is evident in Charles Finney's insistence that producing a revival was just as scientific an enterprise as

[8] Henry F. May, *The Enlightenment in America* (New York: Oxford University Press, 1976), xvi and passim.
[9] Theodore Dwight Bozeman, *Protestants in an Age of Science: The Baconian Ideal and Antebellum American Religious Thought* (Chapel Hill: University of North Carolina Press, 1977), 72 and passim.

producing a crop of corn) and as a basis for Christian apologetics. So in the first heyday of evangelicalism in the United States, objective scientific thought was not tinged with the guilt of fostering secularism. Rather it was boldly lauded as the best friend of the Christian faith and of Christian culture generally.

This cordial relationship between Christianity and a scientifically based culture in the United States was, moreover, not a recent invention of the nineteenth century. Rather the synthesis of the Didactic Enlightenment was a matter of restoring a long-standing marriage briefly threatened by revolutionary passions and infidelity.

Faith and reason

We should consider, however, the character of this well-known marriage of faith and science if we are to understand what went on later. Concerning its beginnings, we know, of course, that the Puritans cordially supported the new science of the seventeenth century. Although, on the one hand, the scientific outlook might have seemed to create a tension with the Puritans' providential readings of nature, on the other hand, the Puritans were so preoccupied with their understanding of God as an orderly lawgiver that they welcomed and fostered investigation of that orderliness.

By the eighteenth century, however, the tension between providential and natural law explanations was becoming a major struggle for thoughtful Protestants of all sorts.[10] Probably it is safe to say that even many of those who were theologically orthodox adopted a world view that, in effect, had Deist tendencies. They viewed the universe as a machine run by natural laws, and in practice distanced the Creator from their understandings of the everyday operations of creation.[11] They also made a sharper distinction between the natural and the supernatural. Those who remained more or less orthodox tended simultaneously to view natural events in two ways, which they considered simply complementary perspectives.[12] Because God was the author of all that was, what he revealed

[10] James Turner, *Without God, Without Creed: The Origin of Unbelief in America* (Baltimore: Johns Hopkins University Press, 1985), 39, provides a nice example of James Boswell's personal wrestling with this issue in 1764.

[11] Jonathan Edwards is an example of someone who took the opposite approach, as in his "Dissertation Concerning the End for which God Created the World."

[12] Turner, *Without God*, 39–40, illustrates this dual outlook in the remarks of Charles Chauncy on the New England earthquake of 1755 as both a law-governed natural event and warning from God. Turner, although sometimes given to hyperbole, furnishes a helpful version of the present thesis.

through natural law would always harmonize with special revelation. The two revelations, indeed, paralleled each other, as Bishop Butler argued. Moreover, as William Paley eventually put it in what became its classic statement, empirical science supported Scripture by providing irrefutable evidence of design.

By the end of the eighteenth century, American Protestants of almost all sorts had adopted this two-tiered world view, founded on an empiricist epistemology, with the laws of nature below, supporting supernatural belief above. They thus had worked out a modern version of the Thomist synthesis of reason and faith. Or, in H. Richard Niebuhr's categories, they had worked out a "Christ Above Culture" intellectual framework in which the realism of science and faith could not conflict.[13]

We can get a glimpse of how this harmonious two-tiered world view worked if we look for a moment at late eighteenth-century Christian views of what we today would call the social sciences. At the time of the American Revolution in the eighteenth century, most Americans viewed political thought as an empirically based scientific discipline, in the tradition of John Locke. What is striking about the eighteenth-century evangelical Christian views of the matter (especially if we contrast them with the immense twentieth-century literature of Christian views of politics) is that there is no distinctly Christian view of political science in the revolutionary era. Rather (excepting perhaps the sectarians) eighteenth-century American Christians offered no distinct perspectives on revolutionary theory.[14] Patriotic Christian Americans could accept without criticism the political theories of Jefferson or Paine. When it got to the realm of "spiritual" questions, they would, of course, part ways. But on mundane matters they assumed that political science was identical for the Christian and the non-Christian. Moreover, many of the truths found by natural law could be confirmed by supernatural revelation. The self-evident injustice of taxation without representation, for instance, confirmed the divine revelation, "Thou shalt not steal." Locke's contract theory of government was, in practice, sufficiently like the Puritan covenant that no one in the revolutionary era seems to have thought it significant to criticize its essentially secular theoretical base.

This modern Protestant counterpart to the Thomist synthesis of sci-

[13] H. Richard Niebuhr, *Christ and Culture* (New York: Harper & Row, 1951).
[14] Mark A. Noll, *Christians in the American Revolution* (Grand Rapids, Mich.: Christian University Press, 1977).

ence and faith was preserved and expanded in the days of American evangelical intellectual hegemony during the first half of the nineteenth century. Francis Wayland, the Baptist author of the most popular college textbooks of the era, provides a typical example. In his *Elements of Moral Science* (1835) he argues that ethics is as much a science as physics, each discovering laws of sequences of cause and effect. Inductive science, however, can go only so far in discovering moral principles. So God's additional revelation in the Bible is necessary to supplement what reason tells us (adding, for instance, information about the Incarnation or the Atonement) and to point us to some moral principles built into nature (such as the value of one day's rest in seven) that we might not have noticed otherwise. Scripture and rational moral science operating independently will reveal completely harmonious principles. The harmony of these two independent sources of truth, says Wayland, constitutes firm evidence for the Christian religion. "So complete is this coincidence," he exclaims, "as to afford irrefragable proof that the Bible contains the moral laws of the universe; and hence, that the Author of the universe—that is of natural religion—is also the Author of the Scriptures."[15]

Consistent with this two-level approach to truth, Wayland could take an entirely different approach in his subsequent text *The Elements of Political Economy* (1837). Although he acknowledges that most topics in political economy could be discussed also in moral philosophy, he writes that "he [Wayland] has not thought it proper to intermingle them, but has argued economical questions on merely economical grounds." Political economy, in other words, is a pure science and has "nothing to do" with ethical questions.[16]

In retrospect, Wayland's approach has been seen as part of a subtle process of secularization in American life. Martin Marty, for instance, points out that secularization typically took place through a peaceful separation of "religious areas" in American life from the secular and the scientific. When this division of labor took place, the two realms were seen in perfect harmony, and true science was always the base of proof

[15] Francis Wayland, *Elements of Moral Science*, edited by Joseph Angus (London, ca. 1860 [1835]), 219–20.
   I have used this example and those in the next four paragraphs in another context (and in a place where only philosophers are likely to see them) in "The Collapse of American Evangelical Academia," *Faith and Rationality*, edited by Alvin Plantinga and Nicholas Wolterstorff (South Bend, Ind.: University of Notre Dame Press, 1984). A few other of the themes in this essay are found also in that one.
[16] Wayland, *The Elements of Political Economy* (Boston, 1860 [1837]), iv.

for true religion.[17] Once the disciplines were declared autonomous and separated from explicit Christian reference until after they had drawn their conclusions, however, it was easy for a later generation to omit altogether the latter step of reference to Christianity.

In the natural sciences, the pattern was both similar and more dramatic. The Baconian methodology in the natural sciences provided the model that the emerging social sciences attempted to imitate. In the natural sciences, however, it was more difficult to see what relationship Christianity would have with most of the technical aspects of the enterprise, even if one wished to relate the two. Generally, evangelical American scientists assumed the total objectivity of their enterprise, but then related it to their Christianity by noting the harmonies of scientific truth and truth in the higher realms of religion and morality. Perhaps the most common way of relating Christianity to science was the "doxological." One should emerge from one's scientific inquiries into nature praising God for the marvels of his creation.[18]

Closely related, but more important for our purposes, was the apologetic use of natural science. In addition to the foundational argument from design, these arguments pointed out the harmonies between what was known in the natural world and what was known in the moral and spiritual world. "*The theology of natural science*" declared Lewis W. Green, in 1854, in a typical statement of the day, "is in perfect harmony with *the theology of the Bible.*" Each of these, plus our moral intuitions, told us of a wise, benevolent, and orderly governor of the universe. The harmonious fit of the Bible with what was discovered by objective science in these other areas was the crucial question for the evangelical apologists. Their principal opponents were Deists who shared their beliefs that the natural and moral order pointed inescapably to a wise deity. The Bible, the evangelical apologists were convinced, could be shown to fit exactly with objective truths discovered in these other areas. As Mark Hopkins, the best-known evangelical teacher of the era, put it in summarizing his apologetics: "There is a harmony of adaptation, and also of analogy. The key is adapted to the lock; the fin of the fish is analogous

---

[17] Martin E. Marty, *The Modern Schism: Three Paths to the Secular* (New York: Harper & Row, 1969), 98.

[18] Bozeman, *Protestants in an Age of Science;* George H. Daniels, *American Science in the Age of Jackson* (New York: Columbia University Press, 1968); Herbert Hovenkamp, *Science and Religion in America, 1800–1860* (Philadelphia: University of Pennsylvania Press, 1978); E. Brooks Holifield, *The Gentlemen Theologians: American Theology in Southern Culture, 1795–1860* (Durham: Duke University Press, 1978).

to the wing of the bird. Christianity, as I hope to show, is adapted to man." Given such parallels and harmonies in the two sources of revelation, said Lewis Green in 1854, Christians had nothing to fear if astronomy discovered new worlds, geology new ages, or anthropology extinct races and species. Rather would "the Christian welcome joyfully, and appropriate each successive revelation."[19]

The Darwinian challenges

The reception of Darwinism, which eventually became pivotal in shaping and symbolizing evangelical attitudes toward scientific culture, has to be understood in this context. By 1859, evangelicals, both scientists and theologians, thought they had discovered an impregnable synthesis between faith and reason. Scientific reasoning, the kind they most respected, firmly supported Christian faith. In principle they were deeply wedded to a scientific culture, so long as it left room (indeed a privileged place of honor) to add on their version of Christianity.

Given this commitment, it is not surprising that the evangelical reaction to Darwinism was, as numerous recent studies have shown,[20] far more ambivalent than the stereotyped story would suggest. The stereotyped story, so convenient to those of us who lecture about modern culture, has been framed by the metaphors of warfare. According to this story, Darwinism marked the triumphant assault of modern scientific culture against the last remaining citadels of the premodern religious culture. In England, the story goes, the fulminations of Bishop Wilberforce typified the consternation of the befuddled defenders of traditional religion. Thomas Huxley, however, destroyed Wilberforce's position in their famed debate of 1860. After that it was a mopping-up operation, although fundamentalists remained here and there, especially here in America, for many years after. This version of the story has been tagged "1859 and All That."[21] The implication of the story is that Darwinism

[19] Lewis W. Green, *Lectures on the Evidences of Christianity* (New York, 1854), 463–64; Mark Hopkins, *Evidence of Christianity* (Boston, 1876 [1846]), 75.
[20] E.g., James R. Moore, *The Post-Darwinian Controversies: A Study of the Protestant Struggle to Come to Terms with Darwin in Great Britain and America, 1870–1900* (Cambridge: Cambridge University Press, 1979); Neil C. Gillespie, *Charles Darwin and the Problem of Creation* (Chicago: University of Chicago Press, 1979); Peter J. Bowler, *Evolution: The History of an Idea* (Berkeley: University of California Press, 1984); John Durant, ed., *Darwinism and Divinity: Essays on Evolution and Religious Belief* (Oxford: Basil Blackwell, 1985); Ronald L. Numbers, "Science and Religion," *OSIRIS,* 2d series, 1985, 1:59–80.
[21] James R. Moore, "1859 and All That: Remaking the Story of Evolution and Religion,"

brought the decisive culmination of a long-standing struggle between modernity and prescientific religious faith.

In fact, because evangelicalism and the scientific culture had been so deeply intertwined throughout the first half of the nineteenth century, the reactions to Darwinism were far more complex. One evidence of this is that opinions about Darwinism did not immediately split exactly along conservative and liberal theological lines. Although it is possible that lay opinion among strict Bible-believers was largely negative regarding biological evolution,[22] the conservative intellectual leadership was divided. While various conservative leaders pointed out a number of problems with reconciling Christianity and Darwinism, others (just as conservative) proposed ways of surmounting these problems.

The first of the problems for conservative Bible-believers was that of reconciling biological evolution with a literal interpretation of early Genesis. This question, however, did not cause the polarization that (in light of current discussion by "creation scientists")[23] we might expect. The way had been prepared during the first half of the century by extensive intraevangelical debates over how to reconcile Genesis with the seemingly inescapable evidence for geological evolution[24] and the more speculative, but popular, nebular hypothesis for explaining the natural origins of the universe.[25] Although there were holdouts,[26] the predominant opinion among the American conservative evangelical leaders was that Genesis was susceptible to some reinterpretation in the light of modern scientific discovery. By the time *Origin of Species* appeared, the commonplace view among biblicists was that the six "days" of creation in the first chapter of Genesis represented vast eons. Moreover, the order of the creation of the species in Genesis fit roughly the Darwinian order. As to whether God might create through evolutionary means, there was no

in Roger G. Chapman and Cleveland T. Duval, eds., *Charles Darwin, 1809–1882: A Centennial Commemorative* (Wellington, N.Z.: Nova Pacifica, 1982), 167–94.

[22] Numbers, "Science and Religion," 73.

[23] I have discussed the shift in fundamentalist attitudes leading to "creation science" in "Creation versus Evolution: No Middle Way," *Nature* 305 (5935) (October 13, 1983), 571–74.

[24] Bowler, *Evolution*, 206.

[25] Ronald L. Numbers, *Creation by Natural Law: Laplace's Nebular Hypothesis in American Thought* (Seattle: University of Washington Press, 1977).

[26] These holdouts were not necessarily obscurantists. See, for instance, the view of Moses Stuart, a champion of modern scientific methods of biblical scholarship as discussed in George M. Marsden, "Everyone One's Own Interpreter? The Bible, Science, and Authority in Mid-Nineteenth Century America," in Nathan O. Hatch and Mark A. Noll, eds., *The Bible in America: Essays in Cultural History* (New York: Oxford University Press, 1982), 92–93.

new problem. If God could guide the natural evolution of mountains, he could create other entities that way.

A second objection was the "dignity of man" argument, proposed by Bishop Wilberforce and many others who were offended by thinking of humans and apes as blood relations. Such initial objections were not confined to biblicists. Biblicist evolutionists, moreover, could easily sidestep the substantive aspect of this objection by proposing that God may have intervened late in the evolutionary process, either to create humans as a distinct species or at least to create the human soul.

A third type of objection to Darwinism was based on scientific considerations. Initially, however, these did not follow conservative-versus-liberal theological lines either. The most formidable American scientific opponent of Darwin was Harvard's Louis Agassiz, a Unitarian. The most formidable supporter was Agassiz's colleague, Asa Gray, an evangelical. Most American evangelicals had a firm commitment to nonspeculative Baconian inductionism, and some objected to Darwin's speculations on those grounds. By the 1870s, however, many evangelical scientists were following Gray in seeing that Darwin's hypothesis explained too many disparate phenomena to be lightly dismissed as a working model.[27]

A fourth objection was more philosophical. It was best articulated by Charles Hodge of Princeton Theological Seminary. Hodge's objection was summarized in conclusion to his 1874 study, *What Is Darwinism?* "What is Darwinism?" Hodge asked. "It is atheism." Hodge's summary so well suits the warfare model for understanding the relation of conservative religion and post-Darwinian science that it has been a favorite quotation supposedly encapsulating the conservative side of the whole affair. In fact, however, Hodge was making some careful distinctions. The idea of evolution, he observed, was not unique to Darwin, nor was that the important point at issue. Neither was the concept of natural selection. What was central and crucial, said Hodge, was that "Darwin rejects all teleology, or the doctrine of final causes." To Hodge, Darwin's intransigence on this point amounted to a practical atheism, because it left us with a chance universe.[28]

The great debate within the American (and British) evangelical community was whether Darwin's total rejection of design was *entailed* by his theories about biological development or whether they were views

[27] Cf. note 20 above.
[28] Charles Hodge, *What Is Darwinism?* (New York: Scribners, Armstrong, and Co., 1874), excerpts in Mark A. Noll, editor and compiler, *The Princeton Theology, 1812–1921* (Grand Rapids, Mich.: Baker Book House, 1983), 145–52.

that were nonessential to true "Darwinism." Asa Gray and Darwin cor-
responded at length on this point and never did agree.[29] Among conservative Protestant intellectuals, however, the prevailing opinion seems
to have favored Gray's view, thus allowing for reconciliation of some
version of Darwin's biological theories with the Bible, and hence design.[30] Liberal evangelicals managed this by adopting ever-looser interpretations of Scripture. Conservatives, however, reconciled themselves to
biological evolution without giving up their trust in biblical reliability.

An important indicator of this degree of acceptance is that only in the
American South did accommodations to Darwinism get conservative
theologians into trouble in the late nineteenth century. The most famous
case is that of James Woodrow, whose views were typical of the conservative evangelical reconcilers. In 1886 Woodrow lost his job at Columbia Theological Seminary, then in South Carolina, for teaching that
God had created the body of Adam through evolutionary means, even
though he taught that God had intervened to create Adam's soul. Woodrow was so much a biblicist that he held that God also intervened to
create Eve from Adam's rib.[31] In the North such combinations of bibli-
cism and evolution seem not to have raised serious problems in conservative circles during these decades. Even at Princeton Seminary, the bastion
of Biblical conservatism where the term *inerrancy* was first used to describe their confidence in exact biblical statements, the door stood open
to accommodations to evolutionary biology. Charles Hodge's own son
and immediate successor, Archibald Alexander Hodge, held such views.
So did B. B. Warfield.[32] James R. Moore, in his impressive study of the
post-Darwinian controversies in the United States and Britain, concludes
that, in fact, some conservative Calvinists were especially prone to reconciling biological evolution and design, because they had a long history of
explaining how God's complete providential control could operate through
secondary natural agencies.[33]

[29] Moore, *Post-Darwinian Controversies*, 269–80.
[30] Cf. note 20 above.
[31] Ernest Trice Thompson, *Presbyterians in the South, Vol. II, 1861–1890* (Richmond, Va., 1973), 442–90.
[32] David N. Livingstone, *Darwin's Forgotten Defenders: The Encounter between Evangel-ical Theology and Evolutionary Thought* (Grand Rapids, Mich.: William B. Eerdmans, 1987), 115–21. Contrary to Charles Hodge, Warfield thought that Darwin's strict natu-ralism was not entailed by his theory but an intellectual quirk because "his absorption in a single line of investigation and inference had so atrophied his mind in other directions that he had ceased to be a trustworthy judge of evidence." "Darwin's Argument against Christianity and against Religion" [1889], in *Selected Shorter Writings*, 141.
[33] Moore, *Post-Darwinian Controversies*, 334.

Certainly the best evidence that total opposition to biological evolution had not become an article of faith for American conservative evangelicals of this period is that *The Fundamentals*, published from 1910 to 1915 by some of the originators of the fundamentalist movement, included articles that, although guarded, still allow some room for theistically controlled biological evolution. Even at those late dates, then, "evolution" had not yet become the almost universal code word among conservative evangelicals symbolizing their discontent with the dominant tendencies of modern scientific culture.

Origins of the conflict

How, then, did the conservative evangelical reaction to Darwinism come to be regarded as though it always had been an all-out warfare, when for a half-century the attitudes among some of the movement's most prominent leaders were, at least, mixed and ambivalent? The answer to this question will give us an important clue to identifying where the real tension point was developing between evangelicals and the new scientific culture.

A number of recent historians of the reception of Darwinism seem largely agreed that, in the early decades after *Origin of Species,* the "warfare" framework for understanding the relationship of Christianity to Darwinism was developed and promoted primarily by ardent opponents of Christianity.[34] A few defenders of Christianity did immediately anathematize Darwinism and some, as in the American South, continued to do so. The anti-Christian polemicists, however, made the most of such opposition, suggesting that traditional Christians had always attacked modern science. In short, they claimed, this was another instance of a long-standing war between faith and science. Soon after Darwin published, his defenders vigorously promoted this warfare metaphor. In 1869, for instance, Andrew Dixon White, the young president of Cornell, lectured a New York City audience on "The Battle-Fields of Science." White's version of the story eventually developed into his two-volume *History of the Warfare of Science with Theology in Christendom* (1896). In the meantime, John William Draper's popular *History of the Conflict between Religion and Science* (1874) had already introduced a large read-

---

[34] Ibid., 19–102; John Durant, "Darwinism and Divinity: A Century of Debate," in Durant, ed., *Darwinism and Divinity*, 9–39; and Ronald L. Numbers, "Science and Religion," each summarize some of the other sources in this growing consensus.

ing public to the warfare model. Both White and Draper projected the warfare into the past. Through dubious reconstructions of the evidence (usually ignoring, for instance, that most of the debates about science had been debates among Christians)[35] they suggested that the intellectual life of the past several centuries had been dominated by the conflict between advocates of religiously based obscurantism and enlightened champions of value-free scientific truth.

One does not have to look far to see what was behind such heavy-handed reconstructions of the past. White and Draper were prophets of a new age in which the scientific quest for truth would finally be freed from religious constraint. As prophets tend to, they saw the issue as a contest between the forces of light and the forces of darkness. The prototype of this company of prophets was "Darwin's Bulldog," T. H. Huxley. Huxley was preoccupied with the metaphors of warfare for describing his efforts. "Warfare has been my business and duty," he declared frankly. Huxley spoke for that band of intellectual "agnostics" (to use his new term) who were convinced that people should not be guided by beliefs they could not know with scientific certainty. They were champions of essentially August Comte's view that positive science must replace inferior ways that civilizations had previously used to find truth. To do this, the essential first step was the reform of science itself, to remove it from any connection with religion. Science must be defined as the investigation of natural causes and nothing else. Science that continued to have the traditional references to religion must be called nonscience. As Neil Gillespie summarizes it, the older "episteme" open to religious truth had to be discredited, because "the very existence of a rival science or of an alternate mode of knowledge was intolerable to the positivist." For a Huxley or a Draper, says Gillespie, "It was not enough to drive out the old ideas. Their advocates had to be driven out of the scientific community as well."[36]

Two well-known points about this campaign should be briefly noted. First, this effort to secularize both science and society was under way before Darwin published. Second, the secularizers accepted Darwin's views so enthusiastically and promoted them so vigorously because they were

[35] David C. Lindberg and Ronald L. Numbers, "Beyond Waar and Peace: A Reappraisal of the Encounter between Christianity and Science" *Church History* 55 (September 1986): 338–54. Cf. by the same authors, *God and Nature: Historical Essays on the Encounter between Christianity and Science* (Berkeley: University of California Press, 1986).
[36] Gillespie, *Charles Darwin*, 152–53.

ideally suited to their campaign. Darwin's massive array of evidence was aimed directly at the concept of design, the link between Christianity and science that had been hardest to dissolve. Once science was freed, civilization could be. As T. H. Huxley said characteristically in a review of Darwin's theory in 1860, "Every philosophical thinker hails it as a veritable Whitworth gun in the armoury of liberalism."[37]

Why many biblicists did not know they were at war with science

Darwinism appeared, of course, at a time when there was a widespread impulse toward secularization in Western culture. It is important to note that so far as secularization was something that was advocated, in addition to something that just happened, it could have two very different rationales. On the one hand, the push to secularize might come from nonreligious people, such as the agnostics, who were convinced that their positivism (using the term loosely) provided a better moral basis for civilization than did Christianity.[38] On the other hand, secularization might be promoted simply as a methodology. That is, various activities might be removed from religious reference not because people sought to promote a non-Christian world view, but simply because people were convinced that the activities could be better carried out without the distractions of religious considerations, however valuable those considerations might be in other contexts. As we have seen, evangelicals in the United States had already been advocating methodological secularization, à la Francis Wayland. Moreover, to return to Martin Marty's point, secularization in this country initially involved relatively little antireligious sentiment.[39] So in the latter decades of the nineteenth century many biblicist Christians might advocate the methodological secularization of science for much the same reasons that they might favor the trend toward more efficient business practices.[40] So they might have been ready allies of the

[37] Thomas Henry Huxley, "Orthodoxy Scotched, If Not Slain," abridged from Huxley, *Lay Sermons, Addresses, and Reviews* (New York, 1871), in Harold Y. Vanderpool, ed., *Darwin and Darwinism: Revolutionary Insights concerning Man, Nature, Religion, and Society* (Lexington, Mass.: D. C. Heath, 1973), 91.

[38] Turner, *Without God*, discusses the conviction of the agnostics that their position was essential to a higher morality, e.g., 203.

[39] Marty, *Modern Schism*, passim. Marty points out, for instance, the contrast with the anticlericalism in French secularization.

[40] Samuel Haber, *Efficiency and Uplift: Scientific Management in the Progressive Era, 1890–1920* (Chicago: University of Chicago Press, 1964) suggests a widespread American enthusiasm (in which conservative evangelicals apparently participated) for "scientific" procedures of all sorts during this era.

militant agnostics in the campaign to get religion out of science, that is, to define science purely naturalistically.[41]

Such methodological secularization was connected with the professionalization of American life. Professionalization involved the isolation of various disciplines. One of the natural implications of this isolation of the disciplines was that theology would have to be isolated from each of them. All this fit with the sentiments to make each discipline more scientific and to define science naturalistically. The trend was reinforced by the need simply to improve scientific study itself. In pre-Civil War America, much natural science, for instance, had been conducted by amateurs, often theologians. A more strictly naturalistic definition of science was thus likely to appeal to those Christians or non-Christians who thought that quality would be improved by developing professional specialties.

The rise of the social sciences followed similar lines. As American universities emerged after the Civil War, the new social sciences were organized on a scientific model. William Graham Sumner provides a familiar example of the new secular outlook. His famous remark—that he put his religious beliefs in a drawer and twenty years later he opened the drawer and the beliefs were gone—illustrates the ease with which a secularized methodology might be turned into a secular world view.

Sumner, however, was not typical of American academics in the 1870s. Rather, both in the natural sciences and in the social sciences, it took a whole generation for the transition to take place. Until at least around the turn of the century, the moral-religious tradition that had been inherited from the amateur practitioners of moral science and political economy retained some momentum. So, for instance, we find the early literature of the American Economic Association, founded in 1886, describing it as a Christian endeavor. Richard T. Ely, the first secretary, declared at the organizational meeting that because "our work lies in the direction of practical Christianity, we appeal to the church, the chief of the social forces in this country, to help us, to support us, and to make our work a complete success, which it can by no possibility be without her assistance." Apparently not all the organizers agreed with this sentiment. Just as important, the papers presented to the early organization were strictly technical.[42] Because the discipline was thus defined as a science, it would

---

[41] Cf. Gillespie, *Charles Darwin*, 13.
[42] "Statement of Dr. Richard T. Ely," *Report of the Organization of the American Economic Association*, Richard T. Ely, Secretary, vol. I, no. 1 (Baltimore, 1886), 18. Cf.

be relatively simple in the next generation to let views such as Ely's simply die out.

Although it would take additional research to establish the point, my working hypothesis would be that before 1900 the apparently benign nature of American secularization kept most conservative evangelicals from seeing what was taking place. One thing that confused the issue was that evangelical Protestantism was now breaking into liberal and conservative camps. So conservatives, who might approve of relating Christianity to social analyses when it was done by conservatives, might disapprove of it when done by theological liberals. Moreover, they were still free in their own circles to promote their own views about Christian economic and social principles, an exercise that may have contributed to the illusion that they were still speaking to the whole nation.[43] Indeed, the alliance between Christian rhetoric and politics was still taken for granted at the center of American public life through the Progressive Era. In the triumph of Prohibition in 1919 the conservative and liberal wings of Protestantism allied for one last nationwide victory, but they, of course, had no way of knowing it was their last. Such victories, or the hopes for them, could keep alive the belief that conservative Christians still had an important voice in controlling the science-infatuated American culture.

And then it was too late

Such continuing influences of evangelical Christianity on public life obscured the degree to which conservative Christians were completely losing their place in some of the crucial centers of the scientific culture. Sometime after 1900, probably after 1910, the isolation of the sciences from religious considerations, especially from the academically discredited conservative biblicist views, had become no longer an option but a strict requirement. The trend had advanced so far that there was no longer any way for conservative Bible-believers to have a voice for their religious views within a scientific discipline. In American academe there

footnote on p. 14 that, although some endorsed his views without reservation, others objected strongly, so that Ely's views did not officially represent the association. Cf. passim.

[43] Gary Scott Smith, *The Seeds of Secularization: Calvinism, Culture, and Pluralism in America, 1870–1915* (Grand Rapids, Mich.: Christian University Press, 1985) documents the close attention that Calvinist leaders gave to national issues and their ongoing hopes to influence them decisively.

was one science indeed, and biblicist Christianity had no part in it. Moreover, by now it had become the intellectual fashion to abandon the Christian faith. So the naturalistic definition of science was rapidly being transformed from a methodology into a dominant academic world view.

This brings us back to the debate between Warfield and Kuyper. The strategy of the American evangelicals, which was built on the assumption that there was one set of scientific truths for the whole race and hence that the best views ought eventually to drive out those that were inferior, set up the American evangelicals for their spectacular intellectual defeat. The attitudes of the Princetonians again illustrate the point. All through the later decades of the nineteenth century they had been noting and deploring the secularization of various areas of American life. A. A. Hodge, for instance, had warned in 1877 against the consequences of removing biblical teachings from public school textbooks, as in eliminating references to Providence and faith in the study of history, or in studying society without regard for biblical principles concerning the moral order. But as Gary Scott Smith has pointed out in his recent study of American Calvinists' response to secularization, such intellectual Protestants did not recognize that equity might demand that major competing world views be given more or less equal places in public life. Rather, their concept of a free republic was one in which one view would triumph in free competition. In economic terms, they would have expected the triumph of a monopoly. Because 90 percent of Americans were Christians, argued A. A. Hodge (in a rare display of generosity to Catholics and liberal Protestants), the government and the schools should be based on explicitly Christian principles. As Smith argues, this attitude that there should be a monolithic public philosophy dominating the public schools opened the door for the triumph of a secular version of such a policy.[44]

The emergence of John Dewey as America's philosopher in the first half of the twentieth century pointedly illustrates the nature of the transition. It is immensely illuminating to realize, as Bruce Kuklick has been emphasizing, that Dewey was a New England Calvinist at heart. His "common faith," promoted through the established school system, can thus be viewed as a secular version of the ideals of the New England standing order.

It is also illuminating to see how Dewey's views changed with the

---

[44] Smith, *Seeds of Secularization*, 40–41, 77, and 93.

academic winds of his era. Until the 1890s, Dewey, like many American academics, related his philosophizing to Christian faith. By the early twentieth century, however, we find Dewey as a champion of a virtual Comtean positivism, praising the triumph of "science" over religious prejudice. Thus Dewey became the archetypal spokesman of his time, marking the triumph of a positivist definition of science that excluded religious reference.[45]

The way in which the seemingly benign nature of American secularization apparently shielded conservative American evangelicals from the imminent triumph of such views until it was too late is most dramatically illustrated in natural science. As we have seen, in the first generation after Darwin, a substantial number of both theologians and scientists were debating exactly how Darwinism might be reconciled with traditional biblical faith. Neil Gillespie argues that during this generation there were two competing "epistemes" within the scientific community, one that viewed such traditional questions of reconciliation of science to the Bible as relevant, and another that saw them as wildly irrelevant and illegitimate.[46] By about 1910, however, the generation of scientists who thought it legitimate to talk about such issues had, in good Kuhnian fashion, simply died out. One of the last to go was Oberlin College's George Frederick Wright, a protégé of Asa Gray, a respected (though amateur) geologist, a conservative reconciler of evolution and early Genesis, and eventually a contributor to *The Fundamentals*. Wright died in 1921 at the age of eighty-three. He was the last of a species.

At the Scopes trial in 1925, Clarence Darrow asked William Jennings Bryan whether he could name any reputable scientist who shared his views. Bryan feebly replied that he thought there was someone named Wright at Oberlin and then named George McCready Price. Darrow was waiting for this part of the answer. Price was a thoroughly amateur proponent of Seventh-Day Adventist Ellen White's view that the Genesis flood explained the earth's geological formations. Darrow could retort with some confidence that "every scientist in this country knows [he] is a mountebank and a pretender and not a geologist at all."[47]

---

[45] E.g., Dewey, "Science in the Reconstruction of Philosophy" (1920), in Loren Baritz, ed., *Sources of the American Mind*, vol. II (New York: Joseph Wiley & Sons, Inc., 1966), 19.
[46] Gillespie, *Charles Darwin*.
[47] Ronald L. Numbers, "Creationism in 20th-Century America," *Science*, 218, no. 5 (November 1982):540.

The fundamentalist war on evolution

The disappearance by the 1920s of biblicist views in virtually all the sciences makes it less surprising that at this point "evolution" emerged among conservative evangelicals (now called fundamentalists) as the almost universal unifying symbol of everything that was wrong. For the fundamentalists, as for the positivists earlier, "evolution" took on truly mythical proportions as the all-explanatory symbol of scientific naturalism.[48] The fundamentalist leaders who opposed evolution recognized that evolutionism had to do with more than just a theory about biology. Evolutionism reflected, and for many champions of secularism long had symbolized, an entire naturalistic world view. In this world view, all talk of absolutes had been dissolved by the widespread conviction that the best way, the only scientific way, to understand things was through historical or developmental explanations. Biblical criticism, which had done so much to discredit traditional evangelical faith, was based on such premises. Conservative evangelical scholars, who a generation earlier had hoped to participate in the science of historical criticism while retaining traditional evangelical faith, were now finding that they had to choose.[49] The thoroughly naturalistic premises of the historicism that had come to dominate the field were consistent only with naturalistic conclusions.

"Evolution," then, became for fundamentalists the chief symbol of their warfare with modern scientific culture. Increasingly, for instance, the fundamentalist subculture would tolerate no concessions to biological evolution. As they almost always made clear, however, they were still not opposed to science as such. They favored what they regarded as true objective science, and they opposed only the biased, false, naturalistic-historicist science that dominated the age.[50]

The period from about 1920 to 1950 became a sort of academic dark age for conservative evangelical scholarship. Biblical considerations had been ruled out of bounds in the sciences, so in the northern United States explicitly biblicist evangelical scholars virtually disappeared from those fields. Secularists were enjoying the heyday of positivism, and Jewish

[48] David N. Livingstone, "Evolution as Myth and Metaphor," *Christian Scholar's Review* XII (1983):11–25, expands the theme of the mythological function of evolution in modern culture.

[49] Wacker, *Augustus H. Strong and the Dilemma of Historical Consciousness,* provides a dramatic example of this struggle in a major biblicist evangelical leader of the era.

[50] George M. Marsden, *Fundamentalism and American Culture: The Shaping of Twentieth-Century Evangelicalism, 1870–1925* (New York: Oxford University Press, 1980), especially 212–21.

scholars, emerging as a major force in American intellectual life, understandably had strong interest in eliminating vestiges of "Christian civilization," which they associated with the lethal anti-Semitism of the era. Although traditionalist biblicist Christians held college or university posts here and there, explicitly evangelical scholarship was largely in exile.

The institutional manifestation of this academic exile was the accelerating growth of the Bible Institute movement. In place of the network of colleges dominated by evangelicals in the nineteenth century, fundamentalists during the first half of the twentieth century were building a network of Bible Institutes, practical training centers in which the curricula centered on the Bible alone. In these schools they learned from other disciplines only insofar as these might aid in evangelism and missions. Fundamentalists still talked about being scientific; but in fact they had become almost thoroughly isolated and alienated from the dominant American scientific culture. Warfare was now indeed the appropriate metaphor for understanding their relationship to the scientific culture.

The sequel: Warfield and Kuyper today

The story does not end there. If the era from 1920 to 1950 was a dark age for conservative evangelical scholarship, the period since 1950 has been a time of minor renaissance. After World War II, some of the heirs to fundamentalism consciously attempted to promote an intellectual comeback.

Most roots of the resurgence can be traced to the tradition of the Princeton theologians, the one group in the fundamentalist coalition who had insisted on rigorous scholarship. J. Gresham Machen, a New Testament scholar respected even by many of his opponents, had led the Princeton movement during the years of fundamentalist-modernist controversies. Eventually, in 1929, Machen had been forced out of Princeton Seminary and had founded his own theological school, Westminster Theological Seminary in Philadelphia. In the 1930s most of the few serious scholars who remained in fundamentalism had some connection with Machen. These inspired a new generation of fundamentalist intellectuals who began to emerge by the early 1940s. A notable number of these aspiring academics did graduate work at Harvard. Many of these scholars were associated with the National Association of Evangelicals (NAE), an agency founded in 1942, primarily to foster intrafundamentalist unity, to promote evangelism, and to try to regain a hearing in American life.

The leadership of the NAE realized that fundamentalists, or "evangelicals" as they now occasionally called themselves, needed to meet the intellectual challenges of the age if the movement was to have a lasting impact. The most substantial outgrowth of this interest was the founding in 1947 of Fuller Theological Seminary in Pasadena, California. Funded by radio evangelist Charles E. Fuller but run by intellectuals, the new seminary became a center for scholarly fundamentalists who sought to influence American intellectual life. Most of their scholarship, and that of their counterparts at a few other schools, was in Christian apologetics or biblical studies. In both areas they attempted to drop some pat fundamentalist formulas and to identify themselves with the broader tradition of Augustinianism and Protestant orthodoxy. Harold J. Ockenga, founder of the NAE and first president of Fuller, tagged the new emphases "the new evangelicalism." The "new evangelical" intellectuals by no means abandoned evangelism, however. To the contrary, they were among the most influential allies of Billy Graham.

Graham lent his influence to another major intellectual project, the founding in 1956 of *Christianity Today* to be an evangelical counterpart to the liberal *Christian Century*. Under the editorship of Carl F. H. Henry, formerly of Fuller Seminary, *Christianity Today* served during the next decade as the rallying point for "the new evangelicalism." In the meantime, both Graham and the "new evangelical" intellectuals broke with the fundamentalist right wing. Strict fundamentalists now began insisting on ecclesiastical separatism and on strict, fundamentalist doctrinal statements that allowed no room for deviation. The "new evangelicals" or "evangelicals," while retaining most of the essential beliefs of fundamentalism, softened its militancy and slightly broadened its doctrinal outlook in the name of a truer orthodoxy and better scholarship.[51]

These emphases accompanied important sociological changes in the movement. The evangelicals who were breaking away from strict fundamentalism were somewhat more affluent and, like many Americans after World War II, more interested in college education. Many of their young people were now attending colleges, and by the 1960s substantial numbers were emerging from graduate schools. Some gained university positions and others staffed a growing number of evangelical colleges. By the 1970s "evangelicalism" referred to a wide variety of denominational ori-

---

[51] George M. Marsden, *Reforming Fundamentalism: Fuller Seminary and the New Evangelicalism* (Grand Rapids, Mich.: W. B. Eerdmans, 1987), explores this phase of the movement.

entations. The Christian College Coalition, for instance, reflected this diversity. By the 1980s it was serving some seventy member colleges. Evangelical scholars from these schools and from universities not only participated in the professional societies of their disciplines but also founded their own parallel societies and journals. Of these, the Society of Christian Philosophers, within the American Philosophical Association, has been most impressive, including in its membership some of the leading figures in the field. The collective literary production of evangelical scholars has developed into a minor industry.[52]

If we look at this evangelical renaissance as an intellectual movement, one theme overshadows all others. In virtually every field the principal intraevangelical debate has been the same: Do evangelical Christian scholars pursue their science or discipline differently from the way secularists do? By now the literature on this subject is vast.[53] In almost every field today, evangelical scholars are divided basically into two camps, with some hybrids in between. These camps are the Warfieldians and the Kuyperians, although they do not necessarily identify themselves as such or follow their mentors precisely. The Warfieldians—those who believe in one science or rationality on which all humanity ought to agree—point to the breakdown of any promised consensus in secular twentieth-century thought and claim that evangelical Christians can still argue their way to victory, at least in individual cases. To do so, they must stay on common ground with the non-Christians as long as possible, pursuing the technical aspects of their disciplines with just the same methodologies as their secular contemporaries do, but adding to them Christian moral and theological principles that truly objective people will see are rationally necessary to complete the picture. The Kuyperians, in contrast, emphasize that any discipline is built on starting assumptions and that Christians' basic assumptions should have substantial effects on many of their theoretical conclusions in a discipline. Thus two conflicting world views may be scientific or rational if each is consistent with its starting premises. People who start with premises that exclude God as an explanatory force and people who start with belief in God as among their basic

---

[52] Mark Lau Branson, *The Reader's Guide to the Best Evangelical Books* (San Francisco: Harper & Row, 1982), provides a survey of some of this scholarship. *Evangelicalism and Modern America*, George Marsden, ed. (Grand Rapids, Mich.: W. B. Eerdmans, 1984), provides essays surveying the movement and discussions of evangelical scholarship in science, the arts, theology, biblical studies, and history.

[53] *Christian Scholar's Review*, founded in 1971 and supported by some thirty Christian colleges and universities, has provided one of the major forums of these discussions.

beliefs may be equally rational and may be able to work together on technical scientific enterprises; but on some key theoretical issues their best arguments will simply come to opposed conclusions.[54] There will be two or more sciences. Rationality alone will not be able to settle arguments among them.

At the moment the issues in the intraevangelical debate are far from resolved. The Warfieldians still look back, in effect, to the days of evangelical hegemony in the emerging American scientific culture and still look forward to a time when true science and true Christianity will be compellingly synthesized. The Kuyperians, on the other hand, are frankly more pluralistic in their view of the human scientific community. Their outlook is thus suited to those aspects of the evangelical psyche that see evangelicalism as a minority view in a pluralistic society. Much of the confusion in understanding what popular evangelicals and fundamentalists want vis-à-vis American society today stems from the lack of resolution among evangelicals (and fundamentalists) of these intellectual issues. Do they want to dominate the scientific culture or simply be recognized as one voice, as legitimately intellectual as the next?

Each side in this debate, however, is working at reconciling two of the central forces in the American cultural heritage, evangelicalism and modern science. These grew up together with the culture itself and hence will be much more difficult to keep separated than has commonly been assumed.

---

[54] See Plantinga and Wolterstorff, eds., *Faith and Rationality,* for philosophical discussion of these issues.

3

An enthusiasm for humanity: the social
emphasis in religion and its accommodation in
Protestant theology

WILLIAM McGUIRE KING

Can anything new and worthwhile be said about the religious thought of the social gospel? Some skepticism is certainly understandable, because critics frequently charge that the social gospel represented a superficial moralism and theological naiveté. Interest in the social gospel's pre-World War I relationship to American progressive social thought and reform has generally not been matched by an equivalent interest in the theological legacy of the social gospel.[1] With the possible exception of the writings of Walter Rauschenbusch, the religious thought of the social gospel has been treated as derivative and unremarkable.[2] But Rauschenbusch did not write in a theological vacuum; at the time of his death in 1918, the theological concerns of the social gospel leaders were just beginning to come to mature expression. It is possible that we do not fully understand the mind of the social gospel because we have not probed

[1] General accounts of the social gospel may be found in James Dombrowski, *The Early Days of Christian Socialism in America* (New York: Columbia University, 1936); C. Howard Hopkins, *The Rise of the Social Gospel in American Protestantism, 1865–1915* (New Haven: Yale University, 1940); Henry F. May, *Protestant Churches and Industrial America* (New York: Harper and Row, 1949); Robert Moats Miller, *American Protestantism and Social Issues, 1919–1939* (Chapel Hill: University of North Carolina, 1958); and Peter Frederick, *Knights of the Golden Rule* (Lexington: University of Kentucky, 1976). Two excellent anthologies are also readily available: Robert T. Handy, ed., *The Social Gospel in America* (New York: Oxford University, 1966) and Ronald C. White, Jr., and C. Howard Hopkins, *The Social Gospel* (Philadelphia: Temple University, 1976).

[2] On Rauschenbusch, see Dores R. Sharpe, *Walter Rauschenbusch* (New York: Macmillan, 1942); Vernon P. Bodein, *The Social Gospel of Walter Rauschenbusch* (New Haven: Yale University, 1944); Max L. Stackhouse, ed., *The Righteousness of the Kingdom* (Nashville: Abingdon Press, 1968); and Winthrop Hudson, ed., *Walter Rauschenbusch, Selected Writings* (New York: Paulist Press, 1984).

deeply into the theological perspective of those twentieth-century intellectuals who were strongly committed to social gospel principles.

I must admit my own bewilderment in sorting through the claims made about the social gospel and in trying to fit together the seemingly disparate pieces of the social gospel puzzle. Two convictions shape my own evaluation. The first is that the "neoorthodox" reaction against the social gospel, so prominent in the 1930s and 1940s, needs to be viewed with some caution. That was a period of intense self-criticism, and intellectual realignment and distinctions often got overstated and relationships ignored. The term *social gospel* itself became a vague catchword for the supposed sins of liberal Protestantism.[3] Therefore, a fresh examination of the sources is in order.

My second conviction is that current interpretations of the social gospel have arrived at a dead-end. Further progress awaits a fundamentally different interpretive paradigm. Explanations of the thought of the social gospel have almost universally stressed its derivative character, as if it were the last vestige of some phase of nineteenth-century thought: evangelical postmillennialism, Bushnellian liberalism, social romanticism, or political populism. In each of these cases, the underlying assumption is that modern Protestant thought really began with the demise of the social gospel and the advent of the Niebuhrian era.

Is this assumption correct? Did the social gospel represent the "end of an era," or was it a new phase of theological reflection? The social gospel theologians certainly viewed their own work as the beginning of a new age of theological reconstruction and religious reorientation. They may have been wrong; but any attempt to explain the social gospel in terms of its precedents, and not in terms of the unprecedented, does violence to the self-understanding of the social gospelers themselves. In fact, on this point, I am convinced that the social gospel should be taken at its word, that a dynamic paradigm should replace the genetic one. My interest, of course, is not in resurrecting a movement but in placing it in a more appropriate historical framework. That framework is the twentieth century itself, and my thesis is that the direction of modern religious thought in the United States was decisively shaped by the social gospel. John Bennett, disciple and critic of the social gospel, made a telling remark when

---

[3] In an article on "The Social Gospel and After," Ralph Read described the confusion within the ranks of the social gospel movement in the 1930s: "Some desert to the right and some to the left, while still others only appear to desert." *World Tomorrow* (January 4, 1934): 15.

he noted that "very often the critics of the social gospel owe to it a great debt."[4]

Looking at the social gospel as an incubator of new emphases, rather than as a termination of old ones, forces one to take seriously its religious and theological dimensions. Often the social gospel is treated as merely a social service movement, buttressed by a vague humanistic philosophy. Curiously enough, one of the earliest books about the social gospel, written by a foreign observer with extensive ecumenical ties to the American social gospel community, presents a different picture. Visser 'T Hooft, in a critical study of the social gospel, claimed that the social gospel is "something distinctly new" and has come "to mean something more specific than merely the application of Christian ideals to society and its problems."[5] The social gospel's "modification of theology," he argued, is its most important contribution. "Those whose views we are to consider are not merely trying to apply the old theology or the old ethics to the social order; they are also constantly re-considering their theoretical position on the basis of the social experience that they gather in doing so."[6] And he was right; what set the social gospel apart was the way that its understanding of the social dimension of human experience was used to rethink the categories of Christian theology. Writing in 1928, Visser 'T Hooft concluded that the social gospel perspective had found "its way into all realms of the intellectual and spiritual life of American Christianity."[7]

H. Richard Niebuhr, another influential critic, accepted the genuine religious and theological integrity of the social gospel (although not always consistently). In a paper on the social gospel Niebuhr wrote:

It is fallacious, I believe, to call the social gospel humanistic; it carried with it too great a heritage of faith in God; it reinterpreted the democratic, humanistic ideas of modernism too much in the light of the New Testament, to allow for such a reduction. . . . God was always the religious object; the social gospel was as dependent on the religio-empirical theology as on teleological ethics.[8]

The social gospel, said Richard Niebuhr, was dependent on a "religio-empirical theology" and a distinctive biblical hermeneutic; and he, too, was right. Curiously enough, Niebuhr even argued that the essential ele-

[4] "The Social Gospel Today," in White and Hopkins, *The Social Gospel*, 285.
[5] 'T Hooft, *The Background of the Social Gospel in America* (Haarlem: H. D. Tjeenk Willink & Zoon, 1928), 18.
[6] Ibid., 16.
[7] Ibid., 31.
[8] Richard Niebuhr, "The Kingdom of God and Eschatology (Social Gospel and Barthianism)," undated manuscript, 2, Niebuhr papers, Yale Divinity School.

ments of the social gospel would survive the changing of the theological guards in the 1930s and survive with renewed vigor. The imperative note of the social gospel, he argued in 1931, would remain the starting point for future theology. The social gospel's understanding of "the radical ethics of Jesus" and its commitment "to man as a social being and to society as a sphere of sin and salvation," he argued, "must form an integral part of any theological system which grows out of the contemporary reading and interpretation of the Christian revelation." Future theology must include the social gospel "in its premises" or it will "fail to relate theology vitally to one of the sources of religious life in the present."[9]

Thus the theological orientation of the social gospel cannot be understood apart from the social gospel's perspective on religious experience. The latter formed the basis of the former. "I claim," said Walter Rauschenbusch, "that social Christianity is by all tokens the great highway by which this present generation can come to God."[10] Charles Clayton Morrison insisted that "the social gospel is primary to the personal gospel," not an alternative.[11] Eugene Lyman argued that at the heart of the social gospel's understanding of Christianity is a religious experience that is "recuperating, healing, reconciling, unifying, liberating in its effect upon the person who has it; and it means also that such experience is kindling and elevating, bringing enthusiasm in the pursuit of the good, heightening and sustaining moral energy."[12] The ebullience of such a sentiment suggests that the social gospel was not prescribing a generic religiosity or a secular placebo. All the adherents of the social gospel spoke of Christianity in pentecostal terms as an experience of "power"—and none more eloquently than Harry Emerson Fosdick, whose poem "God of Grace and God of Glory" still captures the brooding, soaring spirit of social gospel piety.

Indeed the popularity of preachers like Fosdick and Ernest Fremont Tittle and of journals like *Christian Century* and *World Tomorrow* testifies to the strength of the social impulse. Books in the social gospel tradition continued to appear after 1932: John Bennett's *Social Salvation* (1935),[13] Douglas Clyde Macintosh's *Social Religion* (1939),[14] Walter

---

[9] "The Social Gospel and the Liberal Theology," *Keryx* 22 (May 1931):13.
[10] Rauschenbusch, *Christianizing the Social Order* (New York: Macmillan, 1912), 118.
[11] Quoted in Kirby Page, *Living Triumphantly* (New York: Farrar & Rinehart, 1934), 89.
[12] Lyman, "Can Religious Intuition Give Knowledge of Reality?" in *Religious Realism*, edited by Douglas Clyde Macintosh (New York: Macmillan, 1931), 260.
[13] Bennett, *Social Salvation* (New York: Charles Scribner's Sons, 1935), cf. 90–95.
[14] Macintosh, *Social Religion* (New York: Charles Scribner's Sons, 1939).

Marshall Horton's *Can Christianity Save Civilization?* (1940),[15] F. Ernest Johnson's *The Social Gospel Re-examined* (1940),[16] and Henry Sloane Coffin's *God Confronts Man in History* (1947).[17] Moreover, through the work of Bennett, G. Bromley Oxnam, H. P. Van Dusen, and others, the social gospel had a significant effect on the formation of the social thought of the World Council of Churches.[18] And finally, who could miss the social gospel overtones of Martin Luther King, Jr.'s *Strength to Love?*[19]

But if there was a specific "direction" to the religious and theological orientation of the social gospel, what was it? In what ways was it related to the intellectual concerns of other progressive intellectuals? And how did these concerns translate into specific social and political commitments? It is precisely at these points that previous descriptions of the social gospel have not entirely disclosed what the movement was all about. The concepts of progress, immanence, or even "Kingdom of God" do not, I believe, represent the fundamental religious mythos of the social gospel, important as they are. Few people are stirred by a call to worship at the altar of progress, and no one in the mature social gospel movement ever issued that kind of altar call.

In fact, one of the curious features of the social gospel is the central importance accorded to the concept "person." It may well be that references to "personality" and the "personal" occur as frequently as references to any other set of concepts. If that is true, it is certainly an unexpected and puzzling fact. And yet I believe that those references will help us unlock the mystery of the social gospel. They are not merely inadvertent references.

The social gospel view of the self

The fundamental claim of the social gospel was that the way to a profound personal experience of God in the modern world follows the highway of "social religion," that religious self-realization manifests itself as a religious enthusiasm for humanity. We first discern God, wrote Wash-

---

[15] Horton, *Can Christianity Save Civilization?* (New York: Harper & Brothers, 1940), cf. 250–53.
[16] Johnson, *The Social Gospel Re-examined* (New York: Harper & Brothers, 1940).
[17] Coffin, *God Confronts Man in History* (New York: Charles Scribner's Sons, 1947), cf. 125–51.
[18] See Paul Bock, *In Search of a Responsible World Society: The Social Teachings of the World Council of Churches* (Philadelphia: Westminster, 1974).
[19] King, *Strength to Love* (New York: Harper and Row, 1963).

ington Gladden, "in the common life of man."[20] In a sense, therefore, practical social reforms were really only penultimate goals in the social gospel. They were the necessary means to a larger end: the vision of God and the vision of the shared life of humanity in God. "The question is often raised in religion," noted Harris Franklin Rall, "is the final end self-realization or service? Or were the fathers right when they said it was to glorify God? But these ends are not opposed or exclusive. On the contrary, each involves the other."[21] Early in his career, the religious psychologist and social gospel theoretician George Coe reminded young Christians that the experience of God "is not self-suppression, but self-realization. Its advice is to be completely human, to be completely ourselves, but to remember that this is possible only through participation in the life of our fellows."[22]

But what kind of language was this? It was not nineteenth-century individualism, with its stress on character development through imitation and habit.[23] That is why the words *personal* and *individual* were often distinguished in the vocabulary of the social gospel. The social gospel's concern for "enriching personality," wrote F. Ernest Johnson, "is quite true if its meaning is not vitiated by an identification of the two concepts, individual and person, for the two are in an important sense opposed." Individuality "is a property of anything that has separate existence, whereas personality is a spiritual quality. Personalization is a socializing process, an aspect of community." All talk of personality, therefore, is meaningless unless "we have brought into the picture the ongoing communal life in which the individual finds his meaning."[24]

Whereas previous generations of theologians had been preoccupied with concepts of nature, substance, and character, the social gospel theologians were focusing their attention on the historicity and temporality of selfhood. This "modern" orientation was noticed by Visser 'T Hooft, who suggested that one of the main features of the social gospel was that "it takes the idea of *time* seriously" and that it has worked out the meaning of temporality for understanding God and the Christian life.[25] Essen-

---

[20] Gladden, *Where Does the Sky Begin?* (Boston: Houghton, Mifflin, 1904), 14.
[21] Rall, *A Working Faith* (New York: Abingdon, 1914), 173.
[22] Coe, *Religion of a Mature Mind* (Chicago: Fleming H. Revell, 1902), 172.
[23] See D. H. Meyer, *The Instructed Conscience* (Philadelphia: University of Pennsylvania, 1972).
[24] Johnson, *The Social Gospel Re-examined*, 143.
[25] Visser 'T Hooft, *The Background of the Social Gospel in America*, 43.

tially the same point was made in a 1951 dissertation on the social gospel by Harold Allen Durfee.[26] All experience and knowledge had a temporal character, and it was this sweeping awareness that made the social gospel part of the cultural transition into modernity. "It is no surprise," writes theologian Langdon Gilkey, "that modern philosophy—of almost all sorts, naturalistic, idealistic, existential—has emphasized process, change, and the temporality of being. . . . This has been the modern experience of whatever being they knew."[27] Similarly, Peter Berger has recently noted that the "least misleading" generalization that one can make about the process of modernization is that it is "a transformation in the experience of time."[28]

This suggestion is not particularly new. The notion of temporality within the social gospel has received scholarly attention, especially in terms of the social gospel's philosophy of history, or "progress."[29] My suggestion, however, is that there was a much more primary religious concern in the theological orientation of the social gospel than the question of progress. It was a concern about the structure of concrete personal experience and about the emergence and preservation of meaning within the self. "The task of the present," wrote George Coe, "is to restore the unity of the living experience."[30] But this unity must be revealed from within the processes of living and willing, not superimposed on those processes. "In this experience of *ownness*," claimed Coe, "the past, the present, and the future are bound together and standards of value are attached thereto." The temporality of the self could not be clearer. "One's self enters into the flow of events," wrote Coe; therefore "personality is not a static thing that is first here and then, later, noticed. It has its start and its continuing existence in acts that have the quality of self-awareness."[31] The fundamental thing about "selves," observed Eugene Lyman, a colleague of Coe's at Union Theological Seminary, "is that they can bring both the past and the future to bear upon the present." The self emerges and grows through creative, purposive interaction with the world around it. That is why,

[26] Durfee, "The Theologies of the American Social Gospel" (Ph.D. dissertation, Columbia University, 1951), 193–94.
[27] Gilkey, *Society and the Sacred* (New York: Crossroad, 1981), 94.
[28] Berger, *Facing Up to Modernity* (New York: Basic Books, 1977), 73.
[29] An excellent overall discussion is Langdon Gilkey, *Reaping the Whirlwind: A Christian Interpretation of History* (New York: Seabury, 1976), cf. 209–38.
[30] Coe, "Can Religion Be Taught?" Inaugural Address, Union Theological Seminary, November 16, 1909, 16.
[31] Coe, *What Is Christian Education?* (New York: Charles Scribner's Sons, 1930), 70.

Lyman noted, "time is the necessary form of all inner, psychic life." Time "is the indispensable form of moral living, with the discovery of ideals and its purposeful activity for their realization."[32]

What characterizes human experience is not an abstract set of feelings or a permanent "character profile" that one builds for oneself. Human experience is a field in which the past structures the present, while future possibilities shape the ability of the self to respond creatively and purposefully in the present. Discovering that it is environed in a specific sociotemporal matrix, the self discovers that it is not self-sufficient. Personal identity, wrote Coe, "lies not in something that is done and finished." Personal identity "is a flowing thing, like time itself." The self discovers its reality in its social activity. "Personality is marked," explained Coe, "not by scattering but by gathering. It binds together its own past and future; it holds to meanings in the flux of events; by redirecting its experience it creates meanings where otherwise none would have been."[33]

The social question, for the social gospel theologians, derived its urgency from the problematic of personal existence—the task of integrating the self. Because the self is not a substance but a creative center of meaning, its emergence and characteristics depend on its interaction with other selves and its participation in the shared task of fashioning a social environment that embodies personal values. A self "is a subject of experience, an active purposive experiencer," wrote Eugene Lyman; it is characterized by an ability "to bring to bear upon the present that which exists no longer (the past) and that which does not yet exist (the future) and to act as a whole; it is therefore a non-mechanical originative whole." Through social action, the self becomes "aware of itself in relation to other similar wholes and to its general environment."[34] Only through such creative transcendence of the past does personal self-awareness become possible. And it is society that mediates the forms and opportunities for such transcendence. "All too slowly does the truth lay hold upon the church," remarked Harry Emerson Fosdick, "that our very personalities themselves are social products, that we are born out of society and live in it and are molded by it, that without society we should not be human at all, and that the influences which play upon our lives, whether redeeming or degrading, are socially mediated."[35] A "person," said Harris Franklin

[32] Lyman, *The Meaning and Truth of Religion* (New York: Charles Scribner's Sons, 1933), 359, 374.
[33] Coe, *What Is Christian Education?*, 74.
[34] Lyman, *Meaning and Truth*, 363.
[35] Fosdick, *Christianity and Progress* (New York: Fleming H. Revell, 1922), 100–101.

Rall, "is a conscious center of life, but one whose actual living in terms of what he does and feels and thinks, is mainly a life shared with others. No individual could ever reach a human, personal life except in the social matrix."[36]

This argument was not deterministic or crudely environmentalist. On the contrary, freedom and contingency everywhere mark the self. That is why personal life is not fixed or finished, and that is why social action is a genuine act of transcendence. Such self-transcendence, remarked Harris Franklin Rall, comes "by way of action." The knowledge of personal selves is always concrete, never abstract. Knowledge of self, of other selves, and of God comes through commitment. "There is no knowledge without action," argued Rall and his fellow social gospel colleagues; for "no one can really know who remains simply an onlooker." Indeed, "unless we enter into life, unless we give ourselves in interest and action, we cannot know."[37]

Religion is therefore an attempt to explore the sociotemporal concreteness of human experience. "No wall of partition separates religious values from other values, religious experience from other experience," insisted George Coe. "Human consciousness as such is religious consciousness." All genuine religion "appears as a phase of the whole struggle for existence. . . . Religion—the essence of it—is to be looked for in the dust and noise, the sweat and the blood, or, as the case may be, the music and the laughter of our actual living."[38] If spiritual life is not to become an "unreality" for modern man, wrote Henry Churchill King, it must be looked for "not as something apart from life, but in the very midst of it, knit up with the call and with sex, with all human relations and employments and tendencies and strivings." Does not a spiritual life pressed into "a water-tight compartment," he asked, "proclaim its own impotence and falsity?"[39] Yes, answered George Coe, for "religion is continuous with whatever makes human life human."[40]

The social gospel and secular social theorists

For the social gospel, therefore, social criticism and social action had a double religious goal: to enable others to discover the personal fulfill-

---

[36] Rall, *A Faith for Today* (New York: Abingdon, 1936), 265–66.
[37] Ibid., 79.
[38] Coe, "Can Religion Be Taught?" 23–25.
[39] King, *The Seeming Unreality of the Spiritual Life* (New York: Macmillan, 1908), 27–29.
[40] Coe, "Can Religion Be Taught?" 25.

ment of authentic human relationships and to enable oneself to find a personal center of meaning. Both goals were intertwined in the minds of the social gospel theologians. "To change social environments which oppress and dwarf and defile the lives of men," remarked Harry Emerson Fosdick, "is one way of giving the transforming Spirit a fair chance to reach and redeem them."[41] Such reform would be religiously sterile, however, if it lacked that transforming Spirit, ethical creativity, and religious awareness of the ultimacy of interpersonal values. "To develop the ethical aspect of religion," commented Harry Ward, "is not to reduce it to a system of ethics or to a set of ethical principles." Religion treats the ethical development of the self "as a continuous process of experience, by viewing it as the continued unfolding of the possibilities of human living, by using it as the key to the solution of the riddle of the universe, following it as the path that leads from man to God and from God to man."[42] If religion is to help modern persons to live creatively, it "must perceive and aid the increasingly organic relationship between the individual and society, must be aware of the social nature of the self, and all of its teaching and program must root in this knowledge."[43]

Such convictions were quite compatible with the views of many other progressive reformers in the early twentieth century. Jane Addams, for example, in referring to the "subjective necessity" for social settlement work, spoke in distinctly religious terms about the "great desire to share the race life," which characterized the aspirations of her generation. This "is not philanthropy nor benevolence," she claimed, but "the sense of humanity." She spoke of this commitment as "a Holy Communion" by which a reformer "fecundates all his faculties." The feeling is fundamentally Christian, she claimed, discovering "in love a cosmic force" and experiencing "the joy of finding the Christ which lieth in each man, but which no man can unfold save in fellowship." She said she felt "something primordial about these motives." They are a "spiritual force," a "very religious fervor," existing wherever life has "new meaning to unfold, new action to propose."[44]

Robert Crunden has recently argued that "religion provided the central motivating force" in the formative years of many progressive reformers. In contrast to historical arguments that interpret progressivism as a

[41] Fosdick, *Christianity and Progress*, 100.
[42] Ward, *Which Way Religion?* (New York: Macmillan, 1931), 111.
[43] Ibid., 79.
[44] "The Subjective Necessity for Social Settlements," in *The Social Thought of Jane Addams*, edited by Christopher Lasch (Indianapolis: Bobbs-Merrill, 1965), 35, 41–42.

"secularization" of American religious aspirations,[45] Crunden argues that it is "the subsequent secularization of modern culture" itself that has largely "obscured the importance of religion in forming the minds" of the progressive generation.[46]

These religious connections put a somewhat new perspective on the relationship between the Protestant social reform community and the "secular" progressive movement. The social gospel advocates were eager to build bridges between the religious and secular social agencies of the progressive period.[47] Similar bridges were built in the intellectual realm, and many social gospel intellectuals were quick to ally themselves at the beginning of this century with the work of social theorists like Richard Ely, Simon Patten, Edward A. Ross, and John Dewey.[48]

It would be too facile, however, to conclude that the social gospel was merely capitulating to the secular spirit of the times. Although the interests of the social gospel and other progressive forces often coincided, allowing for cooperation and coalition activity, on a more fundamental level of conviction, the social gospel remained resistant to a purely "social engineering" approach to social issues. There certainly were some social engineers among the social gospelers, like Charles Ellwood, the "Christian sociologist" at the University of Missouri; but they were not part of the mainstream. "Social efficiency," wrote Harry Ward in 1919, "involves more than social engineering. It depends also upon a social philosophy, a social ethics, and a social religion."[49] The testimony of Ward, chairman of the American Civil Liberties Union in the 1920s and professor of Christian ethics at Union Theological Seminary, is noteworthy because he was one of the most radical and secularly oriented of the social gospel leaders. Yet even for Ward, the fundamental issue was the religious value of each individual person:

It does not lie within our present purpose to define personality, but simply to point out that the new [social] order must recognize and attempt to realize its supreme worth and value. It must be said, however, that personality is increasingly defined in social terms, its values are discovered and realized in fellowship.[50]

---

[45] For example, Jean Quandt, "Religion and Social Thought: The Secularization of Post-millennialism," *American Quarterly* 25 (October 1973):390–409.

[46] Crunden, *Ministers of Reform* (New York: Basic Books, 1982), 40.

[47] May, "The Social Gospel and American Progressivism" in his *Protestant Churches and Industrial America*, pp. 204–34.

[48] In addition to Dombrowski, Hopkins, and Handy, cited in note 1 above, see Sidney Fine, *Laissez Faire and the General-Welfare State* (Ann Arbor: University of Michigan, 1956).

[49] Ward, *The New Social Order* (New York: Macmillan, 1919), 123.

[50] Ibid., 137.

In the area of political reform, the social gospel advocates shared many of the goals of other progressive reformers. Yet even in this area, the characteristic emphasis of the social gospel was on the enrichment of human personality. High priority was given in social gospel statements to the creation of political and economic structures that promoted "co-operation," that is, that promoted broad participation in decision making and sharply restricted any sort of arbitrary power, especially economic power.[51]

"The development of democracy," wrote Ward, "is a process of the continued emancipation and expansion of personality. On the one hand it enlarges personality by continually extending the control of all individuals over the functions of the state, on the other hand it progressively emancipates personality by the continued overthrow of repressive institutions."[52]

Most social gospel advocates viewed property in frankly instrumentalist terms, not as a "natural right" but as a social instrument to be used only for the development of the human dignity of all members of society—especially the least fortunate. "The increase of personality becomes the supreme object of social organization while property falls into its proper place as the base upon which man stands to derive from it the nourishment for his spiritual development."[53] In fact, Ward and many other social gospel proponents in the 1920s accepted a distinction between property for use (for personal needs) and property for power (capitalism), advocating the socialization of the latter.[54] During the 1920s, many social gospel leaders were committed to the principle of economic planning in order to enlarge the "democratic" control of economic institutions. Many supported Norman Thomas in the 1930s, and most favored an economic system that would be an "experimental" mixture of private and public enterprises, with emphasis on the latter.[55]

Finally, by 1920 the social gospel reformers had become disillusioned with nationalism and urgently sought to broaden the conception of social relations to embrace an inclusive international community. "It is only as we break through first the natural and then the artificial barrier of na-

[51] Social statements of the churches before 1930 may be found in *The Social Work of the Churches,* edited by F. Ernest Johnson (New York: Federal Council of Churches, 1930). See also Miller.
[52] Ward, *The New Social Order,* 142–43.
[53] Ibid., 153.
[54] "Therefore the distinction between property for power and property for use does give us a workable basis for the removal of the intolerable inequalities of our present property system." Harry F. Ward, *Our Economic Morality* (New York: Macmillan, 1929), 210.
[55] See Miller, *American Protestantism and Social Issues.*

tionality, class, and race," wrote Ward in 1919, "that we really come to the largest expression of our own personality."[56] Or as Eugene Lyman explained in 1933, social religion "brings to the social struggle *the standard* of the intrinsic and infinite worth of the human personality, which when translated into social terms means that our ultimate standard must be a community of creative personalities which shall be world-wide." Lyman added that "this standard is a searching principle of criticism with respect to our existing institutions. It forbids that property should be put above personality, whether in law, in economic policy, or in a particular situation of social strain." This standard also means that Christians must "persistently seek the abolition of war, whether by refusal to participate in it or support it, or by resisting military training and service, or by promoting organization for peace."[57] Liberal Protestant support for pacifism between the two world wars, as well as its strong advocacy of international cooperation, economic justice, missionary service, and ecumenical advance can all be traced to this growing internationalistic perspective.[58]

Social gospel advocates felt at home in many progressive causes because their view of the self and society was not unlike that articulated in progressive social theories. Progressives in general viewed "society as the inevitable theater in which men's problems and aspirations must be resolved."[59] For many progressives, individuals were defined in terms of their social relationships. According to R. Jackson Wilson, progressives like Charles Peirce, James Mark Baldwin, G. Stanley Hall, Herbert Croly, Josiah Royce, and John Dewey "began with the primary assumption that a man is defined by his relations with other men and that whatever a man can or should become depends on his membership in a functioning community."[60] Some social scientists, such as Richard Ely, Simon Patten, G. Stanley Hall, Charles Cooley, and Edward A. Ross even advocated the maintenance of "social religion" as an essential function in society.[61]

---

[56] Ward, *The New Social Order*, 153.

[57] Lyman, *Meaning and Truth*, 443, 451.

[58] In addition to Miller, *American Protestantism and Social Issues*, see Charles Chatfield, *For Peace and Justice, Pacifism in America, 1914–1941* (Knoxville: University of Tennessee, 1971), and also J. Neal Hughley, *Trends in Protestant Social Idealism* (New York: King's Crown, 1948).

[59] R. Jackson Wilson, *In Quest of Community: Social Philosophy in the United States, 1860–1920* (New York: Oxford University, 1968), 173.

[60] Ibid., 67.

[61] According to Wilson, "Ross conceived his mission as something like that of a minister preaching the progressive social gospel. 'Most of all,' he wrote to Ely of *Social Control*, 'preachers will get the book. It throws floods of light on what they are dealing with, viz.,

However, despite an apparent congruence between these views and social gospel views, the social gospel proponents manifested very little actual interest in the work of these social scientists. What is more striking than occasional references and bibliographical citations is the almost total absence in twentieth-century social gospel writings of any serious engagement with sociological or social scientific thought. The reason for that indifference is really not so hard to discover. The focus of social gospel concerns was quite different. The secular social psychologists were interested in religion primarily as a "socializing" force, a force contributing to "social control" and "social equilibrium." According to this conception, the function of the churches in society would be to restrain individualistic impulses and to teach individuals to merge their interests with the interests of society at large. "Morality," explained James Mark Baldwin, "has arisen because it is socially useful. . . . The preservation of a group depends on the character of its inner organization. This requires . . . the subordination and regulation of the individuals."[62] Under the Christian law "of service and self-sacrifice," wrote G. Stanley Hall, "the race, not the self, must become supreme. . . . The old consciousness is sloughed off, and the soul enters, more or less transformed, its mature, imago stage, to live for the race and not for self."[63] The "feature common to all religions," wrote Harvard sociologist Thomas Nixon Carver, is to provide "an ultrarational sanction for the sacrifice of the interests of the individual to those of the social organism."[64]

The social gospel advocates, in contrast, resisted the idea that societies per se, rather than the persons living in a social matrix, are the primary objects of social concern. This was a fine line, but a crucial one if the social gospel was not to be reduced to a program of social reform or social engineering. The religious dimension of *personal* experience and its genuinely creative interaction with its environment had to be preserved. "It becomes increasingly clear," wrote Ward, "that the meaning and end of individual life and of social living is reciprocal and inter-dependent; that each feeds upon, enlarges and completes the other." Therefore, he

the regeneration of men.' " Ibid., 107, note 37. Charles H. Cooley wrote of society's need "of religion in the form of 'social salvation.' " *Social Organization* (New York: Charles Scribner's Sons, 1909), 380. See also Richard Ely, *Social Aspects of Christianity* (New York: T. Y. Crowell, 1889); Simon Patten, *The Social Basis of Religion* (New York: Macmillan, 1911); and Edward A. Ross, *Social Control* (New York: Macmillan, 1901).
[62] Quoted in Wilson, *In Quest of Community*, 69.
[63] Quoted in ibid., 133.
[64] Carver, *Sociology and Social Progress* (Boston: Ginn and Company, 1905), 496.

concluded, "the new order must seek for its chosen end and goal the development of personality."[65] The liberation of concrete individuals was the point of social reform, as far as the social gospel was concerned. Ward and other social gospel leaders realized that progressive social theory could be used for reactionary purposes. There is "a not inconsiderable section of psychology in the universities," he warned, "creating a social environment that inhibits and destroys personality. Without a consciousness of its part in the development of an ethical religion it will make individuals more efficient in maintaining the acquisitive society instead of more effective in transforming it."[66] However much society might need "the method of trial and error at the hands of experts in social engineering," observed Francis McConnell, it needs Christianity to "keep alive . . . the spirit of prophetic radicalism."[67]

This difference in perspective became increasingly clear after World War I, as the relationship between the social gospel and the "secular" social sciences became strained. On the one hand, the desire for professionalism and objectivity in the social sciences broke some of the spirit of collegiality that had existed earlier. On the other hand, social gospel writers became uneasy with the secular drift of social theory.

Harry Elmer Barnes in *The Twilight of Christianity* bluntly expressed the reaction of the "hard" scientist and reformer to the sentimentalism of the religious reformers. "When the writer has listened to preachers like Sherwood Eddy, Harry Ward, and Francis J. McConnell denouncing our current social injustices," Barnes confessed, "he has felt that in such trends as these are to be discerned praiseworthy symptoms which the natural and social scientist alike may well approve and support."[68] But why, he wondered in bewilderment, must they keep bringing in Jesus and Christianity? Harry Ward himself, he insisted, "or Mr. [Kirby] Page himself is an infinitely better informed and more trustworthy guide to religious reconstruction than Jesus and all the Old Testament prophets combined." So far as Barnes could tell, "nothing better could happen to American religion than for progressive young divines in Methodism to forget about Jesus . . . and seek their inspiration in the life and doctrines of Bishop McConnell."[69]

[65] Ward, *The New Social Order*, 137.
[66] Ward, *Which Way Religion?*, 35.
[67] McConnell, *Christian Principles and Industrial Reconstruction* (New York: Association Press, 1919), 18.
[68] Barnes, *The Twilight of Christianity* (New York: Vanguard, 1929), vii.
[69] Ibid., 384.

Even the most liberal members of the social gospel movement responded to this secular trend in social thought by insisting on the importance of a theological understanding of the human situation. In a 1923
article that appeared in the *Journal of Religion,* Shailer Mathews attacked those who "would substitute sociology and psychology for religion." He called on the church and the social gospel clergy to resist "this
pursuit of morals without God, and utopias without repentance," lest
"religion itself is to be [only] a sociology and an ethic."[70]

Nothing demonstrates this widening division more than the general
indifference of the social gospel proponents to the writings of Charles
Ellwood in the 1920s. In a series of books, Ellwood called on the church
to join hands with social science and *"to act as an agency of social control."* Religion, said Ellwood, is primarily a product of group life and "is
essentially a social rather than an individual matter." *"It thus harmo-
nizes man, on the side of will and emotion, with his world."*[71] In a 1922
review of Ellwood's work, Harry Ward derided Ellwood's view of religion. Can this "appeal to reason," asked Ward, really "secure the avoid-
ance of evil?" He warned that "those who put their trust in [reason's]
capacity to keep collective humanity out of the broad road that leads to
destruction have yet to reckon with the nature of the crowd, with the
vast irrationality of life." All that sociology can give us without some
"deeper" religious conviction, Ward continued, is a "faith that is already
within us" instead of a faith that can change the world. Ellwood's religion "remains static, or becomes reactionary."[72] What sociology has difficulty speaking about is sin; as Eugene Lyman observed, "The evils of
society are too deeply seated in human nature and social institutions to
be overcome except as also all the resources of religion for personal and
social redemption be drawn upon."[73]

Ward's friend George Coe attacked more directly the methods and
assumptions of some of his colleagues in the social sciences, especially
their pretensions to objectivity in the study of religion and human experience. In a 1926 article on "What Constitutes a Scientific Interpretation

[70] Mathews, "What May the Social Worker Expect of the Church?" *Journal of Religion* 3
(November 1923):638.
[71] Ellwood, *The Reconstruction of Religion* (New York: Macmillan, 1922), 41–42. See also
Ellwood, *Christianity and Social Science* (New York: Macmillan, 1923) and *Man's Social
Destiny in the Light of Science* (Nashville: Cokesbury, 1929). Ellwood later taught at
Duke University.
[72] Ward, "Social Science and Religion," *Journal of Religion* 2 (September 1922):481, 483,
488.
[73] Lyman, *Meaning and Truth,* 349.

of Religion?" Coe charged that "the light of science does not seem to conduct us into ever more light, but at last into obscurity." Coe did not mean that the religious life cannot be studied by a social scientist; that task was precisely what Coe had made a career out of doing. What he questioned were the positivistic, secularistic assumptions that failed to come to terms with the full reality of human experience. The issue, Coe insisted, was whether "the method of science requires us to abstract from the concrete wholeness of experience." The "concrete wholeness of experience," after all, is where religion is located. "We should distrust any interpretation of religion that allows for no open doors in experience and for no windows in itself." Social psychology, he asserted, has substituted the abstract socialized self for the "uniquely individual experience that is yet a socially shared experience." The primary question in Coe's mind was what sort of values and meanings are demanded by that experience, "whether our values are merely incidental in our universe or whether they are fundamental." But what scientist can take this last step, for it would require "neither observation nor analysis, but a position-taking which might very well be also an entering-in."[74]

The theological core of the social gospel

This dialogue with progressive social thought indicates that, rather than being religiously moribund, the Protestant social gospel rested on an irreducible religious core. What was the religious filter at work in social gospel thinking? Over and over again social gospel writers said that the key religious question was whether there is anything in human experience that *supports* the values and purposes of socially centered selves. This was not a social question but an ontological and theological one. Under a purely mechanistic, or deterministic, view of the universe, wrote Eugene Lyman, "the empirical world remains intrinsically aimless."[75] When "purpose disappears from the universe," he wrote in 1910, "we are destined to be haunted by the spectre of the aimlessness of the world."[76] This is a question of "alienation from what is meaningful in one's world—whether through complete moral and intellectual frustration . . . or through being reduced to futility and utterly broken by fate." Such existential

[74] Coe, "What Constitutes a Scientific Interpretation of Religion?" *Journal of Religion* 6 (May 1926):226–27, 232–33, 235.
[75] Lyman, *Theology and Human Problems* (New York: Charles Scribner's Sons, 1910), 120.
[76] Ibid., 117.

"estrangement in its tendency . . . toward sheer desolateness or numbness of spirit is the antithesis of religion."[77]

How to prevent numbness of human spirit was the vital religious question. Society itself, of course, could be reshaped to help support the deeper, cooperatively oriented values of the self. And much of the practical social program of the churches was geared to fostering just such structures.

But social programs could not be ends in themselves, for they could not in themselves answer the more fundamental personal question: the *reality* and permanence of the social values that the self discovered. The fundamental religious question, according to social gospel writers, is whether the total "cosmic environment" in which personality and society emerge ultimately supports and conserves human good. The basic issue was the reality of God and whether one can speak of a divine will that supports the struggle of humanity to liberate the human spirit. "We shall not attempt to dip out the ocean with a cup," remarked Henry Churchill King in a criticism of secular social service, "and we shall not enter on a boundless social task in which there is no hope of accomplishing any permanent and large result."[78] "The problem of social living," noted Coe, "does itself lead on to the question of a possible unity or reconciliation between the natural and the social."[79] We need to know that we work "with the grain of the world," observed John Bennett.[80] Indeed, the issue, according to Harris Rall, is whether the world itself is as "personal" as we are:

Our social program to-day is putting the personal first. We have put down human slavery and political autocracy; now we are putting down industrial autocracy. The personal is supreme to-day: men and women and children. How can we hold such a program for society if it does not rest upon a corresponding faith? And that is this: the ultimate reality of this world is personal.[81]

Only a faith like that, wrote Coe, can support the deepest religious convictions of our personal selves: that "life as a whole is enterprise within a universe that contains nothing eternally finished and final, but rather invites us to be part creators of its flowing destiny."[82]

The search of the social gospel, in other words, was not a search for a utopian community to replace a lost idyllic past. It was a genuinely reli-

[77] Lyman, *Meaning and Truth*, 74–75.
[78] King, *Seeming Unreality*, 185.
[79] Coe, *The Psychology of Religion* (Chicago: University of Chicago Press, 1916), 214.
[80] Bennett, *Social Salvation*, 215.
[81] Rall, *A Working Faith*, 57.
[82] Coe, *Education in Religion and Morals* (Chicago: Fleming H. Revell, 1904), 35.

gious search, a search for meaning and value within the structures of modern experience that support human aspirations in the midst of the tension between freedom and destiny. "Religion has a field of experience," said Lyman; "this field is our experience of the underlying relations between reality and value."[83] In trying to come to terms with the nature of that field of experience, the social gospel writers turned to history rather than the social sciences. "Only as we heed the wisdom of the past," warned Coe, the psychologist, "can we escape a narrow individualism or a shallow up-to-dateness."[84] The past is part of the destiny of all concrete human experience. However much the past may bear creative future possibilities, remarked Lyman, "the notion that the past may be ignored and forgotten is a sure recipe for spiritual smallness."[85] Rather than cutting themselves off from historic Christianity, the social gospel theologians affirmed that "present religious experiences and active social devotion, if they are not rooted in great sacred memories, are apt to be like the seed sown in the thin soil, which springs up quickly but as quickly withers away."[86]

It was natural, therefore, that the social gospel theorists relied heavily on a "socio-historical" method for appropriating scripture and religious tradition. Although this method is most commonly associated with Shailer Mathews, Shirley Jackson Case, and the "Chicago School,"[87] it actually characterized the interpretive stance of the entire social gospel movement. It was surely implicit, for example, in the exegetical and historical work of Rauschenbusch and Francis Greenwood Peabody.[88] This method is sometimes mistakenly described as a capitulation to historical relativism, for it attempts to describe how each "age" interprets its religious experience in terms of the dominant social patterns and paradigms of its culture.[89] In actuality, its theological intention was just the reverse: to escape from the trammels of relativism. The socio-historical method was a hermeneutical procedure designed to disclose the fundamental ontological structures of human experience. The intention of this hermeneutic,

[83] Lyman, *Meaning and Truth*, 83.
[84] Coe, "Can Religion Be Taught?" 16.
[85] Lyman, *Theology and Human Problems*, 109.
[86] Lyman, *Meaning and Truth*, 40.
[87] See William J. Hynes, *Shirley Jackson Case and the Chicago School* (Chico, Calif.: Scholars Press, 1981).
[88] See William M. King, "The Biblical Base of the Social Gospel," in *The Bible and Social Reform*, edited by Ernest R. Sandeen (Philadelphia: Fortress, 1982), 59–84.
[89] See, for example, Shailer Mathews, *The Growth of the Idea of God* (New York: Macmillan, 1931).

wrote Mathews, was to show "that the gospel has been brought into dynamic relations with each successive and essentially new social mind," thus demonstrating "the continuity of the spiritual content of human experience through historical changes." Indeed, its explicit theological purpose was "to find equivalents for the successive organs of spiritual self-expression," not through a mere repetition of dated symbol systems, but through discovery in religious history of "the points of contact at which the spiritual life of one age realizes its unity with and draws inspiration from the spiritual life of the past."[90] If anything, Mathews was an historical realist, who derided a purely functionalist, or "empty revolver," interpretation of religious history. "History that has lost its historicity becomes . . . of equally dubious value."[91] One misjudges the social gospel if one neglects this orientation to the past and the relevance of historical memory in personal experience. For example, even the iconoclastic radical Harry Ward, in discussing the sins and follies of capitalism, felt compelled to admit the historical contributions and past virtues of the capitalist ethic.[92]

But what was the social gospel looking for in its interpretations of history? The received wisdom about the social gospel is that its fundamental religious "mythos" was the myth of "Progress."[93] It was certainly an important part of any discussion of history and temporality—and in disguised forms it still is today. The difficulty with calling the idea of Progress the fundamental myth of the social gospel is that the evidence turns out to be less conclusive and more ambiguous than it is supposed to be. There was a firm conviction in a certain kind of progress, but it was not "evolutionary" in a biological sense, nor was it particularly "shallow" in its optimism.

When twentieth-century social gospel theologians thought of "history," they did not have in mind a self-explanatory, automatically evolving mechanism, which took care of itself and whose shape could be traced as a smoothly ascending curve. Progress took place, but it was episodic. Moments of victory emerged only out of a web of suffering and tragedy. "At the first glance," wrote Mathews in 1910, "this process appears full of contradictions. It is not steady or unbroken. It has its eddies and its

---

[90] Mathews, *The Gospel and the Modern Man* (New York: Macmillan, 1912), 81.
[91] Ibid., 93.
[92] Ward, *Our Economic Morality*.
[93] Cf. Gilkey, *Reaping the Whirlwind*.

counter currents. Progress is sometimes more than offset by degeneracy." Mathews recognized the "apparent atomistic, divisive character of change." Indeed, from a naturalistic or mechanistic (or abstract) point of view, he conceded, "the world of nature as well as of history seems full of unrelated and, to any science we as yet possess, unrelatable movements and counter-movements." History is not self-explanatory. "There is no such patent evolution as some enthusiasts assume."[94] As early as 1902, for example, George Coe had warned against "a hazy conception of universal progress that associates itself with the notion of organic evolution." That, he added, "is an utter misunderstanding."[95] Similarly, in 1914, Harris Rall criticized the "shallow optimism in our thinking to-day." The trouble is, he noted, that "it is so easy to assume that evolution means progress, that there is a sort of natural drift to the higher and better." On the contrary, "the natural drift is in the line of selfishness and laziness and too often evil passion."[96] And just after the war, Harry Emerson Fosdick reiterated the point that "evolution is not an escalator" automatically moving upward. The fact is, he said, "that human history is a strange blend of progress and regress." Indeed, "even when advance has come, it has come by mingled progress and cataclysm."[97]

Fosdick's complaints about "a soft gospel of inevitable progress" reminds one of Rauschenbusch's sober warning that "the coming of the Kingdom of God will not be by peaceful development only, but by conflict with the Kingdom of Evil. We should estimate the power of sin too lightly if we forecast a smooth road."[98] For some reason, however, commentators persist in explaining this remark as a product of wartime disillusionment. Yet in 1912, in *Christianizing the Social Order,* which is often characterized as his most optimistic work, Rauschenbusch cautioned that "the doctrine of gradualness may be overworked." And then he added that "no matter how just a social change may be, the social class affected by it will resist it." In fact he worried that "the capacity of the nation to throw off injustice and go through a social transformation is lessening in many ways," for "our nation is losing its youthful elasticity and crossing the dead line of middle age." Lest anyone miss his meaning he warned—in 1912—that "recent events have already thrown the shadow

[94] Mathews, *The Gospel and the Modern Man*, 39–40.
[95] Coe, *Religion of a Mature Mind*, 146–47.
[96] Rall, *A Working Faith*, 52–53.
[97] Fosdick, *Christianity and Progress*, 29, 38.
[98] Rauschenbusch, *A Theology for the Social Gospel* (New York: Macmillan, 1917), 226.

of social terrorism across the future of our country. It is certain to come, for America itself breeds it."[99]

Now this is not to say that the social gospel had no doctrine of progress. Eugene Lyman tried to explain the difference by distinguishing between "a *belief in progress* and a *belief in the possibility of progress.*" The distinction was crucial. There is no "natural law which renders progress secure and certain." Nor is there any ultimate elimination of sin and evil in human existence. Rather, said Lyman, the Christian faith calls for "the hope of progress in the future, because it rests on the faith that men may become instruments of God in the positive and cumulative realization of spiritual value in history."[100] Such faith did not rest on empirical experience alone, nor on wishful thinking, but rather on those "sacred memories." "History," wrote Shailer Mathews, "is more than events in time." What religious faith looks for is a "spiritual order that gives coherency to all our experience," and this order is revealed only in "the unity of process rather than that of states."[101]

I suggest that the fundamental mythos of the social gospel was not the idea of Progress but belief in a "God of Battles"—a God of creative power who "bears down" on history as the ground of possibility. God, wrote Fosdick,

undergirds our endeavors for justice in the earth with his power; who fights in and for and with us against the hosts of evil; whose presence is a guarantee of ultimate victory; and whose effect upon us is to send us out to war against ancient human curses, assured that what ought to be done can be done.[102]

It is "in this world of sorrow and sin" that "we must find God at work," wrote William Adams Brown, "manifesting his presence in spite of its tragedy and heartbreak."[103] God "is the ground of our optimism," exalted H. F. Rall. "That is why we dare to talk of banishing disease and driving out poverty and overthrowing oppression."[104] We do all these things, said Eugene Lyman, knowing that it is "God who toils and suffers with us," who "welcomes each toiling and struggling soul into the august fellowship of his age-long labors." In fact, he added, "the deepest motive in the current liberal theology of our land" is the belief that "the struggle

[99] Rauschenbusch, *Christianizing the Social Order*, 29, 38.
[100] Lyman, *Meaning and Truth*, 340; see also his "The Kingdom of God and History," in *The Kingdom of God and History*, edited by H. G. Wood et al. (Chicago: Willett, Clark and Company, 1938), 75–104.
[101] Mathews, *The Gospel and the Modern Man*, 41–42.
[102] Fosdick, *Christianity and Progress*, 43.
[103] Brown, *Is Christianity Practicable?* (New York: Charles Scribner's Sons, 1916), 153.
[104] Rall, *A Working Faith*, 54.

with evil is one in which [God] really shares."[105] "God confronts man in history," wrote Henry Sloane Coffin. It was the same God who, in the famous poem by Frank Mason North, made haste "to heal these hearts of pain" and "tread the city's streets again." "The pursuing love of God," wrote Kirby Page, leads us "against poverty and exploitation, racial discrimination and segregation, violence, and war," all of which are but "parts of God's age-old struggle to create a suitable habitation on earth for his sons and daughters."[106]

But what kind of God was this and how was God known? To describe that God as immanent is to miss the most important note in the social gospel. The God of Battles was transcendent, not "supernatural" in the old sense of that word, as William Adams Brown carefully explained.[107] Our experience of historical reality, said Lyman, forces us to speak "of a God who is both transcendent and immanent."[108] Neither nature nor history is a mechanically determined process; on this ontological point the social gospel theologians were unanimous. "Novelties"—unprecedented moments or events in time—"are constantly coming to pass." Such novelties enrich the world, according to Lyman.[109] "While there is an aspect of causal sequence in phenomena," wrote F. Ernest Johnson, "there is also an aspect of discontinuity, of novelty, of 'irruption,' if you will." And the ground of that novelty is personal. "Personality literally 'breaks into' the temporal order of events with creative power."[110]

That "personality" is God. "What we have is a Will, a Purpose, a Goodness, a personal God," wrote Rall, "not the sum of all things but their ground, their explanation, their end, himself always more than the world which has its being in him."[111] Eugene Lyman agreed with Rall that "while we must think of God as realizing his purposes under temporal conditions . . . we must think of him also as transcending the world." After all, he argued, "we cannot rightly speak of God as immanent in the world-process unless we conceive of him as also transcending it. For otherwise it is the world-process itself, or some aspect of it, concerning which we really are speaking and the idea of the immanence of *God* is lost."[112] Lyman was echoing what Mathews had earlier said: that *God* is not the

---

[105] Lyman, *Theology and Human Problems*, 18, 175.
[106] Page, *Living Triumphantly*, 6, 28.
[107] Brown, *Is Christianity Practicable?*, 79.
[108] Lyman, *Meaning and Truth*, 343.
[109] Lyman, *Theology and Human Problems*, 125–134.
[110] Johnson, *The Social Gospel Re-examined*, 47.
[111] Rall, *A Faith for Today*, 106.
[112] Lyman, *Meaning and Truth*, 433.

"Process," but "the source and guide of all progress," the "cosmically personal."[113] As Rall put it, "if nature is to be more than a mere mechanism and history more than a tangle of events," then "we must believe in a God who is more than nature, in whom purpose and meaning have their reality."[114] That is, we must believe in a God who brings the future.

This God was not "supernatural" in the old sense of the word, "not something apart from the natural, added from without."[115] Nor was God supernatural as existing alongside the realm of cause and effect—a subjective "ethical" reality—as in the thought of Horace Bushnell or Albrecht Ritschl. The supernatural is rather the "emergence" in nature and history of "personal" centers of meaning and value. What the social gospel religious consciousness does, wrote F. Ernest Johnson, "is to bring the creative aspect of life into an empirical framework—to domesticate religion within the common life. The *deus ex machina* is displaced by an informing creative force. Supernature becomes the self-transcending aspect of nature and of man."[116] To discover "God at work," said Brown, "is to discover in the flux of chance and change something splendid and enduring which lifts us above ourselves and introduces us into a wonderful new world."[117] It is to discover ourselves within a socio-temporal matrix whose structure is not a destiny but freedom and creativity. In the moment of "self-realization and self-expression," said Mathews, "a man is volitionally at one with an environing God from whom he has been separated by sin."[118]

One final note is in order. The social gospel terms *higher* and *best* in reference to the self were not, strictly speaking, moral categories at all. They were references to levels of self-transcendence. The Christian gospel, maintained Mathews, is "more than a graduate lecture course in Christian ethics." It is above all a "sense of the reality of sin," and sin "is evidently something more than wrongdoing. It is a violation of the will of God. It is an attack upon the God of the universe." Self-transcendence begins, therefore, with repentance. "It is a fearful thing for an unloving man to fall into the hands of a loving God," he quipped. "The past is irrevocable except as its consequences are overcome by the very powers

---

[113] Mathews, *The Gospel and the Modern Man*, 82.
[114] Rall, *A Faith for Today*, 18–19.
[115] Brown, *Is Christianity Practicable?*, 79.
[116] Johnson, *The Social Gospel Re-examined*, 76.
[117] Brown, *God at Work* (New York: Charles Scribner's Sons, 1933), 8.
[118] Mathews, *The Gospel and the Modern Man*, 276.

that are making a different future."[119] For George Coe, the sense of belonging to a divinely grounded socio-temporal reality produces "a certain divine discontent that spurs men on to seek and find even higher unity of themselves and their world." This "opposition that religion seeks to solve is within man as well as between him and nature." For that reason, "man never regards his present state as properly final; self-judgment pursues him."[120]

The emphasis on self-transcendence, rather than socialization or self-realization, is what separated the social gospel community from many of its scientific and humanist friends. "It is very evident," wrote Macintosh, "that this merely human social transcendence is not adequate. Social psychology cannot give us the final word as to reality." The reason is that personal life fully emerges only "when there has been a 'transvaluation of values,' and life is interpreted in its highest terms as the spiritual development and efficiency of the individual and society."[121] "Our loyalty," remarked Rall, "is not simply to our groups, or even to a total humanity as such, but to that humanity as seen in the good purpose of this God." It is to persons, for "the object of our [social] aspiration is not an imperfect and idealized *we*, but a perfect *Thou*."[122]

For George Coe, too, the distinctive note in religion was self-transcendence, a "revaluation of values." That revaluation "is the function that characterizes the confessedly great turning points of religious consciousness in individuals and in groups." When we speak of society, he cautioned, we must be careful; for "society is a reciprocal attribution of value to 'I's' and 'thou's'; it is a matter of persons." This means that none of us "is a mere echo of others." Society is not "a complex of reciprocal imitations"; it is rather a "mutuality in which precedents and the unprecedented are everywhere present and interfused."[123]

Thus society is not saved by socialization but by radical transformation. "It will not do to identify all sociality with religion," Coe wrote, "for the very point of religion at a given historical period may lie in the opposition of a fuller toward a less full realization of society." One finds religion "in our sociality chiefly when it becomes radical," when it "finds

---

[119] Ibid., 173, 175, 178–79, 183.
[120] Coe, *Psychology of Religion*, 201, 206.
[121] Macintosh, "The Reaction Against Metaphysics in Theology" (Ph.D. dissertation, University of Chicago, 1911), 79, 81.
[122] Rall, *The Meaning of God* (Nashville: Cokesbury, 1928), 52.
[123] Coe, *Psychology of Religion*, 236; *What Is Christian Education?*, 98–99.

itself in the profoundest discontent with things as they are." This is a love that "asserts itself as demand for justice (which is the recognition of persons as finalities for thought and action)." Justice is the issue, for only justice can create "reflective loyalty" and "mutuality." Justice "cannot measure welfare by averages; it cannot forget, as science often must, the individual in the general. A fully socialized religion . . . is therefore the most dangerous thing in the world."[124]

The legacy of social gospel thought

What happened to the social gospel after the 1920s? I have argued that the social gospel did not really "die," except as a self-designation. But that is hardly surprising. There had never been any great attachment to what was an awkward term at best—no "Fellowship of Social Gospel Christians." Nor had anyone thought to draw up a "Social Gospel Manifesto" in order to separate true believers from fellow travelers. But it is also true that there were too many liberal theologians "changing minds" in the 1930s and pointing fingers at the social gospel to allow us to pass over the question so glibly.

It seems fair to say that whenever the social gospel was castigated in the 1930s, it was generally defined in the broadest and most imprecise sort of way. Frequently, when critics of the social gospel got down to specific individuals—a Rauschenbusch, a Brown, or a Lyman—they suddenly changed their tone and started making qualifications. In addition, although there were important changes in theological methods and modes of discourse, some of the changes turned out to be somewhat cosmetic. The appeal to pragmatic warrants for religious belief were definitely gone, but faith still demonstrated its power by its effect on life. Certain kinds of language, like "Cosmic Creative Power," lost their glamour, although one could speak of the "*kairos*" without embarrassment. Personalist language was out, but existentialist language about self and selfhood was mandatory. Transcendence had to be mentioned before presence, rather than vice versa. The word *progress* was definitely removed from the theological vocabulary, but approximations of the kingdom could be found.

I do not mean to deny the importance of the changes that were taking place in the 1930s. Schubert Ogden seems correct when he speaks of the

[124] Coe, *Psychology of Religion*, 241.

1930s as a "self-critical" phase of American liberalism, rather than a revolution.[125] Why that was happening, I believe, still needs to be explained. I suggest that the rumblings of this period are traceable to the mid-1920s. They came at first not as a response to European neoorthodoxy but as a response to the "humanist" movement in America, and to the naturalistic premises on which it rested. However diverse and ambiguous on religious matters these naturalist and humanist writings were, members of the movement were agreed in regarding the concept of a "personal" God, a God of Battles, as a hopeless projection and wish fulfillment. Many of the social gospel theologians felt particularly betrayed by Dewey's Gifford Lectures, *The Quest for Certainty*, which seemed to undermine the pragmatic warrants for religious belief on which they had depended. Philosophical and social scientific alliances that had been built up over two decades were suddenly severely strained. Thus, between 1926 and 1933, a spate of books and articles by social gospel writers appeared in response to the humanist "challenge."

However carefully those responses were phrased—for the social gospel advocates did not wish to repudiate humanism per se—the undertone of anger and betrayal was difficult to hide. And the responses were all pretty much the same. How can one existentially devote oneself to human values and accept self-sacrifice in the process without a corresponding belief in the objective reality of values and meaning in the world, that is, a personal God? "It substitutes human capacity for God," replied Shailer Mathews. Humanism is naively optimistic: "What God cannot do; where faith has failed, science will succeed." Humanism lacks any genuine appreciation of the religious qualities of human experience, and thus it is guilty of treating experience too abstractly. Indeed, the humanist view of human experience has a fatal flaw—it overlooks the reality of sin. "One might describe sin as an attempt of a man to live," wrote Mathews, "as if the forces that produced him had ceased to exist." What the humanist calls "religious," said Mathews, is no such thing; "he undertakes to label ethics and sociology religion." And worst of all, he makes society itself into a kind of ultimate reality. "For even if the individual be submerged in the social quest," argued Mathews, "society is certainly not the frontier of human existence." Indeed, "as individuals we know only too clearly that society is not an end, but a means for the development of the per-

---

[125] Ogden, "Sources of Religious Authority," *Journal of the American Academy of Religion* 44 (1976):410.

sonal values of the individual."[126] Eugene Lyman complained that Dewey's naturalism had confined religion "wholly to the field of psychological and social processes and values."[127] William Adams Brown was most upset by Dewey's claim that one could be religious while abandoning religious "certainty."[128]

In the context of this paper, this debate is interesting because it reveals just how isolated Protestant liberals had begun to feel by the end of the 1920s. They were no longer part of a like-minded progressive generation. Invariably they felt the need to establish their own professional autonomy and to find stronger intellectual warrants for theological discourse. Brown welcomed the increasing interest in professional theological study. And Walter Marshall Horton revealed the mood of the liberals in the early 1930s when he called on theology to become a science and to stake "her claim to possess a subject matter peculiar to herself," while protesting "against the view that sociology is the last of the primary sciences."[129]

What is even more noteworthy, however, is that the very charges that the social gospel writers leveled against the humanist movement in the 1920s came back to haunt them in the 1930s. Theology, claimed H. Richard Niebuhr, is now, at last, "turning away from psychological and subjective views of religion toward objective, theological definitions of its content.[130] The social gospel, he asserted, was "characterized by the conviction that social units of every sort are the primary human realities"; hence the social gospel focused only upon "the social individual— the citizen, class-member, race-member . . . rather than upon the individual for the [sake of] the individual." Moreover, the social gospel was guilty of assuming "that religion as such has no direct bearing on social life." Instead, it put its faith in man rather than in God "as the moving force in history."[131] And "the final fruit of this development," he concluded, "is modern humanism."[132]

The intellectual atmosphere in which theology worked had changed.

---

[126] Mathews, "Can We Have Religion Without God?" in *Humanism: Another Battle Line*, edited by William P. King (Nashville: Cokesbury, 1931), 135, 138, 141, 143.

[127] Lyman, "Can Religious Intuition Give Knowledge of Reality?" 248.

[128] Brown, *Beliefs That Matter* (New York: Charles Scribner's Sons, 1930), 6–7.

[129] Horton, "Authority Without Infallibility," in *Religious Realism*, 287–88.

[130] Richard Niebuhr, "Religious Realism in the Twentieth Century," in *Religious Realism*, 423.

[131] Richard Niebuhr, "The Attack upon the Social Gospel," *Religion in Life* 5 (Spring 1936):176–77, 179, 181.

[132] Richard Niebuhr, "Religious Realism," 416.

As Walter Rauschenbusch once noted, "humanity must reconstruct its moral and religious synthesis whenever it passes from one era to another. When all other departments of life and thought are silently changing, it is impossible for religion to remain unaffected."[133] Although H. Richard Niebuhr was more aware of his own indebtedness to the social gospel than the preceding citations would suggest, he wrote in an age of analysis, not synthesis, of discontinuity, not continuity.

It is still fair to say, however, that if the neoorthodox movement in America was really a "self-critical" form of liberalism, then that "self-critical" modality began to take shape in the social gospel era. It was then that the theological wrestling with the problem of temporality began. It was then that liberal theology realized just how seriously it had to struggle with the socio-historical matrix of experience. It was then that the role of *praxis* and the influence of social orientations in determining theological thought was stressed. "God cannot be proven," remarked Harris Rall; "he must be lived."[134] And, finally, it was then that the necessity of resisting "secularity" by preserving a genuine Christian humanism was outlined. "It is one of the curious perversions of a great faith," remarked John Bennett, "that there ever arose the confusing division between personal and social Christianity."[135]

[133] Rauschenbusch, *Christianizing the Social Order*, 120.
[134] Rall, *A Faith for Today*, 85.
[135] Bennett, *Social Salvation*, 65.

4

John Dewey, American theology, and
scientific politics

BRUCE KUKLICK

This essay has two parts. The first and more substantial part explicates
some of John Dewey's ideas. The second part is more sketchy and speculative but emerges naturally out of the first; it examines how a version
of some of these ideas became common cultural assumptions.

The first part outlines the origins in American theology of Dewey's
thought. I also want to suggest, however, how Dewey transformed his
heritage in enunciating his well-known instrumentalist philosophy. Although Dewey's work before 1900 must be understood in the context of
the philosophy of religion of Trinitarian Congregationalism, he shifted
the axis of learned debate as he grew away from the faith of his fathers.
At the same time it is useful to trace continuities between his earlier ideas
and his later ones, that is, those elaborated in New York City from the
turn of the century until his death in 1952.

The second part of this essay suggests how what I call a "scientific
politics" became integral to American life and how Dewey contributed
to this development. In elaborating how Dewey's ideas gave some people
a faith to live by, I again hope to demonstrate continuities between earlier
religious ideas and later "secular" ones.

From 1740 until 1880, religious thought in most New England centers
of culture was dominated by the work of Jonathan Edwards and his followers. These men contributed to the most sustained intellectual tradition in this country, a peculiar set of Calvinist ideas widely known as the
"New England theology," and established themselves in schools of divinity throughout the Northeast. The divines defended the Calvinist essentials of depravity and grace, the fall, the natural sinfulness of man, and

78

the need for redemption. These doctrines were intricately connected for all reform Protestants, but American divines focused on the problems raised by the absolute responsibility of individuals for their behavior even when they were evil by nature and could not resist grace. God's omnipotence rested uneasily with man's accountability, especially when grace was clearly supernatural. Bringing the distinct realms of God and man and nature and the supernatural into appropriate relation became critical. The theologians again and again displayed an interest in an idealistic metaphysics that might bridge these two chasms.

It was not until the 1880s, however, that Calvinist philosophers of religion were able to appropriate a modest version of Hegel to attack these perplexing dualisms. At the Andover Theological Seminary, the premier graduate institution in the country, a group of Trinitarian young turks came to power. Known as the Andover Liberals, they proclaimed a "New Theology," "Progressive Orthodoxy." From the viewpoint of Calvinist nonprogressives, however, the antidualistic views of the Liberals left much to be desired and precipitated a long struggle between them and their adversaries for control of the seminary. The Liberals drove an older journal, *Bibliotheca Sacra,* out of Andover and started a new one, *The Andover Review,* to promote their ideas.

The New Theologians at Andover were successful, but their victory over more orthodox divines turned out to be a palace coup. At the same time, theology of whatever description was giving way to philosophy as the speculative science that was sanctioned by crucial legitimating communities on the East Coast. The end of the nineteenth century was the period of the rise of the modern university system in the United States, the growth of disciplinary scholarship outside divinity, and the emergence of a host of scientifically oriented creeds that responded to Charles Darwin's *Origin of Species.* In this intellectual environment, theology was unable to prosper, and it lost its hold on the literate, upper-middle-class public.[1]

Philosophy came to command the respect of this public at the expense of theology. Philosophy departments attracted the money, talent, and social support that had previously been devoted to theology. In the 1890s, at Harvard, President Charles Eliot built "the great department" that a non-American of the stature of Bertrand Russell recognized as "the best

---

[1] The substantive textual issues raised in the first part or this essay are treated at length in my *Churchmen and Philosophers: From Jonathan Edwards to John Dewey* (New Haven: Yale University Press, 1985), where extensive citations can be found.

in the world."[2] At the same time, Andover Seminary went into a sharp decline, immediately following its period of radicalism, and shortly thereafter it merged with Harvard. At Princeton, James McCosh asserted the primacy of philosophy over theology after the dominance of the seminary over Princeton's college for fifty years. At new universities like Chicago philosophy became preeminent, while divinity was relegated to a secondary status.

This is the context in which it is appropriate to account for the career of John Dewey. He was born into an orthodox Congregational Calvinist family in Burlington, Vermont. The most formidable influence on his life was his mother, who often made old-fashioned fear and degradation the core of religious life. Dewey's religion was also shaped by the work of the Congregational minister in Burlington, Lewis O. Brastow, who later taught at the Yale Divinity School. Brastow enunciated in Vermont a popular blend of beliefs similar to what was being propagated by the Andover Liberals. Dewey underwent a conversion experience when he was in his early twenties, taught Congregational Sunday School, and was an active church member until he went to teach at the University of Chicago in his mid-thirties. As he later put it, he had suffered as a young man from the "inward laceration" of his "heritage of New England culture" that isolated "self from the world, . . . soul from body, . . . nature from God."[3]

Dewey had two academic mentors. H. A. P. Torrey, the professor of philosophy at the University of Vermont, and George Sylvester Morris, of Johns Hopkins, where Dewey took an early doctorate in philosophy. Both Torrey and Morris had been graduate students of divinity, but both had given up the Congregational ministry—Torrey actually left a pulpit—for careers in academic philosophy. Both were philosophic defenders of a Protestant Christianity based on German thought, and Dewey, their student, took up their concerns.

As a philosopher of religion, Dewey believed that the New Theology of the Andover Liberals had an inadequate philosophical base. Andover had not fully escaped the careful logical categories of Edwardsean Calvinism. In particular, Progressive Orthodoxy had no compelling way of disputing the older Calvinist dualisms between God and man, and the

[2] Russell, *Autobiography,* vol. 1 (New York: Little, Brown and Co., 1967), 326.
[3] John Dewey, "From Absolutism to Experimentalism," in *Contemporary American Philosophy,* 2 vols., edited by George P. Adams and William Pepperell Montague (New York: Macmillan, 1930), vol. 2, 19.

natural and the supernatural, although the progressives did denigrate these dualisms. The German belief on which Andover had fallen back, thought Dewey, was still too dualistic. Hegel relied on a dichotomy between absolute and individual spirit—between God and man—and Kant distinguished between the phenomenal and noumenal worlds—nature and the supernatural. Dewey wanted to reconstruct German thought on antidualistic lines and thus to provide a solid philosophic base for Progressive Orthodoxy. Much of his early writing appeared in the *Andover Review,* the journal that had replaced *Bibliotheca Sacra* at Andover.

Commentators have regularly noted that the young Dewey was a Hegelian, and although this is a bit of a distortion it is near enough to the mark. What they have ignored is that Dewey's "Hegelianism" promoted a philosophy of religion designed to fortify the latest developments in Trinitarian Congregationalism. Dewey had little to do with the pragmatism of Charles Peirce and William James. He was a disciple of Morris at Johns Hopkins, and avoided Peirce, who also taught there; Dewey believed that Peirce's "formal" logic typified just the sort of dualism that was erroneous. Although Dewey did find much to aid him in William James's *Principles of Psychology,* the book appeared in 1890, after Dewey's own position had been formulated, and James had previously poked fun at Dewey's ruminations. At the same time James saw what many later commentators have neglected in regard to Dewey. Writing in 1880 James said that the resurrection of Hegel in America was due to the fact that he gave to liberal theology what it needed and had lacked in the United States—"a quasi-metaphysic backbone."[4]

In the 1880s Dewey argued that we could not separate God and man, absolute and finite spirit. God *was* only as individual selves realized him; the dynamic evolution of self-consciousness in human beings in history was God. Dewey also denied a cleavage between the natural and the supernatural, phenomenal and noumenal. The two worlds were one; spirit was in nature; nature was a symbol of spirit. The physical world evolved into the spiritual; it had spiritual potential in it. Nature *became* moral and religious.

In both these attacks on philosophic dualisms Dewey developed his own philosophical dialect, a German teleological vision of Darwinian science. Then, in the late 1880s and early 1890s, he abandoned the language of German idealism for a more explicitly scientific vocabulary. In-

[4] Ralph Barton Perry, *The Thought and Character of William James* (Little, Brown and Co.: Boston, 1935), 2 vols., vol. 1, 674.

stead of talking about the union of man and God, Dewey spoke of the intrinsic meaningfulness of experience and the ability of men, using the scientific method, to uncover greater and greater syntheses of meaning. Rather than writing of the human realization of God, Dewey wrote of science as progressively increasing human harmony and tranquility through the growth of meaning.

Dewey also ceased to write of the connection between the natural and the supernatural worlds. Instead, he wrote that the scientific method had previously been applied to nature but could now be applied to the social world. The spheres of nature and morality were of a piece, and the method perfected in physics could be used in the arena of culture. Questions about nature and supernature were transformed.

Dewey's concerns of the early 1890s are the recognizable ones of "our" Dewey. One way to construe these changes is cosmetic, as changes in rhetoric. The issues for Dewey in the late 1870s and early 1890s were the same; the mode of expressing them altered. Why did Dewey alter his linguistic strategy? In part, like most other American intellectuals, he was captured by the ideal of applied science. He was only the most prominent among American thinkers who read Darwin in a benign way that promoted a new way of thinking about man and the world. In part Dewey was also a man on the make. He knew that systematic theology was no longer a sure route to success. He wanted to be a respectable theoretician in his culture, and this desire meant coming to terms with science.

Whatever we make of this mix of motives, it is well to remember that Dewey did not *merely* change his language. He was also a creative genius. In casting older problems of the philosophy of religion in a new set of formulas, he shifted the axis on which intellectual problems were conceived. Dewey recognized this process in his own way in his famous essay on the impact of nineteenth-century science on philosophy. He said that we did not solve intellectual problems but that we got over them.[5] He had begun his career by intending to shore up Andover liberalism. The changing milieu in which Dewey wrote meant that he came to maturity as the founder of modern American thought.

Commentators argue that Dewey naturalized German thought by stressing the concrete growth of cultures and the interaction of organisms in their environment. What is more important, however, is that Dewey

[5] "The Influence of Darwinism on Philosophy," in *The Middle Works of John Dewey, 1899–1924* (Southern Illinois University Press: Carbondale and Edwardsville) (hereafter *MW*), Vol. 4: 1907–1909 (1977), 14.

began his professional life as a certain sort of philosopher of religion. Although he shifted the contours of thought in the United States, his philosophy bore the tell-tale marks of his older interests. The locus of the divine shifted from the supernatural to the natural, and science could be applied to what was formerly supernatural. But there was still a godly residue in things. Jonathan Edwards had argued that man was redeemed only through grace. For Dewey man was still redeemed, but the instrumentality was the ostensibly areligious technique of science.

By the early twentieth century, science came to serve, for Dewey, what in the nineteenth century was plainly a divine purpose. Until that time it is easy enough to trace the family resemblance between his Andover philosophy of religion and what came to be known as his "instrumentalism"; thereafter, although the resemblance exists, the set of Dewey's mind turned away not merely from philosophical theology but also from its Hegelian buttress. The new language Dewey adopted enabled him fully to become a theorist of the burgeoning social sciences. Indeed, the theoretical message was consistent from the turn of the century until his death. Scholars are well aware of the issues in the works of the 1920s—*Reconstruction in Philosophy, Human Nature and Conduct,* and *The Quest for Certainty,* whose tenth chapter is still required reading for those interested in the foundations of moral judgment. Yet these ideas, little altered in the 1920s, were promoted much earlier. A long essay of 1903, "The Logical Conditions of a Scientific Treatment of Morality," is his most sustained treatment; Dewey had it reprinted virtually unchanged in 1946.[6]

Dewey defined the scientific method as a means of controlling the assertion of certain statements. To use the method was to assert a statement H as a conclusion that gained support from and was grounded by certain antecedents that had been established as H itself was being established; the consequences derived from H, in the manner in which H itself was derived, constituted the meaning of H. Dewey's view was that this method could be applied to moral concerns.

He urged that science rested on the commitment of the scientific community to judge truly. All scientists accepted this value or "attitude"; hence, to assume that science dealt with facts and morality with attitudes would not serve to distinguish science from ethics. Science presupposed certain attitudes.

[6] See Darnell Rucker, "Introduction," to *MW, Vol. 3: 1903–1906* (1977), xii.

Dewey acknowledged that there was *now* a distinction between scientific and moral judgments. The distinction did not lie in some easy cleavage between fact and attitude, but that did not entail that there was no distinction. The problem was that in scientific judgments the individual attitudes of the scientist were presupposed, were indifferent, or affected each judgment equally. Because every scientific researcher was, for example, committed to telling the truth, this attitude, although critical to the scientific enterprise, was not an issue in asserting any scientific proposition.

When people made moral judgments, the situation was different. From Dewey's perspective the attitudes relevant to making warranted—that is, scientific—ethical judgments were out of control.

Many critics have pointed out that Dewey's elaboration of his ideas was often programmatic, always vague, and unusually dense. Nonetheless, he did repeatedly try to express what it would be like to get control over ethical judgments. Judgments of the sort "I ought to do X" not only propound that X be done but also give me a reason for doing X. If all goes well, I will act in a certain way. That is, enunciating a moral judgment shapes my character. What I *do* makes me what I am; and what I *am* further shapes what I am likely to do, what sorts of moral judgments I will make in the future.

The trouble was that people were shortsighted and often confused about what they ought to do. They did not recognize with any clarity what would be the consequences of deciding in alternative ways. Moreover, they did not have a sense of whether they would like the consequences even if they had some idea of what they were. In these circumstances, Dewey wrote, the attitudes involved in moral judgment were not under control. People made decisions not in malicious ways but in ignorant and unwitting ways; the result was conflict, the idiosyncrasies of personal moral choice, and interminable and unproductive argument about what course of action should be undertaken.

The novel "reflective morality" for which Dewey called in "Logical Conditions of a Scientific Treatment of Morality" and other writings had two initial requirements. First, it demanded what Dewey perceived as a sociological component: that people had knowledge of their options—the consequences that would ensue from different sorts of behavior. Second, it had a psychological component: that people had knowledge of what they wanted, given that they knew what their options were.

Dewey stressed that invoking sociology and psychology exemplified "the continuity of scientific judgment" in ethics. The invocation was "the postulate of moral science." Dewey's key concern was spelling out what was confusedly apparent to people when they made their usual misguided moral judgments. What people were after was a sense of what was likely to occur *and* what they individually wanted. As an analyst Dewey had to explicate what was involved in asserting these judgments and to explore how they could be warranted.

Now a postulate is an assumption, and the assumption here was not just that moral judgments were about the consequences of behavior that people desired. Dewey was also arguing (1) that it was possible for people to gauge the outcomes of certain kinds of behavior and to attribute causality correctly and (2) that in such rehearsals people would be able to figure out what it was that they wanted. The notion is that the essence of moral judgments can be verified in experience. The human sciences can provide us the wherewithal for making more adequate judgments.[7]

It must be stressed, as Murray G. Murphey has pointed out, that for Dewey there were no really nontrivial ethical questions to be answered once the empirical inquiries were settled. Some of his significant critics have argued that this analysis is off the mark. Assume people might know how to bring X into existence *and* want to bring X into existence and be justified in saying that they would continue to want to have X. A sociological examination could explore the consequences of actions and a psychological one could demonstrate that people desired one set of consequences and would continue to do so. But, critics add, it could still always be asked if people *ought* to have X. Such critics accept that the sociological and psychological matters are determinate; but they say that agreement on the facts bears no relation to the question of morals. Critics may be right about this issue, but they have not seen that their understanding of things makes no sense to Dewey. Once the theorist worked out the consequences of alternative decisions and learned which ones people desired, Dewey believed moral dilemmas were solved. There was no further issue of whether something genuinely "ought" to be done. Dewey assumed there was no criterion of what ought to be desired beyond its experimentally validated tendency to lead people to consequences that they in fact desired.[8]

[7] "Logical Conditions of a Scientific Treatment of Morality," in *MW*, Vol. 3, 3–35. My description of the content of this paper strays from the language that Dewey uses; I have tried to convey his meaning more colloquially and simply.
[8] See Murray G. Murphey, "Introduction" to *Human Nature and Conduct* in *MW*, vol. 14 (1983), xxii.

Dewey's ethical theory was in this sense rationalist. People were all alike under the skin, and once their intellectual confusions were removed by the helpful instrumentality of science, their attitudes would automatically come under control. That is, similar dispositions would guide moral judgments, just as such dispositions aided in justifying scientific ones.

For Dewey, the world and the individual were *transparent*. Ambiguity, irony, and paradox were not part of his universe. He had no sense that people might not like what they wanted once they got it, if their wants were experimentally justified. Nor could he sense that people might not be able to spell out the consequences of alternative schemes of actions in any way that would distinguish what they desired from what they would not desire.

Let me elaborate this point. Dewey and his main critics argued over whether a certain set of facts were morally relevant; they argued whether some empirical generalization of sociology and psychology would help settle ethical disputes. Dewey said yes; the critics said no. But both Dewey and his critics thought that there were—or could be—facts of the matter; both believed that the consequences of actions and human wants were peculiarly specifiable, or could be made so. What I have called the transparency of Dewey's notions was widely shared. The human psyche was not tormented or ambivalent, and science had the power to fathom this psyche's connections to the world.

The Edwardsean tradition separated God from man and the natural from the supernatural, and Andover liberals opposed these dichotomies with notions derived from German idealism. Nonetheless, Dewey believed that the accepted German idealism was itself dualistic. To provide an adequate ground for the Andover position, he asserted that individual consciousnesses could not be distinguished from the absolute consciousness and that the natural world had spiritual potential in it—natural and supernatural were no more distinct than man and God. When Dewey gave up the language of his own antidualistic idealism, there were nonetheless continuities in his thought. The idea that human experience had within it latent and ever-growing harmonies of meaning to be uncovered by science was the later analogue of the earlier view that individual and divine consciousness were of a piece. The idea that the scientific method could be applied to the moral as well as to the physical world was the later analogue of the earlier view that nature and the supernatural were of a piece.

After the turn of the century, Dewey became a high-powered theoretician of the sciences of man, but in his mature works one can still detect versions of these two youthful axioms at work. The belief that the consequences of behavior were determinate and that people's preferences could be clarified was his final rendering of the notion that growing harmonies of experience were waiting to be constructed—that God and man were one. The belief that empirical findings ended significant moral inquiry stemmed from the conception that physical and moral science were comparable—that the natural and the supernatural were joined.

By the 1920s and 1930s when Dewey was regarded as a preeminent American thinker, social science academics and the men of ideas socially connected to institutions of higher learning were a varied lot. Nonetheless, it is fair to say that most of these scholars and theorists took Dewey's ideas seriously, and scholarly studies have had an easy time in linking these thinkers to a Deweyite climate of opinion in the 1930s.[9]

Some of these intellectuals were positivists who claimed that their work was value-free and had no implications for social policy. Many others adopted what has been called scientific naturalism, for which they often called on Dewey for support. The naturalists contended that social science was objective and scientific, and hence different from the work of the moralist. Yet naturalists also asserted that the conclusions of their research would have beneficial consequences for society. This sort of view was the credo of the *New Republic,* the *Nation, Common Sense,* and *Plan Age,* as well as people like Thurman Arnold, Adolph Berle, Bruce Bliven, Stuart Chase, Morris L. Cooke, Paul Douglas, Freda Kirchway, Max Lerner, Harold Loeb, Lewis Lorwin, Robert Lynd, Gardiner Means, George Soule, and Rexford Guy Tugwell.[10] Edward Purcell, in his study of social scientists and the problem of evaluation, writes that these people actually enunciated their own ethical precepts under the guise of being impartial experts. They were able to claim neutrality for their moralistic social science because they confidently believed in the existence of an

[9] See William E. Akin, *Technology and the American Dream* (Berkeley: University of California Press, 1977); Guy Alchon, *The Invisible Hand of Planning* (Princeton: Princeton University Press, 1985); Barry D. Karl, *Charles E. Merriam and the Study of Politics* (Chicago: University of Chicago Press, 1976); R. Alan Lawson, *The Failure of Independent Liberalism (1930–41)* (New York: Capricorn Book Edition, 1972); and Edward A. Purcell, Jr., *The Crisis of Democratic Theory: Scientific Naturalism and the Problem of Value* (Lexington: University of Kentucky Press, 1973).

[10] See Robert Westbrook, *John Dewey and American Democracy* (Ithaca: Cornell University Press, forthcoming), chapter 9.

essentially good and orderly universe. They unconsciously assumed the validity of certain values and could not imagine their rejection. That they embraced these values—for example, efficiency and administrative expertise—was not evidence of moralism but of rationality, intimated in loose and antiseptic phrases.[11]

Some historians have claimed that Dewey's philosophy did not really credit this popular "managerial elitism." Indeed, Dewey's call for a scientific morality has been minimally construed as a plea for the use of a democratic scientific intelligence in the formation of public policy.[12] But Dewey's ideas were so viscous that his plea could easily buttress social scientific mandarinism, and it was often used to do so.

In 1931, at the height of the Depression, Stuart Chase, the popular economist, wrote that the greatest need was not for philosopher kings but for "philosopher engineers."[13] In his 1932 effort, *A New Deal,* he argued that successful New Deal reforms would follow a road lit by "a torch . . . borne by another class [than the business class], one hitherto unknown to history: the men and women who have grasped the hand of science."[14] Chase parodied Dewey, but social scientists in general found the philosopher to embody their attitudes. Although these would-be managers of the state could not pass as academic interpreters of Dewey, they drew from him (and others) a teaching that was not entirely antithetical to his texts. This class believed that power in the modern world rightly belonged to the intellectuals, and that power would be exercised dispassionately, impartially, and objectively only if they had control. As one acute interpreter has written, "A more self-interested theory cannot be imagined."[15]

The concern of these scholarly types for Dewey was the most important way his ideas became part of the baggage of intellectuals. I want to emphasize here, however, an even more amorphous societal development. These ideas were put into action by practical scientists, but they were also incorporated into the way the educated public thought about politics and recent American history.

The development I want to get at was a long process that got its start in the Progressive Era and picked up steam with the notions of adminis-

[11] Purcell, *Crisis of Democratic Theory,* 25, 27, 46.
[12] Westbrook, *John Dewey and American Democracy.*
[13] Chase, *The Nemesis of American Business* (New York: Macmillan, 1931), 107.
[14] Chase, *A New Deal* (New York: Macmillan, 1932), 179.
[15] John Oliver Crompton Phillips, "John Dewey and the Transformation of American Intellectual Life, 1859–1904," Ph.D. dissertation, Harvard University, 1978, 309.

trative progressivism and efficiency with which Herbert Hoover was associated in the 1920s. But the most important period was the mid-1930s when the Rooseveltian political revolution occurred. I call the transformation the emergence of the idea of a scientific politics; perhaps more familiarly it is that transformation by means of which some commentators have perceived that philosophical pragmatism became pragmatic liberalism in politics.

It is a perception that is still with us today, and to flesh it out I want to quote at length some remarks from a 1985 essay by Marcus G. Singer, a noted philosopher who has also recently edited a volume on American thought. Pragmatism, writes Singer, is not unreasonably regarded as "typically American"; the "unconscious pragmatism of American life" was given public expression by Franklin Roosevelt himself. The president, says Singer, was "the William James of American politics," and he goes on to draw "parallels" between the two.[16] Now it would be better for my purposes if Singer had said FDR was the Dewey of American politics, but the comparison is close enough. Singer's basic idea is that somehow, in the 1930s, certain true theoretical ideas became successfully and usefully incarnated in our civic life. At minimum, however, what happened was that Roosevelt's presidency was a vehicle through which the rhetorical stance of Deweyite social scientists became part of our political parlance.

In the late nineteenth century, political morality was secured by the truths of religion, truths that, in politics, were put to work in the world. By FDR's era, such a justification of political virtue was old hat. Instead there was a new, scientific justification. Social investigation could determine what the costs and benefits of alternative decisions were and what decisions would satisfy in the long run. Men of knowledge thereby became instrumental to successful statesmanship. Politics became pragmatic, requiring social scientific expertise.

It is commonplace for some commentators, like Singer, to write of this evolution as simply a benign, progressive development. But I want to raise the issue of this sort of writing as *itself* a subject for historical exploration. Surely today most historians are more dubious than some philosophers about handing the mantle of Dewey (or James) to FDR. Historians have long conceded that Dewey's "instrumentalism" had little to

---

[16] Singer, "Moral Issues and Social Problems: The Moral Relevance of Moral Philosophy," *Philosophy* 60 (1985): 9–10. *American Philosophy* (London: Macmillan, 1986) is Singer's edited volume on American thought.

do with the politics of the 1930s.[17] Yet I think it is wrong to assume that the notion of pragmatic politics is merely shorthand for an assumed lack of ideological commitment that is not opportunism; pragmatic liberalism, that is, is not just a nice way of being more or less unscrupulous in public life. The ascendancy of the discourse common to Singer and others did have something to do with Dewey. As I have tried to imply, however, the issue was rhetoric and rationale, not, as Singer suggests, the fruition of a more rational and beneficial politics under Roosevelt.

In a 1932 speech FDR urged that the nation needed "bold, persistent experimentation." He went on, "It is common sense to take a method and try it; . . . if it fails, admit it frankly and try another."[18] Historians have concluded that these words were not Dewey in action. As Arthur Schlesinger, Jr., noted sometime ago, Dewey vehemently rejected what he described as the New Deal view that politics ought to be about "messing around . . . doing a little of this and a little of that in the hope that things will improve." Dewey, Schlesinger wrote, was not a believer in "trial-and-error pragmatism" but a "theoretical experimentalist," advocating "experimentalism in a restricted and special sense." Dewey, Schlesinger contended, was rigid and ideological in his pragmatism.[19] For Schlesinger and for others, FDR was by no means a speculative metaphysician, but the conception lingers that Roosevelt at least pointed politics in a scientific direction; trial-and-error is better than nothing. Roosevelt described himself as a quarterback who would not call a future play until he saw how a previous play had turned out. The president also said that although he did not expect to get a hit every time at bat, he wanted to achieve the highest possible batting average. Cartoonists pictured him as a baseball and football player, and as a prize fighter. These analogies hinted that political skills led to measurable achievement in which causal connections could be adumbrated. This view of Roosevelt and of the nature of politics after him was adopted by the educated upper middle class.

The view was corroborated in the ideas formulated by the social scientific epigoni of Dewey. If politics was somehow like sports, it could be aided by the sort of applied scholarship that social scientists could provide. The college educated and politically concerned believed that experts

---

[17] See the discussion in William Leuchtenburg, *Franklin D. Roosevelt and the New Deal, 1932–1940* (New York: Harper and Row, 1963), 344.

[18] Franklin D. Roosevelt, *Looking Forward* (New York: John Day Co., 1933), 51.

[19] Arthur Schlesinger, Jr., *The Age of Roosevelt: The Politics of Upheaval* (Boston: Houghton Mifflin, 1960), 155.

might figure out the consequences of alternative possible policies and that policy questions could be resolved when these empirical disputes were settled.

The intelligent citizen became committed to assessing the rational formulation and implementation of publicly beneficial policies that went beyond what was offered by actually practicing politicians. Political leaders were judged by a sort of nonpartisan standard, a vision that politics should be about reasoned accomplishment discernable to the intelligent and knowledgeable, about the possibility of the progressive evolution of "reform" by the use of human intelligence.

I have traced continuities in Dewey's ideas as they altered over the years. Popularizing social scientists picked up the divinely tinged notions (1) that the consequences of human behavior and human preferences were determinate and (2) that this empirical information was all that was necessary to settle moral disputes. These postulates are those at work in the conception of politics since the time of Roosevelt: it is possible to assign responsibility for the implementation and consequences of policy and to assess whether the policy produces general social benefit. This, I think, is what people mean by liberal pragmatic politics, and it does have a connection to philosophical pragmatism.

Surely a religious, quasi-Hegelian progressive sense of the meaning of America had been part of the consciousness of some Romantic historians since the middle of the nineteenth century. I have, however, tried to locate with greater precision how this constellation of perceptions achieved its modern foundation.[20] By the 1930s high religious thought had permanently gone out of fashion with the educated upper middle class, and politics became the place where matters of ultimate commitment lodged.

In effect the theoreticians of social science functioned as the theologians of another age had done. As a high priest, Dewey provided the grammar for a common faith in an era when old-time religion was no longer compelling for intellectuals. To say that Dewey was the chief exponent of posttraditional secularism is unnuanced. He, rather, trans-

[20] At the end of 1933 the Englishman John Maynard Keynes wrote an open letter to Roosevelt. He said that FDR had made himself "the trustee for those in every country" who wanted "reasoned experiment" in social change between "orthodoxy and revolution" (quoted in Leuchtenburg, *Franklin D. Roosevelt*, 337). Obviously, what appear to be vintage ideas of Dewey were part of the world view of Western capitalist intellectuals, as has been argued by James Kloppenberg in *Uncertain Victory: Social Democracy and Progressivism in Europe and America, 1870–1920* (New York: Oxford University Press, 1986). My concern is to locate the ideas in a specific American milieu.

formed religious concerns into a new language acceptable to his contemporaries, because it allowed them to avoid ancient problems and look at new ones—and because it gave them a creed to live by. It is certainly arguable that what many intellectuals took from Dewey was a distortion, or that they would have come to their ideas regardless of what Dewey said. It is still true that Dewey's words and approximations of his ideas were commonly used in the discourse of the era. More than anyone else he at least provided the lingua franca for those in the knowledge professions who sought power. A Dewey-like creed, in a form suitably allied to the political categories of the New Deal, became part of the views of an influential class of Americans.

Let me expand on this issue. The Reformed Protestant theologian Reinhold Niebuhr was the man scientific naturalists loved to hate in the 1930s. Niebuhr made them uncomfortable because he insisted to a large audience that social scientific rationality was something like a fiction or a metaphor, useful for the interest of an intellectual class attempting to mobilize certain kinds of support. But "reason" was also naive, said Niebuhr, and could not plumb the paradoxes of existence in a way that Reformed Protestantism could. From time to time Dewey powerfully responded to Niebuhr, forcing a choice between the admittedly imperfect notions of social science and, in Dewey's mind, the fatally flawed faith in religion.

In his recent biography of Niebuhr, Richard Fox has suggested that if their political positions and the rationales for their positions are carefully examined, Dewey and Niebuhr appear to have been really close on many issues.[21] Because Dewey's roots were almost as much in Calvin as were Niebuhr's, I would not dispute this appraisal; I would add that Niebuhr was able to be a formidable enemy of Dewey because he couched his "similar" ideas in language that reflected a more complex view of man and of the potential of science. I would also suggest, however, that we shift our focus from the content of ideas and the substance of political debate—and therefore questions about who was right and who was wrong—to the structure of political world views. Overall, Niebuhr was on the losing side; he made a gallant last stand in trying to have overt religious conceptions dominate the polity. In this sense Dewey defeated him: scientific politics became the accepted mode of addressing public

[21] Richard Wightman Fox, *Reinhold Niebuhr* (New York: Pantheon Books, 1985).

questions. But this does not mean that scientific politics was true or that it was without elements of faith.

On one occasion Dewey criticized Niebuhr uncharacteristically. Dewey wrote that "the exaltation of intelligence and experimental method" might be an "illusion." But this "illusion" was worth a trial, was more worthy of commitment, than the "collective illusion in the past." "Illusion for illusion," wrote Dewey, social science might be better than religion.[22]

Dewey quickly took back what he had said by arguing that the case for the experimental method in social matters was *not* yet illusory; nonetheless, in this passage he leaves me with a feeling of triumph. For Dewey hinted here that somewhere deep down in his soul he recognized that his call for experimental intelligence might be no better than the Calvinism it had replaced for him. In each case we are dealing with mumbo-jumbo, but not the mere "bloviating" of Warren Harding that intellectuals could not stomach. Paradoxically, the mumbo-jumbo was profound; it provided the essential framework for collective human endeavor.

At the end of the nineteenth century there was a revolution in our grasp of religious history, and religious movements began to be studied insofar as they manifested struggles for power, worldly perquisites, and psychic gratification. Avoiding a commitment one way or another to the truth of religion, historians analyzed the function of religion on Earth and achieved a different perspective on the subject, distancing themselves from its categories. We have no such distance from the categories of the peculiar politics bequeathed to us by the Roosevelt presidency and the popularization of pragmatism. We believe that politics is about reasoned accomplishment. This is not to say that our political views are unbelievable. Rather, it is to say that one of Dewey's accomplishments was to move our common faith from the supernatural to the natural. Our political views are about as equivalently tied to the empirical evidence as the views they have replaced and about as believable as the cartoons depicting FDR as a physically active athlete.[23]

---

[22] Dewey, "Intelligence and Power," *New Republic* 78 (25 April 1934): 386. See also the discussion in *Churchmen and Philosophers*, 256–61; and in Fox, *Niebuhr*, especially 136–41.

[23] For helpful comments on an earlier version of this paper, I would like to thank the participants—especially Robert Westbrook—in the Woodrow Wilson Center's conference on Science and Religion in March 1986.

5

The Niebuhr brothers and
the liberal Protestant heritage

RICHARD WIGHTMAN FOX

If the average historian knows one thing about the development of twentieth-century American religion, it is this: the idealistic liberal Protestantism of the early part of the century gave way by the 1940s to the realism
of Reinhold Niebuhr. The liberal belief in human goodness—and in historical progress through the spread of goodwill and scientific method—
was routed by Niebuhr's potent preaching on sin, tragedy, and the irreducible irrationality at the heart of human life. There is enough truth in
this conventional view to keep it current in textbook treatments of recent
intellectual history. But it conceals and distorts as much as it reveals. The
very fact that it was Reinhold Niebuhr's own view of his historic place
should put us on guard. Indeed, it is one sign of Niebuhr's enormous
impact on twentieth-century intellectual life that his self-image as the
crusader against liberalism should have cemented itself so solidly in our
historical memory.[1]

In fact Niebuhr was always a liberal, however fiery his rhetorical dis-
missals of liberal "sentimentality" or "utopianism." Despite his reputation as a "neoorthodox" theologian, he spent his entire career battling
Barthian neoorthodoxy, which he rightly viewed as a threat to the liberal
Protestant tradition of Harnack and Troeltsch. Despite his perennial

---

[1] Robert Wiebe's contribution to Bernard Bailyn et al., *The Great Republic,* 2d ed., Lexington, Mass., 1981, 874, is typical in counterposing the "realist" Niebuhr to the "idealist"
Dewey. But that polarity merely restates Niebuhr's own view of the situation and does
not probe the enduring links between those two liberals. Arthur Schlesinger, Jr., has been
more responsible than anyone else for cementing Niebuhr's reputation as crusader against
liberal idealism. See his "Reinhold Niebuhr's Role in American Political Thought and
Life," in Charles W. Kegley, ed., *Reinhold Niebuhr: His Religious, Social, and Political
Thought* (New York: Macmillan, [1956] 1984) and my own discussion in "Reinhold Niebuhr's 'Revolution,' " *Wilson Quarterly* 8 (Autumn, 1984): 82–93.

carping at the "scientists," the "Deweyans," and the "educators" for their supposedly naive faith in the power of reason to solve human problems, he was fundamentally in accord with them in their appeal to experience as the ground of truth. Like his brother H. Richard Niebuhr, who also dissociated himself from Barth, Reinhold Niebuhr was deeply committed to what might be called the scientific frame of mind: relativist, historicist, critical. True, like his brother he was very suspicious of the pretensions of some segments of the scientific community, and scoffed at those who presumed that science had rendered inherited faiths anachronistic. But both Niebuhrs believed that science, rightly understood, posed no threat to religion. Indeed, a mature religion had to be more than merely tolerant of science; it required a scientific foundation. The scientific frame of mind was a necessary, though not a sufficient, condition for modern religious belief.[2]

Richard Niebuhr was much more perceptive about Reinhold's role than Reinhold himself was. It was in Richard's life-long campaign to carve out his own niche—safe from the domination of his famous older brother—that he carefully defined the character of Reinhold's liberalism and sketched out a standpoint that challenged it. He saw that, although Reinhold pushed liberal ethics to its limit, he never seriously doubted liberal theology. Richard, by contrast, took liberal theology to the limit. Whereas Reinhold was fascinated by Marxism as an ethical resource, Richard was tempted by Barthianism—and ultimately drawn toward Catholicism as an uncompromising faith. Yet each stepped back from his respective precipice and reaffirmed a fundamentally liberal, modernist commitment. Together they offer a case study in the continued potency of liberal Protestantism in the mid-twentieth century—a time when it was supposedly in decline and disarray.

---

[2] Students of religion have done better than historians at grasping the persistent liberalism in the Niebuhrs' works. William Hutchison, "Liberal Protestantism and the 'End of Innocence'," *American Quarterly* 15(1963):126–39, stresses continuities between the Niebuhrs and the previous liberal generation. David Tracy, *Blessed Rage for Order* (New York: Seabury Press, 1975), 27–31, suggests that the Niebuhrs and even Barth himself are best seen as part of the liberal tradition. "Neoorthodoxy" in Tracy's usage is a label for those "postmodernists" who shared the nineteenth-century liberals' distaste for historic orthodoxy but detected deep flaws in the liberal perspective. In this view, Barth, Brunner, Bultmann, Tillich, and the Niebuhrs all become in-house critics of liberalism. But Tracy's classification skews the Niebuhrs' historic place by minimizing the gap that separated them from Barth. Both Niebuhrs—Reinhold in particular—were much closer to the liberal modernists than Tracy allows. Reinhold, for his part, self-consciously rejected the label "neoorthodox." See my *Reinhold Niebuhr: A Biography* (New York: Pantheon Books, 1986), 214.

It was the conviction of both Niebuhrs, following the lead of their chief intellectual mentor Ernst Troeltsch (on whom Richard wrote his doctoral dissertation at Yale), that biblical religion had a key role to play in modern scientific culture. Yet religion had to respect the established epistemological framework of the time. Like the liberals before them, from Schleiermacher and Ritschl to Bushnell and Rauschenbusch, they felt obliged to respect the cultural achievements of the modern era. There could be no return to the simple assurances of a prescientific time. Revelation could no longer be viewed as an unimpeded communication between God and the believer through the flawless mediation of the Bible. A reader of the Bible confronted a vast web of historical contingencies and relativities. Religion provided no direct access to truth. For the Niebuhrs, religion was a faith and a trust that, beyond the relativity that conditioned human knowledge and beyond the realm of scientific reason, God truly was acting to reconcile the world to himself. That faith was subject to no rational, risk-free validation. But belief was justified by its fruits: its capacity to make sense of the ultimate mysteries and perplexities of human life.[3]

When Reinhold Niebuhr took to the warpath against liberal Protestantism in the 1920s, he was launching a civil conflict, a battle within the liberal ranks themselves. He had been a confirmed liberal modernist even before going to Yale Divinity School in 1913, and the Yale experience had deepened his liberal convictions. "Love" was the principle of the individual Christian life and the solution to the social disorder of the capitalist marketplace. Like other liberals, Niebuhr was scarcely a naive sentimentalist. He knew that the world did not immediately or automatically bend to the will of the Christian forces. Nor did he assume that history was inevitably and irreversibly moving toward justice, peace, and social harmony. When in the 1920s he began to castigate liberal Protestantism for holding precisely those indefensible views, he was caricaturing his own earlier beliefs, as well as the beliefs of his former colleagues.

The liberal Protestantism of the late nineteenth and early twentieth century *was* sometimes simplistic and utopian. Lyman Abbott and Henry Churchill King, for example, were excessively sentimental in their rhapsodic hymns to human potential. But more representative figures, from Washington Gladden and George Gordon to Walter Rauschenbusch and

---

[3] On the Niebuhrs' intellectual relationship with Troeltsch, see the analysis by their close friend Wilhelm Pauck (who studied with Troeltsch), in *Harnack and Troeltsch* (New York: Oxford University Press, 1968).

the young Niebuhr himself, were a good deal more sophisticated. Their distinctive stance cannot be reduced to "optimism" or "utopianism." It might be better defined as confidence in culture, openness to the world. Liberals believed that the secular world was not merely a field for religious action. It was itself a source of value, indeed, a realm of the sacred. The role of religion was not so much to convert the world as to join the world in deepening the religious spirit of "personality" that had already penetrated it. What all liberals shared—whether they were "social gospelers" committed to the progressive transformation of society or individualists wedded to a laissez-faire political economy—was a zeal to promote personality by breaking down the boundaries between the religious and the secular.[4]

It was not simply that each of those realms enriched the other, but that they really formed only one realm. The liberals were captivated by the interdependencies that linked all spheres of life: the individual and the collective, the scientific and the literary, the natural and the spiritual. What held everything together was the overarching power of the "personal." It was precisely their commitment to modern science—the critical study of the Bible, the systematic investigation of society, the empirical analysis of human origins and human behavior—that provoked their stress on personality. They realized that their embracing of the secular and the natural posed certain risks, among them the chance that human beings might come to be viewed as just one species among many, and the chance that Christianity might come to be viewed as just one religion among many. The notion of personality helped to neutralize those risks. What distinguished human beings from other animals was their spiritual capacity as persons; what distinguished Christianity from other religions was the perfect manner in which Jesus embodied the personality ideal.

It is essential to stress that when they spoke of the personal, the liberal Protestants had nothing in common with the secular success advisers who, already in the early twentieth century, were glorifying the well-groomed "personality." There is a superficial resemblance, because both groups saw personality as something vital and dynamic. But for the Protestants, personality was still an arena of unpredictable encounters between God and man; it was not just a resource for more effective self-presentation.

[4] William Hutchison, *The Modernist Impulse in American Protestantism* (Cambridge, Mass.: Harvard University Press, 1976), 186–91, (on Abbott, King, and Gordon). Hutchison estimates that "among the thirty-three most prominent leaders of theological liberalism in the period from 1875 to 1915, about one third took no discernible part in the Social Gospel."

Indeed, personality was an ideal that put self-giving ahead of self-aggran-
dizement. It stood for the "dying to self" to which Christians aspired. It
represented what human beings were at their best: social creatures who
had the capacity to put the interests of others ahead of their own. Personality made people more than merely natural beings whose behavior could
be grasped (and ultimately predicted or managed) scientifically. The concept therefore allowed liberals to commit themselves to scientific analysis
because it posited a privileged, undetermined sphere of existence that lay
beyond the reach of scientific investigation. Not that liberals feared science. On the whole they cherished it as a revelation of the creativity of
human culture. But they realized that science had a certain imperial potential. It might easily claim the exclusive right to provide authoritative
knowledge about the human condition.[5]

For liberal Protestants personality was a social as well as an individual
reality. More exactly, it was a reality that presupposed a communal context. It demanded self-giving interaction among persons for its realization. Human society had an unbounded potential for the realization of
personality. So did human history. The future was a realm of indetermi-
nate possibility. There was no guarantee of progress, but there was no
structural impediment to a spiral of improvement. The individual capacity for spiritual growth was matched by the social capacity for harmonious fellowship. Edward Bellamy's phenomenal best-seller *Looking Back-
ward* (1888) was a classic expression of that liberal Protestant conviction.
When it is read in the 1980s, it seems fantastically simple-minded in its
depiction of a society transformed, without conflict, into a vast fellowship. But Protestant readers in the 1880s did not find it simple-minded.
Bellamy's "religion of solidarity" appeared to be the essence of common
sense. There was a fundamental fit between individuals, their society, and
their history. There were no ineradicable surds in human existence.

[5] To my knowledge there is no adequate examination of the concept of personality in Victorian or Progressive American culture, either religious or secular. Warren Susman's essay
"Personality and the Making of American Culture," in his *Culture as History: The Transformation of American Society in the Twentieth Century* (New York: Pantheon Books,
1985), is very suggestive, but by contrasting "character" to "personality" it constricts the
meaning of the latter to its sense of winsomeness. In fact "personality" was widely used
by religious and even secular writers in the early twentieth century in its "spiritual" sense:
a capacity for disciplined, long-term self-giving, as in leadership, friendship, love, or self-
sacrifice. A prime case in point is Randolph Bourne, who develops that meaning in *Youth
and Life* (Boston: Houghton-Mifflin, 1913), 294. Susman (281) quotes Bourne on personality but assumes him to be talking about winsomeness when he is really talking about
spirituality.

The full story of Reinhold Niebuhr's evolution in the 1920s, when he turned vigorously against some features of his liberal heritage, is too involved to recount here. His encounter with Henry Ford, himself a notorious "liberal" idealist, had a great deal to do with Niebuhr's insight into the deceptive potential of religious idealism. National and international politics—especially the conflict between labor and capital and the French occupation of the Ruhr—made him doubt the adequacy of liberal pacifism in the social arena. Similarly, the pervasive political apathy of middle-class Americans persuaded him that liberal Protestantism lacked "energy," "vitality," "motive force." Religion could provide that energy, but only if it went beyond preaching love and goodwill as the solution to social problems.

Niebuhr's vociferous rejection of reasonableness as an ethical strategy beginning in the late 1920s has led one historian after another to conclude that he was giving up on liberalism, joining Barthian neoorthodoxy in its dismissal of human reason as a primary resource in the quest for ultimate meaning. But Niebuhr's attack on liberalism was in a precise sense rhetorical. Liberalism, he believed, needed a new rhetoric if it was to become potent in the social sphere. Like the literary realists of the Progressive period—Stephen Crane, Lincoln Steffens, and others—Niebuhr was disgusted by the sincere, long-winded, flowery conventions of Victorian writing. He thought them effeminate and vowed to combat them with muscular, hard-hitting prose. Readers were not to be "cultivated" through languorous, wordy indirection, but awakened and mobilized by straightforward shooting from the hip. Liberalism had to be toughened, streamlined. Niebuhr was not abandoning the liberal view that reason and experience were the only possible foundations for truth-seeking in the modern era. But he was condemning those like John Dewey who he thought were too optimistic about injecting reason into the body politic, too patient and gradualist in their political rhetoric. The combative voice was an indispensable part of his program for creating a leaner, tougher liberalism.[6]

Moral Man and Immoral Society (1932) was Niebuhr's declaration of

[6] The work of Christopher Wilson is very important in clarifying the cultural meaning of literary realism. See his "The Rhetoric of Consumption: Mass-Market Magazines and the Demise of Gentle Reader," in Richard Wightman Fox and T. J. Jackson Lears, eds., *The Culture of Consumption in America, Critical Essays in American History, 1880–1980* (New York: Pantheon Books, 1983) and Christopher P. Wilson, *Labor of Words: Literary Professionalism in the Progressive Era* (Athens, Ga.: University of Georgia Press, 1985).

independence from the coterie of liberal idealists with whom he had associated for much of the previous decade. By page three he had already vilified John Dewey—with whom he had worked in various New York political groups since 1929—as a "platitudinous . . . analyst who has no clear counsels about the way to overcome social inertia." Niebuhr knew how to overcome it. The liberal goal of justice for all could be attained only if progressive forces "believe rather more firmly in the justice and probable triumph of their cause than any impartial science would give them the right to believe." Sufficient morale could be created only if intellectuals helped to create "the right dogmas, symbols, and emotionally potent over-simplifications." Moreover, it might well be necessary to use occasional violence in the social struggle. Niebuhr heaped scorn on namby-pamby liberals who imagined that nonviolent "force" was as far as moral men could go. He insisted that there was no absolute distinction between violent and nonviolent coercion; he invoked Mohandas Gandhi himself as an authority, because that advocate of nonviolence had himself supported the British effort in World War I.[7]

Not only did the liberal goal of a just society require a willingness to countenance antiliberal means—propaganda, coercion, and even violence—but also the liberal idea of justice itself had to be reinterpreted. Niebuhr forthrightly disposed of the long-standing liberal Protestant notion that the social-historical realm was an arena of potential fellowship and harmony. Human beings in groups did not have the same moral potential that individuals did: a single person really did have the capacity to subordinate his or her own interest to that of others, while a group like a nation or a class did not. The quest for a Kingdom of God on Earth, in either its religious or secular forms, was futile. It ignored the structural incapacity of social entities to put love above interest. The proper social goal was justice, not love, and justice was to be viewed as a perpetual balancing act among contending forces, not a static future state in which all citizens or all nations would achieve social or political parity.

Niebuhr's sneering repudiation of the liberal strategy of goodwill and the liberal vision of a final fellowship caused a furor in liberal ranks. His former comrades took turns excommunicating him from the Christian community. He himself insisted on keeping the Christian label but delighted in rejecting the liberal one: he called himself a "Marxian" Christian, a "prophetic" Christian socialist. By emphasizing the obstacles to

---

[7] Niebuhr, *Moral Man and Immoral Society* (New York: C. Scribner's Sons, 1932), xiv–xv.

achieving justice and the necessity for endorsing the use of power in trying to achieve it, Niebuhr had taken liberal politics and liberal ethics to their limit. Most of his critics thought he had renounced liberalism altogether. But Richard Niebuhr, a strong private critic of *Moral Man* in two remarkable letters, understood that for all the militance and all the skepticism about society, his brother had in fact reaffirmed the central point of the liberal vision.

Richard distinguished himself, at the outset, from "the good democrats, liberals, orthodox believers in the efficacy of goodwill and intelligence" who were "horrified" by *Moral Man* "because their dogma is attacked" and "because their dogma is a defense against all disturbances of law and order, by which they profit more or less." He was not interested in defending their idealism. "I hate it with all my heart as an expression of our original sin." But Richard noted that other readers, among whom he included himself, were critical of the book despite the fact that they were "as cynical or almost as cynical and skeptical as you are." Those readers were discontented because they wanted the book to offer a constructive vision of Christian discipleship in a postidealist, revolutionary age. "They await a Messianic word of release which has not been given to our time. You are so much of a Christian that you can understand and appreciate them. . . . These men though they criticize you are your best friends and they would not hurt you were they not wounded themselves."

In Richard's view, Reinhold had been unable in *Moral Man* to go beyond pillorying liberal idealism because he was still too deeply immersed in it. He was "still too romantic about human nature in the individual and in face-to-face relationships." Richard had only to contemplate his own relationship with Reinhold to prove his point. "I am convinced there is quite as much hypocrisy in this idealization of our personal relationships as there is in our collective behavior. Take such a thing as brotherly love. I hate to look at my brotherly love for you to see how it is compounded with personal pride—I taking some kind of credit for the things you do and basking in reflected glory—and with selfish ambition—trying to stand on my own feet, trying to live up to you, being jealous of you, to use a harsh and brutal term. Enough to make one vomit. . . . The moral gift man has is not a gift of goodness, but a gift of judging right and wrong. 'Moral man' if he is moral knows he's bad. Therefore I must dissent from the whole argument that 'individuals (as individuals) have a moral code . . . which makes the actions of collective man an outrage to their conscience.' They have a code which makes their own actions an outrage to their own conscience."

Reinhold had asserted that individuals possessed a natural capacity for goodness—a potential for "personality"—that collectivities lacked. Richard strongly disputed that position. He believed that "what keeps men halfway decent in face-to-face relations is coercion, particularly the coercion of public approval and disapproval." He denied that it was possible to love another person as oneself. Human beings did the opposite: identified themselves "with the other man and loved themselves in him or her." It was in people's "enlightened self-interest" to be polite or charitable in face-to-face contact; the goodness that they managed to display stemmed from no "will to love," but from a conscious or unconscious calculation of advantage. "I do not deny the presence of ideals," he wrote. "I deny their efficacy in influencing action."

For all Reinhold's huffing and puffing about liberal myopia and complacency, he was still, in Richard's view, a liberal in his central assumptions about human nature. The self was still the rational agency of goodwill—the font of personal spirit—even though it no longer enjoyed a fundamental "fit" with the larger social-historical world. *Moral Man* had banished "personality" from society but preserved it in the self. But as Richard proceeded to point out, the book had not even totally dispensed with the liberal Protestant approach to society:

You think of religion as a power—dangerous sometimes, helpful sometimes. That's liberal. For religion itself religion is no power, but that to which religion is directed, God . . . I think the liberal religion is thoroughly bad. It is a first-aid to hypocrisy. It is the exaltation of goodwill, moral idealism. It worships the God whose qualities are "the human qualities raised to the nth degree," and I don't expect as much help from this religion as you do. It is sentimental and romantic.

Religious liberals, like secular liberals, imagined that they were called to transform society. Those like Reinhold who became more militant in the 1930s had not given up the liberal paradigm. They merely detected a gap between liberal goals and liberal power to achieve them; they insisted on stronger measures. Richard rightly argued that the heart of Reinhold's radicalism was thoroughly liberal: in its essence it was not a commitment to class conflict, but a belief in man's capacity to manage, and perhaps master, the social maelstrom:

I agree with you wholly on the amorality of violence and nonviolence. A pacifism based on the immorality of violence hasn't a leg to stand on. But I do think that an activism which stresses immediate results is the cancer of our modern life. It is betraying us constantly into interfering with events, pushing, pulling, trying to wriggle out of an impassable situation, and so drawing the noose tighter around our necks. We want to be saviors of civilization and simply bring down new destruction.[8]

Richard was critical of so much of the liberal tradition that he was able to see it from the outside and to place Reinhold accurately within it. He was not fooled by his brother's antiliberal rhetoric. He understood how completely Reinhold had assimilated the perspective of Ernst Troeltsch—religion was less a divine revelation than it was a human power. Religion was a two-tiered reality: for the individual it offered a perspective from which to make sense of the ultimate mysteries of life, for society it provided energy and vitality to carry on the quest for justice.

During the 1930s Reinhold drastically revised his liberal view of selfhood by appropriating a good deal of Richard's more pessimistic position. He came to see the self as a paradoxical entity at odds with itself. It was no longer merely a dualistic combination of spiritual and natural elements, of "personal" potential joined to "impersonal" impulse. Even in its spiritual essence it was divided: human creativity was constantly undermined by the sin of pride. But Reinhold never did accept his brother's quietistic conclusion that, because human nature was so deeply fragmented, social intervention was futile. He remained devoted to the inherited liberal Protestant faith in building a just society, even as he stressed the fragility of all human constructions. He developed the notion of "responsibility" as an alternative to the more open-ended ideal of "personality." Responsibility implied a worldly wise maturity and a go-slow politics: a willingness to act whenever possible for a better world, but a suspicion that social commitments were always in danger of becoming fanatical. Human beings had an obligation to transform society, but they also had a gift for deluding themselves. Politics was indispensable to the moral life, but only if kept under control.

By the late 1930s Niebuhr had molded the distinctive Niebuhrian position on religion and politics, one that marked him as a liberal in politics just as he was in theology. Religion provided both a motive for political action and a critical corrective whenever that action threatened to become self-righteous. It was energy, and it was a set of limits. Niebuhr knew that American politics had always been suffused with moral and religious convictions. He sensed that without them politics would degenerate into a mere balance of power, into Machiavellian amorality. But he

[8] H. Richard Niebuhr to Reinhold Niebuhr, n.d. [fall, 1932], and n.d. [mid-January, 1933], quoted in Fox, *Reinhold Niebuhr*, 144–46.

also knew that religion was dangerous—it easily became absolutist, intolerant. Politics needed religion, therefore, but "prophetic" religion—in which God was a Judge who condemned not only social injustice but the self-righteousness even of those who battled against it.

H. Richard Niebuhr was firmly antiliberal in his conception of human nature and human history. His intrafamilial preaching played a major part in reorienting Reinhold's perspective on selfhood and politics. The liberal realism—the liberalism within limits—that Reinhold propagated beginning in the late 1930s owed much of its power to the rigor of Richard's analysis. It would be only a slight exaggeration to say that Reinhold was for the rest of his career a publicist for ideas articulated first and with greater precision by his younger brother. More exactly, Reinhold's influential revision of liberalism was a tense balancing act: he kept the liberal commitment to history making but under Richard's prodding dropped the liberal view of the self as an agency of "personal" goodwill.

All this might lead one to believe that while Reinhold was a conservative liberal who went halfway in renouncing his liberal Protestant heritage, Richard himself was a full-blooded conservative who renounced that heritage altogether. There is no question that Richard abandoned the world-transforming activism that had long been the hallmark of the social gospel liberals—and remained at the core of Reinhold's faith. But Richard's social and political conservatism was curiously linked to a thoroughgoing intellectual liberalism. He not only defended liberal theology against the Barthians but also was much more self-conscious than his brother in embracing the "scientific frame of mind" of the liberal tradition. Indeed, it is because he was so strongly tempted by the Barthian alternative that he was able to clarify so effectively the enduring contribution of Troeltsch and other liberal relativists and historicists. Moreover, it is because he was so convinced of the "determined" character of human existence—so persuaded that human beings were not in ultimate control of their fate—that he was able to appreciate even the most "deterministic" of the natural, social, and psychological sciences. While Reinhold was writing articles about "The Tyranny of Science," despite his own fundamental accord with the scientific approach to truth, Richard was commenting admiringly on the devotion, loyalty, and faith displayed by scientists in their communities of detached observation.[9]

[9] Reinhold Niebuhr, "The Tyranny of Science," *Theology Today* 10 (January, 1954):464–

Although it is dangerous to bring an author's personal psychology into a discussion of his ideas, it is not wholly beside the point to note that Richard Niebuhr had developed an "observational" perspective from his earliest childhood. With a dominant father and two dominant older brothers, it may have been natural for him to adopt the posture of apparent passivity—under which there lay a forceful will of his own. From the earliest years it became his vocation to explicate, describe, enumerate: to observe the "action" of his father and siblings, not to try to duplicate it. Like Henry James in relation to his older brother William, Richard knew he could not compete with the worldly ease, the public mastery, of Reinhold. He ceded the world of "pushing and pulling," as he called it, to his brother and focused his own intelligence on the "action" of detached analysis.

Henry James's depiction of the "passive" Ralph Touchett in *The Portrait of a Lady* is a self-description that might well be applied to Richard Niebuhr. James's narrator speaks of "the sweet-tasting property of observation," and notes that "conscious observation" was Ralph's alternative to the "American" involvement in worldly affairs displayed by his banker father. Perhaps one might call Richard Niebuhr's "consuming vision" a means of defense against the threat that his powerful relatives might consume *him*. But if it was a defense it was also an "offense": it produced in him a fundamentally open attitude toward activities such as science that lay outside his normal field of vision. Reinhold's world-transforming outlook produced an argumentative, dismissive bearing toward perceived opponents; Richard's observational pose produced a tentative, receptive stance.[10]

At first glance it might appear that Richard Niebuhr's intellectual development in the early part of his career directly mirrored his brother's. Reinhold's second major book, *Moral Man*, was announced as a refutation of the liberal ethical standpoint enunciated in his work of the late

73; H. Richard Niebuhr, "Science in Conflict with Morality?" 1959 lecture reprinted in his *Radical Monotheism and Western Culture* (New York: Harper, 1960).

[10] Henry James, *The Portrait of a Lady* ([Boston, 1881] New York: Signet, 1979), 38. On the "consuming vision" in James's later work, particularly *The Golden Bowl*, see Jean-Christophe Agnew, "The Consuming Vision of Henry James," in Fox and Lears, *The Culture of Consumption in America*. It would be revealing to compare the earlier James of *The Portrait of a Lady* to Richard Niebuhr. In both cases the observational posture is linked to a fundamentally religious conviction that self-sacrifice, "dying to self," is an appropriate (and possible) life project for the moral "person" in a world of menacing impersonality.

1920s, including his first book, *Does Civilization Need Religion?* (1927). Richard's second book, *The Kingdom of God in America* (1937), was framed as a revision of the liberal standpoint that informed his first book, *The Social Sources of Denominationalism* (1929). *Social Sources* had left him "dissatisfied," he wrote in the preface to *Kingdom,* because it examined the American churches only from the outside, from the standpoint of "sociology." *Kingdom* would try to view the Christian movement from the inside, from the standpoint of faith. The book dwelled on the reality of God's sovereignty, the central element in the faith both of Jonathan Edwards and of the author himself. It dismissed the sentimental perversions of Edwards's evangelical doctrine by liberals who worshipped "love," not "God." Richard's God was not a sweet, pleasant benefactor but an inscrutable Judge. He was the opposite of the liberals' "God without wrath [who] brought men without sin into a kingdom without judgment through the ministrations of a Christ without a cross."[11]

Richard's insistence on God's freedom and independence—his transcendence of all human categories and all human claims upon him—revealed the strong impact that Karl Barth's work had had on Richard during the 1930s. Barth's "confessional" theology was designed to free God from the cultural captivity that the liberal world view had imposed on him. It was also designed to liberate the church from its self-imposed mission of persuading Christianity's "cultured despisers" (Schleiermacher's phrase) that religion was reasonable even in an age of science. Barth largely dispensed with apologetics: the point was not to make Christianity appealing, but to preach the Gospel in all its uncompromising severity. Richard Niebuhr agreed that it was time to stop apologizing for the harshness of the evangelical message: Jesus was not, as the liberals had assumed, "an ethical teacher, proclaiming humanitarian morality and relatively painless progress toward the Family of God, but a prophet of doom and deliverance who sees impending in the events of his time a revelation of the destructive God who is at the same time man's deliverer."[12]

But Barth's kerygmatic theology, especially in the early part of his career, adopted a dismissive posture toward secular culture, toward the human sciences that Troeltsch and other liberals had viewed as indis-

---

[11] H. Richard Niebuhr, *The Kingdom of God in America* (Chicago: Willett, Clark & Company, 1937), 193.
[12] H. Richard Niebuhr, "The Social Gospel and the Mind of Jesus," unpublished manuscript [1933], quoted in James W. Fowler, *To See the Kingdom* (Nashville: Abingdon Press, 1974), 84–85.

pensable foundations for theology itself. Richard Niebuhr thought Barth's rejection of culture unnecessary: he would keep Barth's confessional stance and God-centered theology, but also cultivate the scientific commitment characteristic of the liberal tradition. He was not just arguing that in its proper sphere science was no threat to religion. He was asserting that theology itself needed the critical standpoint of science—not to be persuasive to skeptical modern observers, but to do justice to the real relationship between finite, conditioned human beings and their transcendent judge and companion.[13]

In 1941 the publication of Reinhold Niebuhr's Gifford Lectures, *The Nature and Destiny of Man*, was a major media event; the publication of Richard Niebuhr's Taylor Lectures, *The Meaning of Revelation*, passed almost without notice. Each of the books was a reaffirmation of liberal Protestant theology, each an attempt to reinvigorate that theology by stressing a reality that liberals had ignored. Reinhold emphasized the sin, pride, and imperfection that human beings always exhibited despite their undeniable creative achievements; they were creatures as well as creators, sinners as well as images of God. Richard emphasized the relativity of human knowledge, the imperfection of human perception, and the sovereignty of God. Both strongly asserted the distance between God and man; both expressed an equally strong conviction that human beings possessed, within strict limits, an admirable capacity for responsible knowing and acting.

The Meaning of Revelation was both more and less "liberal" in its theology than *The Nature and Destiny of Man*—less liberal in its insistence that God was truly an actor in history, truly "real" and not simply an "idea" that modern Christians found it useful to embrace because it paid dividends. Reinhold had followed the mainstream of American liberal modernism in interpreting theology not as knowledge of God, but as philosophy of life, as a search for "meaningfulness" in human existence. But Richard was more akin to the liberal tradition than Reinhold in his expressed sympathy for the scientific frame of mind, in his firm embrace of the relativist doctrines of the human sciences. Reinhold the apologist perceived the scientific forces as potential competitors for the loyalty of

---

[13] Richard's essay "Religious Realism in the Twentieth Century," in Douglas Clyde MacIntosh, ed., *Religious Realism* (New York: Macmillan, 1931), 413–28, reveals both his attraction to Barth's uncompromising position and his rejection of it. He turns to Tillich as critical defender of human science and culture. Tillich's standpoint, in Richard's view, manages to do equal justice to man's capacities as knower and to God's ultimate independence from the categories of human experience.

modern believers; as a skilled debater he tried to discredit their supposed claims to ultimate wisdom. Richard the confessor praised the scientific perspective for its capacity to keep believers humble and self-critical, by showing them how "determined" they were. The scientific frame of mind had made modern men relativists, and it was that very foundation that made it possible to recapture a traditional evangelical faith in the sovereignty of God. Human knowledge was severely conditioned; it was fragile, shifting, imperfect. It should come as no surprise then that knowledge of God was partial, that God was hidden from human scrutiny. Human beings lived by faith even in their relations with other persons; it was to be expected that they would come by faith alone to an encounter with God, but—as he put it in *The Meaning of Revelation*—he welded Barth to Troeltsch, the champion of the relativist perspective of the modern human sciences.[14]

The Meaning of Revelation made clear that in *The Kingdom of God in America* Richard had not abandoned the "sociological" perspective of *The Social Sources of Denominationalism*. He had simply set it aside temporarily while pursuing a religious line of inquiry. In *The Meaning of Revelation* he brought the two approaches together. The historical development of individuals and communities could legitimately be viewed either "externally" or "internally," from the standpoint of science or the standpoint of faith. Niebuhr was making a standard Kantian distinction between pure and practical reason, between abstract and personal knowledge. The social scientific approach to society and history discovered facts about human life that were detectable by no other method. It established the inescapable truth that human consciousness was delimited, conditioned by culture. Not only was reason dependent on experience, as the Enlightenment had established. Experience itself was determined by culture and biology; inherited patterns of thought were rooted in language, in custom, and in "nature." The religious approach to society and history, by contrast, expressed the complementary truth that human life was a series of unpredictable encounters among interacting persons. In their responses to one another, those persons displayed a creativity and freedom of which even strictly limited creatures were capable.

In a letter to Reinhold written in 1934, Richard expressed his strong sense of the determined character of human existence:

[14] H. Richard Niebuhr, *The Meaning of Revelation* (New York: Macmillan, 1941), xi.

Nature for you means mostly human nature, to me it means the sun, rain, grass, stars, climate, race, glands. You think in terms of psychology where I think in terms of biology and sociology. You think in terms of the absolute and the relative, where I think in terms of determinism and indeterminism. God for me is not so much the absolute, as he is the determining dynamic. . . . To me the transhistorical, absolute point of reference, the x beyond all x's, has no particular significance. This religion of the absolute remains to my mind an aspiration, not a faith, a trust, a hope, a surrender.

Reinhold knew that human beings were finite and imperfectible, but he was not attracted to scientific conclusions that appeared to reduce the autonomy of human beings or compromised their potential to mold their own historical fate. His God was therefore the absolute ideal to which human beings aspired, while knowing that they would always fall short. Richard regarded human beings' historical fate as beyond molding. His God was therefore "the rock upon which we beat in vain." Richard welcomed the determinist conclusions of "external" observation, even as he insisted on an "internal" analysis that guaranteed human beings' freedom to respond creatively to their own determinedness.[15]

The Meaning of Revelation went beyond juxtaposing the scientific and the religious; it joined them in dialectical interplay. Scientific reason depended on a communal "faith" in inquiry. Scientific work required a commitment that could not be justified on purely scientific grounds. Moreover, reason was never independent of feeling, emotion, even poetry. "Far from ruling out imagination, reason depends upon its development, so that those most ethereal of poets, the pure mathematicians, become the spies of man's intelligence service and the pioneers of his dominion over nature." External and internal analysis nourished one another.[16]

In his later work, particularly the posthumous *The Responsible Self,* Richard drew out the full meaning of his insight: social science at its best came, via "external" investigation, to the same conclusion as "internal" religious history: society was a realm not of discrete human atoms, but of relationships—interactions among persons. George Herbert Mead and others asserted that there was no merely individual existence for human beings. Human life was social by definition; each person was an active participant in a set of communities, and that participation at all times

[15] H. Richard Niebuhr to Reinhold Niebuhr, n.d. [early 1934], letter quoted in Fox, *Reinhold Niebuhr,* 153–54.
[16] H. Richard Niebuhr, *The Meaning of Revelation,* 71–72.

required a combination of faith and reason. In order to live—to respond to the dilemmas and opportunities of life—one had to trust other people, have faith in them. But one also had to analyze them, make accurate calculations about their intentions and actions. "The social self exists in responses neither to atomic other beings nor to a generalized other or impartial spectator but to others who as Thou's are members of a group in whose interactions constancies are present in such a way that the self can interpret present and anticipate future action upon it." The responsible self was part scientific observer and part trusting companion.[17]

A person's relationship with God, in Richard Niebuhr's view, was analogous to the person's relationships with other people. Even in those human relationships there was never full disclosure. Not only with strangers or casual acquaintances, but with those one loved the most, there was unbridgeable distance:

We do not know what we are doing by our aggressions and participations, our inactions and isolations from conflict. We move from day to day, from moment to moment, and are often blown about by many winds of political and social doctrine. What the sources and what the issues of our deeds and sufferings may be remains obscure. In our smaller communities, in our families and with our friends, the same ignorance is our portion. We do not know as parents, save in fragmentary ways, what we are doing to our children. We do not understand what our most intimate friends, or our husbands and wives are doing to us and neither do they know.

In one's relationships with other persons, according to Niebuhr, one lived by faith—the faith that despite the irreducible ignorance on each side, one was nonetheless known, trusted, understood.[18]

Social scientific investigation of individuals and communities did not, in Richard Niebuhr's view, lead one inevitably to faith in God. But it did help believers in God to understand that belief. Richard Niebuhr's confessional, antiapologetic position allowed him to affirm the relativity of his own standpoint. He could fully embrace the religious relativism that nineteenth-century liberals had spawned but also feared: Christianity was indeed one religion among many. That contention appeared to push liberalism to its logical end, but despite his bedrock pluralism, Richard Niebuhr refused to reduce the Christian God to "mythical" status, as he came to feel that Tillich and even Reinhold Niebuhr did. Richard knew his own standpoint to be relative, but that did not mean that the

[17] H. Richard Niebuhr, *The Responsible Self* (New York: Harper & Row, 1963 [published posthumously]), 78.
[18] H. Richard Niebuhr, *The Meaning of Revelation*, 89–90.

object of his worship had to be relative. Relativism required only that he acknowledge the historical particularity of his own tradition, the manner in which his own viewpoint had been shaped by cultural forces beyond his control. He could not freely choose to become the product of some other tradition. There was no logical inconsistency in being a relativist on the one hand, and choosing, on the other, to believe in a personal creator and judge who was the absolute, the unconditioned, the determiner. The existence of such a "person" could not be demonstrated by reason—indeed, the term "God" had no meaning at all from the standpoint of external, scientific reason—but faith in him was legitimate.

The revelation of Jesus Christ, according to Niebuhr, was not the revelation of Jesus's own personality, or of personality itself, or of "love," as the liberal tradition had tended to assume. It was not the revelation of a "self" who was a human self raised to the nth degree. Jesus revealed not himself, but his Father, "the lawgiver whose implacable will for the completion and redemption of his creation does not allow even his most well-beloved son to exempt himself from the suffering necessary to that end. The righteousness of God which is revealed in Jesus Christ is the eternal earnestness of a personal God." That God was known just as other persons were known: through mysterious and half-understood encounters, through faith that, despite one's own ignorance and self-concern, one was truly known by the other. "Revelation means the moment in which we are surprised by the knowledge of someone there in the darkness and the void of human life; it means the self-disclosure of light in our darkness."[19]

The "realism" of Reinhold and Richard Niebuhr was firmly committed to the scientific frame of mind, to the historical relativism that they learned from Troeltsch. They knew, as Richard put it, that "the methods and fruits of Biblical and historical criticism as well as of natural and social science cannot be so eliminated from men's minds as to allow them to recover the same attitude toward Scriptures which their seventeenth century forebears had. . . . We cannot achieve their innocence of vision by wishing for it." Much as they both abhorred the "cultural captivity" of religion—and believed that liberal Protestantism had become a cultural captive in the nineteenth century—they refused to follow the Barthians in a full-scale rebellion against liberal modernism. Each of the brothers

---

[19] H. Richard Niebuhr, *The Meaning of Revelation*, 111.

judged the liberal affirmation of culture a permanent acquisition for religion. In the field of ethics, Reinhold took liberal Protestantism to its limit—by exploring the legitimacy of violence in the social struggle—and then affirmed his pluralistic liberal realism. In the field of theology, Richard took liberal Protestantism to its limit—by exploring the legitimacy of Barthian crisis theology—and then affirmed his pluralistic liberal evangelism. Each of them sought a "responsible" middle ground between his inherited liberalism and the antiliberal movements—Communism or Barthianism—that dominated social and theological discussion during the 1930s.

Another way to put it is to assert that both Niebuhrs dismantled the late-nineteenth and early-twentieth-century liberal synthesis—the confident, unified liberal view of self, society, and history—in order to salvage what they considered the essential kernel of liberalism: its rejection of literalistic supernaturalism, its commitment to critical reason. Richard was the more consistent: when he abandoned the liberal view of human selfhood, he took the next logical step and dispensed with the liberal view of human history as a realm that is subject to the creative intervention and management of human actors. Reinhold was satisfied to rest with a paradox: man was a sinner, unable to control even his own impulses, yet still called to act responsibly in history, to establish justice in human relations.

The distance between Richard and Reinhold on the issue of historical intervention was substantial. In that respect Reinhold was much closer to John Dewey, his secular whipping boy, than to his brother. Dewey was always Niebuhr's favorite example of the myopic sentimentalist who imagined that human society could become a real fellowship. And the Dewey-Niebuhr rift has stood as a linchpin of textbook accounts of twentieth-century American intellectual history. But their polemics concealed a fundamental accord. Actually Niebuhr came very close to acknowledging his common ground in a review of Dewey's *A Common Faith* in 1934. He began by challenging Dewey's naturalistic humanism for its blanket dismissal of biblical religion. According to Niebuhr, Dewey thought Christianity meant miracles, supernatural being. But "profound prophetic religion," Niebuhr asserted, worshiped a God who was "not a separate existence but the ground of existence." Dewey's religion came very close to that prophetic religion, Niebuhr thought, because Dewey "does believe in a world in which the possibility of realizing ideals exists. . . . This is the kind of faith that prophetic religion has tried to express mythically and symbolically by belief in a God who is both the creator and the judge of the world, that is, both the ground of existence and its *telos*." Dewey could be a prophetic Christian if he would just understand that Christian myths were not anachronistic in an age of modern science. They gave voice to ultimate mysteries that science could not address. Niebuhr thought his argument proved how close Dewey was to his position; but it also proved how close his was to Dewey's.[20]

Their starting point was the same: the human drive to realize ideals in history. They both viewed religion as a human power, a resource for the quest for justice. They both believed that supernatural religion diverted men from the life of historical responsibility. Niebuhr put more stress on the obstacles to enacting justice than Dewey did, but by the 1930s Dewey himself was quite aware of the structural obstacles to deep-seated social reform. His continued calls for bringing "intelligence" into the social arena were not, as Niebuhr alleged, innocent assertions that scientific method could have the same impact in rebuilding society that it had in analyzing nature. Dewey was calling for the spread of critical intelligence at all levels of society—the only possible basis for a participatory democratic republic. His republican vision of a democracy of freely interacting participants was a good deal more realistic than the vision Niebuhr imputed to him: the secularized Kingdom of God on Earth, the pure fellowship of love and trust.

Underlying Niebuhr's political and ethical activism there lay a vision of community quite close to Dewey's: despite their intrinsic flaws of pride, jealousy, and deception, human beings had the capacity to work together in the common interest. From Richard Niebuhr's standpoint, that "realistic" position was itself utopian. Richard believed in "community," but it was the restricted community of faith, where a minority of confessing Christians sought repentance and abandoned the quest for worldly mastery. For Dewey and Reinhold Niebuhr, however, the inherited liberal Protestant quest for historical community remained a viable vision even in an era of unprecedented conflicts and tempered expectations.

Postscript

Tracing the development of liberal Protestantism in the work of the Niebuhr brothers is more than a matter of historical interest. The issues with

[20] Reinhold Niebuhr, "A Footnote on Religion," *Nation* (September 26, 1934):358.

which they grappled have once again become pressing. It may be useful to give a brief indication of how their positions relate to the current debate. Over the past decade—roughly since the presidential campaign of Jimmy Carter in 1976—there has been an obvious rekindling of interest in Protestant religion in America. The fundamentalist upsurge, sanctioned in different ways by both Carter and Reagan, has drawn the most publicity, but liberal and even radical activists and intellectuals have become more and more intrigued by religious perspectives. Following the example of religious radicals like Reinhold Niebuhr in the 1930s, they have judged the dominant secularism of the contemporary liberal and radical forces inadequate.

Habits of the Heart (1985), by Robert Bellah et al., is a pivotal expression of this trend: a mini-community of five liberal academics assembling to herald the communal traditions—republican *and* biblical—that twentieth-century liberals have forgotten. Public and private life in America, they argue, is dominated by the language of individualism; people lack a language in which they can express the communal loyalties that they continue to seek and often live out. Following in the tradition of Durkheim (and of Richard Niebuhr), the book asserts that sociology at its best is a "moral" science: its "external" analysis is ultimately inseparable from an "internal" analysis of human value. Yet the Bellah group reverts on the whole to the idealistic liberal Protestantism that the Niebuhrs rejected: it has too much faith that the native goodwill—the personality—of Americans will permit them to develop the right "language" and triumph over the contemporary culture of therapeutic consumption. It tends to view culture as a set of "strands," traditions that can be rearranged according to our conscious will. Richard Niebuhr was much more sensitive than the Bellah group to the ways in which our language itself is determined, delimited by culture.

Christopher Lasch's *The Minimal Self* (1983) bears much the same relation to *Habits of the Heart* as the Niebuhr brothers' work bears to earlier American liberal Protestantism. It is much more realistic than the Bellah volume about the paradoxical mixture of human capacities and incapacities. According to Lasch, it is time for the Left to embrace "what remains valuable in the Western, Judeo-Christian tradition," time to attend to both "our fallen state and our surprising capacity for gratitude, remorse, and forgiveness, by means of which we now and then transcend it." For two decades Lasch's work has been founded on the insight that in the United States the disarray of politics is at bottom a disarray of culture. Twentieth-century liberals and radicals have been cut off from their own past, unable to draw on it—as nineteenth-century reformers typically did—as a resource for confronting the injustices of the present. That twentieth-century cultural failure stems, in Lasch's view, from the erosion of community—the inability of Americans to preserve or cultivate a common tradition. Religion, Lasch is now arguing, is at the heart of the common tradition of the American past. It must be resurrected as a corrective to the secular progressive faith in scientific efficiency—a faith that, in its post-Deweyan formulations, has stressed the expertise of professional technicians, not the participation of broad publics, as the source of social progress. Like Niebuhr, he sees religion both as a democratic social power—a capacity to build community—and as a tragic perspective that acknowledges the perennial failure of human beings to make community endure. Religion allows people to grapple with the human mysteries that neither science nor politics can address. But it also provides a force that science and politics can call on in their effort to understand and transform the social world.[21]

The Bellah and Lasch volumes, along with recent work by Daniel Bell, Michael Novak, Richard Neuhaus, and others, demonstrate that religious traditions and perspectives have penetrated to the forefront of intellectual debate on the Left and on the Right. They demonstrate further that the liberal Protestant heritage, and the development of that heritage by the Niebuhr brothers, are both very much alive. Conservative religious groups—with their antiscientific animus and their uniformitarian, antipluralist view of culture—may still be in the ascendancy. But liberals and radicals are increasingly agreeing that, as Reinhold Niebuhr put it a half-century ago, civilization does need religion. As the Niebuhr brothers insisted, however, if politics and culture need religion, they need a religion that builds on the scientific frame of mind. And a religion that brings not only its energy, but also its self-criticism, into the political and cultural arenas.

[21] Christopher Lasch, *The Minimal Self: Psychic Survival in Troubled Times* (New York: W. W. Norton, 1984), 258–59.

6

Justification by verification: the scientific
challenge to the moral authority of Christianity
in modern America

DAVID A. HOLLINGER

The Christian religion and modern science, it was once thought, present
real obstacles to each other's prosperity. No more, it would seem, except
for fundamentalists and, at the other extreme, a few die-hard village atheists
who don't realize how anachronistically Victorian is the vision of a
triumphant science eventually replacing religion. Scholars and moralists
of a variety of orientations now analyze the historical relationship between science and Christianity as a story not of conflict but of "differentiation" and "divergence."[1] No doubt this is an advance, but caution
is in order as we invite ourselves to feel superior to John William Draper
and Andrew Dickson White. Occupants of separate spheres can remain
preoccupied with each other: Much of modern American Protestant
thought has been reactive to the scientific enterprise, and much of that
enterprise has been propelled by cognitive and moral energies drawn from
the Protestant religious tradition. Moreover, divisions of labor can be
invidious: "differentiation and divergence" may constitute not an alternative to "conflict" but a specification of the process by which conflict
has been engaged. If our recent historiography does not openly reaffirm

[1] This perspective has recently been displayed and consolidated in the important collection
of original essays edited by David C. Lindberg and Ronald L. Numbers, *God and Nature:
Historical Essays on the Encounter between Christianity and Science* (Berkeley: University
of California Press, 1986); see especially the remarks of the editors, 9–10, 14. The most
ambitious and polemical contribution to "neo-harmonist" historiography is James R. Moore,
*The Post-Darwinian Controversies: A Study of the Protestant Struggle to Come to Terms
with Darwin in Great Britain and America 1870–1900* (Cambridge: Cambridge University Press, 1979). I have sought to identify the strengths and limitations of Moore's work
in my "What Is Darwinism? It Is Calvinism!" *Reviews in American History*, VIII (March
1980), 80–85.

the once-fashionable "harmonist" perspective (science and Christianity are ultimately "harmonious"), that historiography is subtly "neo-harmonist" in its dual reluctance, first, to acknowledge that beneath all the newly discovered complexities in the relations of science and Christianity there has persisted an authentic struggle over the epistemic principles that shall shape modern culture, and second, to confront in relation to that struggle the gradual and historic de-Christianization of the intellectual discourse of the United States. In overcoming this dual reluctance, this essay sets forth "neo-conflictist" caveats against the direction of recent scholarship. Hence the story this essay tries to tell is at once a story of aggression and of differentiation, of mutual engagement and of divergence.

The agents in the story are intellectuals eager to vindicate scientific inquiry as a religious calling. A major result of their endeavors in late-nineteenth- and early-twentieth-century America was to complicate the challenge presented to Christianity by science. On its simplest level, as studied by Draper and White and even as constructed by their more sophisticated successors, this challenge was strictly cognitive: What should one believe and on what epistemological basis? Where ended the authority of the Bible and of ecclesiastically supervised religious intuitions, and where began the authority of secular scholarship and science? Around these issues our studies of the Darwinian controversy, for example, properly revolve. The challenge of modern science to Christianity has been primarily cognitive, but not exclusively. This challenge also contained a more subtle, moral dimension to which our historiography has been less sensitive. The moral as well as the cognitive authority of Christianity was often at issue. This moral dimension of the scientific challenge to the authority of Christianity was encapsuled in a remark of T. H. Huxley's: the "ethical spirit" of science, quipped scientific culture's most contentious leader, entails "justification, not by faith, but by verification."[2]

"Justification" in its traditional religious meaning was a process by which the individual soul met God's standard. This was the sense of the term contained in the old Pauline maxim perpetuated by Calvinism and invoked by Huxley, "justification by faith." But the term *justification* later came to mean something quite different. When modern philosophers speak about the "justification of true belief," they do so in an en-

---

[2] T. H. Huxley, "On the Advisableness of Improving Natural Knowledge," as reprinted in Alburey Castell, ed., *Selections from the Essays of T. H. Huxley* (New York: Appleton-Century-Crofts, 1948), 14.

tirely secular, epistemological voice. They do not necessarily imply that the state of one's soul depends on the identification and proper use of the best method for assessing truth-claims. The issue in this second sense of *justification* is indeed "verification." Huxley's juxtaposition of this ostentatiously scientific process with the classical Protestant affirmation of faith implied a religious function for the activity of knowing. Our obligations are not to *believe* as our inherited religious authorities have so long prescribed; our obligations, insisted Huxley, are instead to question and ultimately to *know*. "Blind faith is the one unpardonable sin." And how then are we to be "justified" before whatever powers there may be? By living according to the "ethical spirit" of modern science, by practicing "verification."

Post-Reformation defenders of the doctrine of "justification by faith" had faced the more worldly doctrine of justification by "works" and branded it a heresy—the notorious "Arminian heresy." According to this liberal doctrine, the salient sign of God's grace was not the ability to believe, but the ability to perform good works in the world. Justification by "verification" was a more radical extension of "Arminianism," singling out cognitive conduct as the salient form of "works." Had it been advanced with theological seriousness and inspired a response within the Protestant community, "justification by verification" might have been denounced as "the cognitivist heresy." But this potential drama was never played out within the church. For all the enthusiasm felt for the ethic of science by intellectuals who remained committed to Christianity, the leap was too great. To prove one's religious worth by trying to live according to the Sermon on the Mount was one thing, but to offer as such proof the conscientious application of "scientific method" to the study of nature or even to the problems of daily life was quite another, and one for which it was more difficult to find a warrant in the New Testament. Hence the notion of justification by correct cognitive conduct was not explicitly formulated as a theological alternative; the notion does not figure as a major episode in the history of modern Protestant thought.[3] It

[3] Grant Wacker has reminded me that "correct cognitive conduct" of one kind or another is a standard ingredient in most religious traditions, especially the Judeo-Christian tradition. Victorian ideologists of science certainly inherited from that tradition a sense of the spiritual importance of having a proper, authoritative construction of reality. Justification even by "faith" might count as correct cognitive conduct, if one defines "cognitive" and "conduct" very broadly. But I am construing these terms more narrowly and conventionally in the interests of distinguishing the worldly practice of *wissenschaftliche* knowing

does figure largely, however, in "secularization," if this problematic term can be used to refer to the growth in size and in cultural authority of de-Christianized academic elites, and to the corresponding decline in the role played by churches in public life.

These transitions were facilitated in the English-speaking world of the mid- and late nineteenth century by the conviction that *Wissenschaft* was a religiously significant vocation. The intellectuals who shared this conviction drew on Protestantism's traditional commitment to correct belief, but placed more emphasis on this commitment exactly while responding to the epistemological transformations wrought by the successful programs of modern philological, historical, and natural sciences. What it meant to "know" narrowed considerably under the influence of these programs. Hence for men and women of Huxley's stripe, the activity of *knowing* in the modern, scientific sense came to supplement, if not to replace, the classical Christian activities of prayer, worship, good works, and obedience to ecclesiastical authority. The potential for dissonance was diminished for American celebrants of science by the predominantly respectful stance toward the modern sciences long displayed by the leading denominations.[4] The representation of the ideal scientific edifice as a "temple" became one of the most common metaphorical turns in public discussion of science. "Devotion to science," said America's favorite British philosopher, Herbert Spencer, "is a tacit worship."[5] And in one of the most famous aphorisms of Louis Agassiz, the great American zoologist declared a laboratory of natural science to be "a sanctuary where nothing profane should be tolerated."[6] Woodrow Wilson's most favorable image of science was the image of a nun at her prayers.[7] And the novelist Sinclair Lewis found it quite plausible that a budding scientist

from the varieties of faith preached by churches in the name of Christianity. When Huxley distinguished "verification" from "faith," he took for granted an enormous epistemological divide.

[4] American Protestantism's traditionally positive perspective on modern science is discussed in George Marsden's contribution to this volume. Of the several other works detailing this perspective, a study of "old school" Presbyterians has proved especially influential in recent historiography: Theodore Dwight Bozeman, *Protestants in an Age of Science: The Baconian Ideal and Antebellum American Religious Thought* (Chapel Hill: University of North Carolina Press, 1977).

[5] Herbert Spencer, quoted, for example, in Richard Gregory, *Discovery: The Spirit and Service of Science* (London: Macmillan, 1916; New York: 1926), 41.

[6] Quoted, for example, ibid., 43.

[7] Woodrow Wilson, "Princeton in the Nation's Service," Address of October 21, 1896, in Arthur S. Link, ed., *The Papers of Woodrow Wilson* (Princeton: Princeton University

would offer a distinctive, freethinking "prayer of the scientist" upon being given access to a laboratory.[8]

A host of lesser scientists and writers relied on the same images used by Lewis, Wilson, Agassiz, and Spencer. The representation of science as a religious calling had its own conventions, routinely drawn on in public addresses and in essays on "science and culture." Champions of science made the most of these conventions when seeking to neutralize the suspicion, as the botanist Theodore Gill characterized it in 1888, that science was "an aggressive being and even . . . a demon, shoving and pushing all else away and endeavoring to throttle and kill all else." Gill's own counterimage of science is worth quoting at length because the relevant conventions are so prominent in it:

Science is rather a goddess who is rich in attributes and ready to shower her worshipers, but coy in her gifts; she is generous only to those who worship at her shrine in sincerity and truth, and who. supplement their prayers by continual labor and deeds. To such she distributes her gifts much according to their deserts. Her worshipers are generally content with their several portions, and in her temple enjoy such sweet communion and peace of mind that they envy not the lots of those outside; if at all solicitous for any outsiders they are activated by motives of philanthropy and benevolence alone to invite such to share with them. What other possible motive can there be for proselytism?

Here, then, we find not only prayer and worship within a temple, but also the spreading of the gospel for altruistic motives and the performance of virtuous labor. This hard work, moreover, is rewarded according to merit, and, in any event, assures one's existence in a heavenlike state. Gill's "goddess" of science provides a vaguely pagan variation on the otherwise Protestant theme.[9]

Only in a very loose sense, to be sure, did the celebrants of science's religious character articulate a doctrine of justification. Metaphor, not argument, was the primary mode for indicating the religious function of

---

Press, 1966) X, 31: ". . . calm Science seated there, recluse, ascetic, like a nun, not knowing that the world passes, not caring, if the truth but come in answer to her prayer."

[8] Sinclair Lewis, *Arrowsmith* (New York: Harcourt, Brace & World, 1925; reprint, New York: Signet, 1961), 269: "God give me unclouded eyes and freedom from haste. God give me a quiet and relentless anger against all pretense. . . . God give me a restlessness. . . . God give me strength not to trust in God!"

[9] The logic of this pagan variation was a logic of gender, common to defensive reactions against an "aggressive," "demonic" science which Gill represented first as "it" and then as a male (a "man of straw"). Against this aggression Gill's "goddess," like Wilson's Catholic nun, offers an ample supply of pleasing femininity. Gill's goddess of *science* is clearly a reformulation of the traditionally female *nature;* Gill's worshipers—the actual scientists—were implicitly male. Theodore Gill, "Culture and Science," *American Naturalist* XXII (1888):489–90.

the scientific vocation. The explicit idea that the Judeo-Christian God actually judged individuals on the basis of their cognitive conduct, as he was said to do on the basis of "faith" or "works" in the classical doctrines of justification, was rarely expressed. Even Max Weber's widely quoted assertion that a true scientist believes "the fate of his soul depends" on his cognitive conduct should not be read too literally.[10] Weber partook of the common pattern of secularization, according to which a certain mystification of science accompanied the demystification of traditional religions. Proponents of the vocation of science often employed a set of familiar religious images to convey to themselves, and to their educated and powerful contemporaries, a continuity they sensed between the modern scientific enterprise and the inherited religious culture.

The growth and consolidation of science as a distinctive profession provided a powerful incentive to interpret secular inquiry in terms of an ethic that was congruent with Protestant moral ideals. New professions characteristically generate ideologies by which to justify themselves, but this impulse on the part of scientists was intensified by the resistance of clerical and literary elites, especially in England but also in the United States. The storied debates Huxley carried on with Bishop Wilberforce and Matthew Arnold were simply the most dramatic of many episodes in the struggle of a new scientific elite to establish a larger role for itself in education and public culture.[11] By following the "methods" and "spirit" of science, these scientific enthusiasts prophesied, we shall both advance knowledge and improve society's moral discipline.

The crucial common denominator of all formulations of "the spirit of science" was the basic presumption that science *is* a moral enterprise, that values and obligations *do* attend upon it. The new professional cadre of scientists took the lead in developing this presumption into a major theme of public discourse. In so doing, these intellectuals acted against the widespread suspicion that science was no more moral than the objects it studied. In modern times the knower and the moral agent have often been depicted as contrasting personae, defined to a large extent in opposition to each other. David Hume drew this contrast in the starkest of terms, sharpening a distinction inherited from the seventeenth century and bequeathing to the nineteenth and twentieth a legacy of endless dis-

[10] Max Weber, "Vocation of Science," in Hans Gerth and C. Wright Mills, eds., *From Max Weber: Essays in Sociology* (New York: Oxford University Press, 1946), 135.
[11] On the relation of the professionalization of science to Victorian rivalries between "science" and "religion," see Frank M. Turner, "The Victorian Conflict between Science and Religion: A Professional Dimension," *Isis* LXIX (1978):356–76.

putes about "is" and "ought." The ethic of science spoke directly to this tension between the knower and the moral agent, offering "the Scientist" as a conscientious creature of a demanding ethic. The life of science was a life of *virtue*.

Although many specific virtues were attributed to the scientific enterprise by this or that apologist, some ideals were so consistently affirmed that it is no mistake to refer in the singular to an "ethic of science." The ideal scientist was "disinterested" in the sense that he (or she, technically, but the exemplary Scientist was of course presumed to be male) held critically in check whatever sympathies he might have with one or another potential result of his inquiries. He was "skeptical" in saving his trust for ideas that had received a powerful empirical warrant. It was further incumbent on the man of science to be "objective" by virtue of subjugating private experience to conclusions verified on an intersubjective basis. This intersubjectivity, in turn, served the ideal scientist's "universalism": his commitment to developing a body of truths testable everywhere and ultimately available to all humankind. Hence the ethic of science also entailed "discursiveness," an obligation to share the results of one's inquiries and to take account of the results of the inquiries of others. "Veracity," too, was imperative, as the truthfulness and sincerity of each exchange of information were necessary to the success of the entire, extensive, communitarian endeavor of scientific inquiry.[12] It was primarily to these values that American and British proponents of "the ethical spirit of science" gave homage during the late nineteenth and early twentieth centuries.

Not every adherent of the ethic of science regarded it as a supplement to, or replacement of, a more specifically Christian ethic, but those who did were especially prone to the temple-and-prayer vocabulary for describing science. The most inclusive and decisively biblical of these religious images was that of an urgent message of good news about how to be saved: "the gospel." Richard Gregory, the editor of *Nature*, allowed that his grandfather had "preached the gospel of Christ," his father the "gospel of Socialism," and Gregory himself the "gospel of Science."[13]

---

[12] This construction of the ethic of science differs slightly from, but is essentially in accord with, Robert K. Merton's widely cited "ethos" of science, most easily available in Merton, *The Sociology of Science: Theoretical and Empirical Investigations* (Chicago: University of Chicago Press, 1973), 267–78. I have interpreted Merton's construction in relation to the historical circumstances of the 1930s and early 1940s in my "The Defense of Democracy and Robert K. Merton's Formulation of the Scientific Ethos," *Knowledge and Society* IV (1983):1–15.

[13] Quoted by Hilary Rose and Stephen Rose, "The Incorporation of Science," in Rose and

Critics have sometimes used this and other religious terms sardonically, mocking as "a gospel of research" or "a gospel of fact" the extravagance and intensity of this or that scientific enthusiasm, and condemning as "the new priesthood" the modern scientific establishment. So congenial is this ironic voice in our own time that it is easy to forget the lack of artifice with which even reasonably intelligent members of an earlier generation might have advanced these terms. Without prejudice, we can use the concept of an "intellectual gospel" to refer to the belief that conduct in accord with the ethic of science could be religiously fulfilling, a form of "justification."

The concept of an "intellectual gospel" invites us to recognize and keep in mind the parallels between this persuasion and another, comparable movement that flourished alongside it while drawing on different elements of a common religious heritage, the "social gospel." Our histories speak at length about the social gospel, a broad movement of American Protestants seeking, in the name of religious duty, to reform society along the lines of the ethics of Jesus.[14] Although some theologically conservative critics thought that the social gospel was a recrudescence of the old Arminian heresy, the movement was strong enough to establish itself firmly within several major American Protestant denominations and to find rigorous theological expression in Walter Rauschenbusch's classic of 1917, *A Theology for the Social Gospel*.[15] What I want to call the "intellectual gospel" bears to the hypothetical "cognitive heresy" the same logical relationship that the social gospel bore to the Arminian heresy. But the intellectual gospel was not developed as a program *for the church;* it was "heretical" only in the indirect sense that it appropriated for the legitimation of nonecclesiastical institutions a set of symbols on which churches had relied for the maintenance of their authority. The intellectual gospel was an outgrowth of Protestantism, appealing especially to liberal Protestants and to freethinkers of Protestant origin, but its merits were not debated by congregations and synods. Even Shailer Mathews, the most "modernistic" of the liberal American theologians of the 1920s,

Rose, eds., *The Political Economy of Science* (London: Macmillan, 1976), 27. See also Gregory, *Discovery*, 47.

[14] The social gospel has received more attention from historians than any other aspect of American religious history since the Civil War. Two of the most influential studies of the topic have been Charles Hopkins, *The Rise of the Social Gospel in American Protestantism, 1865–1915* (New Haven: Yale University Press, 1940), and Henry F. May, *Protestant Churches in Industrial America* (New York: Harper & Row, 1949). See also the contribution to this volume by William King.

[15] Walter Rauschenbusch, *A Theology for the Social Gospel* (New York: Macmillan, 1917).

was not accused of defending "justification by verification."[16] When the intellectual gospel was implicitly condemned by Christian believers, it was condemned in the larger guise of "infidelity" or "secularism." In characterizing this extraecclesiastical movement as a "gospel," we need not lose sight of its secularity relative to the social gospel. Yet in failing to so characterize it, or in failing to emphasize in some comparable manner the roots of the scientific ethic in an inherited religious culture, we risk losing sight of the religiosity of that ethic relative to more utilitarian and materialistic affirmations of "science and technology." The intellectual gospel was a distinctive, extremely idealistic construction of the ultimate significance of science.

When admirers of the ethic of science called attention to its religious potential, they most often alluded to one or more of three specific strands of continuity with the religious culture inherited by American academic intellectuals of the late nineteenth and early twentieth century. These might be termed the psychological, metaphysical, and moral dimensions of "the intellectual gospel." The essence of each of these dimensions can be briefly set forth.

Psychologically, the "religious" character of correct inquiry was in its utter seriousness and nobility of purpose, its righteous devotion to a cause that transcends one's immediate, material interests. This psychological dimension was the most general of the three, and the most akin to claims made on behalf of any serious enterprise, including any number of arts and vocations. It was also the least specific to Protestantism and to the Judeo-Christian tradition.

Metaphysically, secular knowledge was a "religious" mode by virtue of its cosmic importance. It constituted an authentic and intense relationship between human beings and whatever powers made the universe what it was. The intellectuals who developed and popularized the ethic of science drew on a venerable tradition of respect for "the study of nature" as a means of access to God, the Creator. Protestantism and the Scientific Revolution had reinforced each other in many phases of the intellectual history of early modern Europe. The idea of "nature" and "scripture" as parallel expressions of the deity was, of course, firmly entrenched in Britain and the United States in the mid-nineteenth century. Especially in the United States both these avenues to God were distinguished from the

[16] On Mathews and the controversies surrounding his work, see William R. Hutchison, *The Modernist Impulse in American Protestantism* (Cambridge, Mass.: Harvard University Press, 1977), 275–82.

notorious "skepticism" of the Enlightenment, which American believers routinely condemned for departing from the pious, cautious, "Baconian" study of nature and scripture in order to speculate in an ill-informed and undisciplined manner. Although the legacy of skepticism was taken up after midcentury by the intellectuals who developed the cognitive ethic, these intellectuals generally sought to assimilate skepticism into this intensely Protestant vision of empirical study as a reverent, religiously meaningful enterprise.

This task of assimilation was made easier by another tradition on which Huxley and his comrades were able to draw: the moral ideals of Protestantism itself, especially as it developed in Britain and the United States. The opportunity to perpetuate certain of these specific ideals was the third, "moral," dimension of the intellectual gospel. The classical "values of science" were far from alien to a religious heritage in which "disinterestedness" and "self-abnegation" had long been praised. Although the genealogy of the ethic of science obviously included stoic stock, as reinvigorated during the classical revival of the Enlightenment,[17] this ethic was a direct and immediate descendant of Protestantism. Hence the moral discipline of science was "religious" because it apparently carried on from the church the task of promoting certain virtues. When critics complained that science was "irreligious," it was de rigueur to respond that devoted scientists were more Christian than most clergymen. Especially was this line taken in regard to the preacherlike Huxley, of whom it was said, without irony, that in this one agnostic there was "so much real Christianity" that if its plentitude were divided up and distributed, there would be more than enough of it "to save the soul" of every person in the British Isles.[18]

The new secular gospel of which Huxley was a prominent symbol transcended the theist-agnostic divide. Huxley himself sometimes implied that Christianity was a thing of the past, to be replaced eventually by something bearing the name of "science." In the United States this view became more and more common in the early twentieth century, especially under the influence of the great secularist John Dewey, but the intellectual gospel was also absorbed by many men and women who were confident that plenty of room was left for other gospels, too, especially

---

[17] A convenient point of access to this episode, although exclusive to France, is Charles B. Paul, *Science and Immorality: The Eloges of the Paris Academy of Sciences (1699–1791)* (Berkeley: University of California Press, 1980).

[18] This characterization was popularized in America by John Fiske. See, e.g., John Fiske, "Reminiscences of Huxley," *Atlantic* LXXXVII (February 1901), 283.

the one preached by Jesus Christ. This was the standard view throughout the late nineteenth and early twentieth centuries even at Johns Hopkins University, the most ideologically intense bastion of the intellectual gospel in the United States.[19] The chemist Ira Remsen, speaking in 1904 as president of Johns Hopkins, doubted that science could ever actually "take the place of religion," which would surely continue to have its own existence even while the ethical precepts of the scientific endeavor do "conform" to "the teachings of the highest types of religion."[20] Three decades later, when Dewey's influence was at its peak, the Harvard historian of science George Sarton still drew the same conventional science-religion line of demarcation, even while quoting Huxley uncritically and while extolling the intensely religious character of scientific inquiry.[21]

The line between science and religion acknowledged by Remsen and Sarton made it all the easier for institutionally responsible Christians to join in the spreading of the intellectual gospel. If even the most "religious" science fell short of becoming a new religion, surely Christianity had nothing to fear from it? Only the most theologically modernistic of the clergy and the seminarians took much interest in the intellectual gospel, but to them the notion of an intellectual gospel parallel to the social can be the least incongruously applied.[22] The support offered by this minority was, in some cases, firm and vigorous. A convenient example is Andover Theological Seminary's George Harris, one of the ablest and most learned of American Protestant theologians at the turn of the century. Harris found in the scholar's vocation "the likest thing there is" to authentic, living "virtue." Virtue itself has various embodiments, suggested Harris in 1896, and the pure, unselfish scholar's devoted, "disinterested" service to truth is the *intellectual* embodiment of virtue.[23] Har-

---

[19] For a helpful account of the atmosphere at Johns Hopkins in the 1880s, see Hugh Hawkins, *Pioneer: A History of the Johns Hopkins University, 1874–1889* (Ithaca: Cornell University Press, 1960), 293–315.

[20] Ira Remsen, "Scientific Investigation and Progress," *Popular Science Monthly* LXIV (1904):301.

[21] George Sarton, *The History of Science and the New Humanism* (Cambridge, Mass.: Harvard University Press, 1937), 116–18.

[22] Hutchison notes in passing (*Modernist Impulse*, 165) that "about one third" of "the thirty-three most prominent leaders of theological liberalism in the period from 1875 to 1915" took "no discernible part in the social gospel." It is interesting that Hutchison's list of nonparticipants in the one liberal gospel includes several who were attracted to what I am saying amounted to a second liberal gospel: Charles A. Briggs, George Gordon, George Harris, A. C. McGiffert, Theodore Munger, and Egbert Smyth. These thinkers were much more responsive to contemporary scientific thought than the conservative Princeton theologians whose claim to be "scientific" is discussed in this volume by George Marsden.

[23] George Harris, *Moral Evolution* (London: Macmillan, 1896), 76.

ris's Congregationalist colleague Newman Smyth insisted that even the study of Jesus Christ was not "truly and profoundly reverent and religious" if carried out in a setting of "prejudice"; a genuinely "religious" approach would have to entail "the desire to find the facts as they are."[24] Of Newton's disciplining of his own preferences, the German Reformed Church's *Mercersburg Review* exclaimed in 1873, amid enthusiastic references to Bacon, Spencer, and John Tyndall, "What religious self-abnegation . . . What a submission of the pride of intellect to the facts of the universe!"[25]

This was exactly the kind of talk William James parodied in *The Will to Believe:* "what thousands of disinterested moral lives of men lie buried" in the "mere foundations" of "the magnificent edifice of the physical sciences, . . . what patience and postponement, what choking down of mere preference, what submission to the icy laws of outer fact are wrought into its very stones and mortar." But James betrayed here an element of sympathy, even while criticizing the positivist epistemology and the agnosticism with which the intellectual gospel was sometimes connected, and while mocking the "robustious pathos of voice" in which it was so often expressed.[26] Unlike the liberal theologians quoted earlier, James was not an institutionally responsible defender of Christianity, but he was his generation's leading champion of "nonscientific" religious experience. His ironic homage to the intellectual gospel was consistent with his career-long prophecy on behalf of a science broad enough to effect what James frankly called the world's "salvation."[27]

Voices more earnest than James's, and more distant from the pulpit than those of the Andover theologians, were of course the chief agencies of the dissemination of the intellectual gospel. Preeminent among these voices were always Huxley and his contemporary British allies—including Herbert Spencer, John Tyndall, W. K. Clifford, and Charles Kingsley—whose utterances of the 1860s and 1870s remained common coin in American academic discourse long after they were joined in the 1890s

[24] Newman Smyth, *Old Faiths in New Light* (New York: Scribner's, 1879), 24. See also Smyth, *Through Science to Faith* (New York: Scribner's, 1902), which opened with a paean to the "pure love of truth" that ideally united enlightened theologians with scientists.

[25] W. Leaman, "The Scope and Spirit of Scientific Research," *Mercersburg Review* XX (1873):532.

[26] William James, *The Will to Believe* (Cambridge, Mass.: Harvard University Press, 1979), 17–18.

[27] I have discussed James's perspective on science and religion in *In the American Province: Studies in the History and Historiography of Ideas* (Bloomington: Indiana University Press, 1985), 3–22.

by a host of native American voices. During the 1870s and 1880s the celebration of modern, secular science in a religious idiom had also gone forward in the United States, but not on the scale seen in the 1890s and in the early years of the new century when the new universities experienced their most explosive growth in size, number, and prestige.[28] Then did John Dewey explain to the Student Christian Association at the University of Michigan that the modern definition of "prayer" was the attitude of inquiry characteristic of science, and that "the building of the Kingdom of God on earth" depended as much on the spread of the ethic of science as it did on anything else.[29] Then, too, did G. Stanley Hall, as president of the new, zealously scientific Clark University, identify the spirit of "research" as the modern voice of "the Holy Ghost." Hall praised the worldwide academic community—incorporating "all groups of students inflamed with the love of truth"—as the modern equivalent of the "Church universal." The "old oracles find new voices," said Hall, "and who would and should not listen?"[30]

The writings of the American academic reformers were brought comfortably together with the foundational writings of Huxley and his British contemporaries in Richard Gregory's *Discovery: The Spirit and Service of Science,* a volume of 1916 that represents the intellectual gospel at its most romantic. Gregory quoted copiously from various and sundry paeans to "the scientific spirit," interspersing the utterances of the Victorians and their successors with inspirational passages from Bacon, Newton, Shakespeare, and Goethe. *Discovery* was brought out in American as well as British editions; it was in its twelfth printing when the kindred *Arrowsmith* appeared in 1925. Gregory himself favored the inherited religious vocabulary as much as did any of the savants whom he quoted. He spoke repeatedly of the "righteousness" and "holiness" of the calling that was the basis for his "uplifting gospel," a "gospel of light." The "temple of science" demands "sacrifices at the altar of knowledge," and "only those with sincere regard for truth will find their gifts acceptable." Entry into "the spiritual city of science" depends on a purity of heart like Sir Galahad, the knight with a "complete vision of the Holy

---

[28] On the articulation of an ideology of "research" in relation to the creation and growth of these institutions, see Laurence R. Veysey, *The Emergence of the American University* (Chicago: University of Chicago Press, 1965), 121–79, especially 149–58, which focuses on the religiosity of many expressions of this ideology. See also my "Inquiry and Uplift: Late Nineteenth Century American Academics and the Moral Efficacy of Scientific Practice," in Thomas L. Haskell, ed., *The Authority of Experts: Essays in History and Theory* (Bloomington: Indiana University Press, 1984), 142–56.

[29] John Dewey, *The Early Works, 1881–1898,* IV, 104–5, 368.

[30] G. Stanley Hall, "Research the Vital Spirit of Teaching," *Forum* XVII (1894):565.

Grail." The truly scientific mind "cannot be brought within the bounds of a narrow religious formulary," explained Gregory, "yet it is essentially devout, and it influences for good all with whom it comes into contact."[31]

Gregory dwelled on the religious piety of great men of science, including Pasteur, of whom a statue for the Cathedral of St. John the Divine had recently been proposed by Henry Fairfield Osborn, director of the American Museum of Natural History. In his pamphlet of 1913, *The New Order of Sainthood,* Osborn used Pasteur as his model for scientific sainthood. Osborn declared that the essential insights of the "faith of our fathers" were stronger than ever as a result of the "constructive, purifying, and regenerating" acts of scientific inquiry during the second half of the nineteenth century. Hence it was in a real rather than a metaphorical church—the new cathedral being built on 110th Street in New York City—that Osborn proposed the recognition of a distinctive order of saints:

Should we not institute a new order of sainthood for men like Pasteur? Could we find one more eminent for consecration, piety, and service in life and character than this devout investigator? . . . Would not a statue of Louis Pasteur . . . proclaim the faith of the modern Church that the two great historic movements of Love and of Knowledge, of the spiritual and intellectual and the physical well-being of man, are harmonious of a single and eternal truth?[32]

Although the tone in which Osborn and Gregory spoke recalled the nineteenth century, which had produced their greatest heroes and their most treasured aphorisms, the Edwardsean-Progressive works of Osborn and Gregory bear great similarity to the only slightly less romantic versions of the intellectual gospel that were enunciated during the more hard-boiled 1920s. A prominent, but insufficiently recognized, theme in the intellectual history of the 1920s is the perpetuation, in regard to *science,* of a religious idealism that was otherwise on the defensive. The intellectual gospel was updated for this proudly skeptical decade not only by the reverent *Arrowsmith,* on the basis of which Sinclair Lewis won his greatest critical acclaim, but also by the works of historians John Herman Randall, Jr., James Harvey Robinson, and Frederick Barry.[33] All pro-

---

[31] Gregory, *Discovery,* vi, 11, 12, 27, 51, 54–55. Gregory did not cite his sources, and sometimes erred in his attributions. For example, he attributed to the University of Pennsylvania chemist Edgar Fahs Smith a rather well-known poem by James Russell Lowell that Smith had used while praising a colleague for his "self denial stern"; see ibid., 17.

[32] Henry Fairfield Osborn, *The New Order of Sainthood* (New York: Scribner's, 1913), 13, 16.

[33] See, as examples, John Herman Randall, Jr., *Our Changing Civilization: How Science and the Machine Are Reconstructing Modern Life* (New York: Stokes, 1931); James Harvey Robinson, *The Mind in the Making* (New York: Harpers, 1921); and Frederick Barry, *The Scientific Habit of Thought* (New York: Columbia University Press, 1927).

claimed science's ability to carry on some of the salient spiritual functions of traditional religion. The same thought was expressed routinely in the popular writings of physical and social scientists throughout the decade. The biologist Winterton C. Curtis speculated in his widely discussed book, *Science and Human Affairs,* that "the scientific habit of mind" would "satisfy the ethical and philosophical desires which have been hitherto formulated as religion and theology."[34]

This was exactly the upshot of Walter Lippmann's *A Preface to Morals,* although this famous book of 1929 was anything but romantic. An instant classic of cultural criticism, *A Preface to Morals* caught the note of jaundiced "disillusionment" that so many American intellectuals of the 1920s associated with themselves. Hence the book's guarded advocacy of the intellectual gospel is all the more revealing an index of this gospel's appeal. Lippmann addressed what he saw as the enduring *religious* needs of his culture. These needs simply could not be met by the existing churches and their religions, he was quick to conclude, for the "acids of modernity" had eroded their foundations; the sophisticated, educated person still had religious yearnings, but intellectual integrity required that such a person turn away from the inherited, popular religions. Lippmann saw promise in what he called the "high religion" of classical philosophy. The essence of this "high religion" was a stoic "disinterestedness" to be found in Lippmann's own day chiefly *in science.* There, more than anywhere else, could one contemplate the "mature" resignation to the limits of one's existence celebrated in *A Preface to Morals.* There, in science, the individual was to modify desire in order to meet "reality":

And so the mature man would take the world as it comes, and within himself remain quite unperturbed. When he acted, he would know that he was only testing an hypothesis, and . . . he would be quite prepared for the discovery that he might make mistakes, for his intelligence would be disentangled from his hopes. The failure of his experiment could not, therefore, involve the failure of his life. For the aspect of life which implicated his soul would be his understanding of life, and, to the understanding, defeat is no less interesting than victory.[35]

"Hypothesis." "Experiment." "Understanding." Lippmann associated his "religion of the spirit" with ancient sages, but as he elaborated on it he spoke more and more of "the spirit of modern science." Not

[34] Winterton C. Curtis, *Science and Human Affairs: From the Viewpoint of Biology* (New York: Harcourt, Brace and Company, 1922), 8. See also, e.g., Edwin Grant Conklin, *The Direction of Human Evolution* (New York: C. Scribner's Sons, 1922), especially 244.
[35] Walter Lippmann, *A Preface to Morals* (New York: Macmillan, 1929), 209, 329.

only did he prescribe detachment, neutrality, tolerance, universalism, and skepticism; he explicitly identified "pure science" as "high religion incarnate." The high religion has "hitherto" been "lyrical and personal and apart," but now "the scientific discipline" could bring it "down to earth and into direct and decisive contact with the concerns of mankind." Moreover, this religion was uniquely capable of surviving any and all changes in our specific knowledge about the world: "the religion of the spirit does not depend upon creeds and cosmologies; it has no vested interest in any particular truth." It alone could "endure the variety and complexity of things," because it aimed higher. "Its indifference to what the facts may be is indeed the very spirit of scientific inquiry." He smiled at those whose view of science was so naive as to make a religion out of any given, specific set of scientific results; such people did not understand the provisional character of scientific belief, had not absorbed the insight that the religious significance of science was in its "inward principle," its spirit. To support his view of science, Lippmann quoted an essay that Charles Peirce—one of America's most forthright and consistent champions of the ethic of science—had published in *Popular Science Monthly* in 1878.[36]

Lippmann had praised "the discipline of science" long before 1929, but with a very different, more exuberant demeanor. This discipline was to promote "mastery," to enable the men and women of the twentieth century to control their fate, Lippmann had argued in 1914. Fifteen years after he had invoked the "scientific spirit" in his upbeat, bring-on-the-world *Drift and Mastery*—no less a classic of "Progressivism" than was Lippmann's book of 1929 an enduring monument of the intellectual preoccupations of that time—Lippmann called on the same device to help people adapt to "reality."[37] Scholars have noted the emotional gulf Lippmann crossed between these two books, but they have not paid sufficient attention to the fact that in both cases Lippmann turned to "the spirit of science" for his solution. The intellectual gospel admitted of formulations running across a spectrum from heady exuberance to chastened resignation, and Lippmann himself had occupied both extremes by the time he was forty.

John Dewey invites attention here because he never moved so far as

---

[36] Lippmann, *A Preface to Morals*, 129, 131, 239, 327–8. Lippmann quoted Peirce's "How to Make Our Ideas Clear." He cited it as reprinted in the collection of Peirce's writings edited by Morris R. Cohen, *Chance, Love, and Logic* (New York: Harcourt, Brace, 1923).

[37] Walter Lippmann, *Drift and Mastery* (New York: Kinnerly, 1914); on this early work of Lippmann's, see my *In the American Province*, 44–55.

Lippmann did toward the "resignation" end of that spectrum, yet he continued throughout the 1920s and 1930s to depict the life of inquiry as an essentially religious mission. Never had Dewey been more explicit and forthright about this than he was in 1934, in *A Common Faith*. This work was a reaction, in part, to a popular disillusion with science deeper than that registered by Lippmann's *A Preface to Morals*. Lippmann had given up on the idea of reconstructing society, whether by science or by any other means, but remained loyal to the ethic of science as the most defensible source of religious fulfillment. Others had reacted more sharply against the secular, humanistic currents associated with the ethic of science. Orthodox Christianity was then being affirmed against these currents by T. S. Eliot, John Crowe Ransom, and Reinhold Niebuhr.

Dewey would have none of this new orthodoxy. In *A Common Faith*, Dewey renounced once again all varieties of supernaturalism and insisted that inquiry itself could properly be described as a "religious" object. He also rejected as excessively passive the stoical outlook of Lippmann. "Faith in the continued disclosing of truth through directed cooperative human endeavor," Dewey explained, "is more religious in quality than is any faith in a completed revelation." Dewey distinguished sharply between any and all particular *religions,* which he declared to have outlived their usefulness and to have produced many destructive results, and *the religious,* a quality that might inhere in our relation to any object. The unification of the self and its harmonization with the Universe define "the religious," and this unification and harmonization can be more than "a mere Stoical resolution to endure unperturbed throughout the buffetings of fortune." This unification and harmonization can take place in relation to a systematic effort to understand and change the world. Religion is an "element" in life that must be liberated from "religions," Dewey insisted, in order that people can be free to develop this element in healthier contexts, including, above all, the practice of inquiry.[38]

The intellectual gospel did not end with Dewey any more than the social gospel ended with Rauschenbusch. The notion that conduct in accord with the scientific ethic was a form of religious fulfillment continued to be invoked, especially by people who sought to explain the nature of science to a popular audience or to defend secular cultural institutions against charges of insensitivity to the moral and religious needs of society. But the intellectual gospel was a less important feature of American intellectual life during the second third of the twentieth century than it

[38] John Dewey, *A Common Faith* (New Haven: Yale University Press, 1934), 16, 19, 26, 57.

had been during the previous fifty years. This change had a number of sources.

The very success with which cultural institutions had been secularized diminished the need to preach this particular gospel. Intellectuals who were "irreligious" in the sense of professing neither Christianity nor any other of the historic religions were generally more comfortable with their irreligion, and less moved to construct their secularity in terms that called attention to a religious heritage. Intellectuals who remained committed to a Protestant church or to Catholicism were more comfortable with varieties of neoorthodoxy that resisted the open accommodation with "science" favored by the Protestant theological elite of the previous era. The increasing proportion of American intellectuals who had Jewish, rather than Protestant or Catholic, antecedents helped move public discourse about science away from the terms developed by WASP intellectuals in the nineteenth century. The intellectual fashions among educated Americans moved yet more decisively away from the extreme idealism of which the intellectual gospel was, in the 1920s, already an anomalous remnant. The worldwide political crises of the 1930s and 1940s drew proponents of the scientific ethic toward its democratic implications, rather than toward the religious virtues that had seemed so important during the Victorian "crisis of faith." The atomic bomb gave new credibility to the suspicion that demonic forces were somehow entangled in science no less than were the more wholesome forces attributed to it by the intellectual gospel. Finally, the scientific enterprise came under more critical, empirical scrutiny, rendering less plausible and less responsive to current concerns the constructions of science's religiosity popularized by Huxley and Dewey.

During the era in which the intellectual gospel flourished, however, the intellectual gospel and the social gospel divided their common religious heritage between them. Each took up and developed in relative isolation one of the two themes mentioned by Henry Fairfield Osborn, when extolling the sainthood of Pasteur: Love and Knowledge. In proposing a statue of Pasteur in the Cathedral of St. John the Divine, it was natural for even a proponent of the intellectual gospel to envisage a symbolic unification of knowledge with love, but Osborn was primarily a spokesman for an ethic not of love but of science. The social gospel accentuated and developed love as a religious ideal, trusting that other movements would pursue knowledge; the intellectual gospel accentuated and developed knowledge as a religious ideal, trusting that other movements would practice love.

The social gospel and the intellectual gospel deserve to be remembered as siblings, if not as twins. Just as the social gospel was a major tributary to the river of social reform that became a conspicuous feature of the historical landscape of the United States in the late nineteenth and early twentieth century, the intellectual gospel fed the current of academic reform that resulted in the reorganization of American culture around universities devoted largely to research. Just as the social gospel enabled a man or a woman to feel that work in a settlement house or in a Progressive's political campaign helped to bring about the Kingdom of God, the intellectual gospel enabled a man or a woman to feel that work in a university or a laboratory helped to bring to maturation spiritual seeds planted in the Bible and nurtured by Christianity. Just as the social gospel provided religious sanction for the liberal reforms carried out by the bourgeoisie in the face of tensions created by industrial capitalism, the intellectual gospel rendered a religious mission the production of the new knowledge on which the technologically sophisticated social order of modern times was increasingly dependent. Just as the social gospel inspired many church members to believe that the essence of their Christian birthright was a set of moral teachings not dissimilar to those found in other religions, the intellectual gospel inspired many intellectuals to believe that an aura of divinity accompanied the secularization of public doctrine in response to the content, scope, and dynamic character of modern scientific knowledge. Just as the social gospel encouraged its adherents to interpret their labors in society as signs of a right relationship with God, the intellectual gospel encouraged its adherents to interpret their labors in the laboratory and the archives as signs of a right relationship with whatever gods they recognized.

But where, in the intellectual gospel, was Jesus Christ? For all its striking similarities to the social gospel, the intellectual gospel was not explicitly preached in the name of a unique Christianity. In the social gospel, men and women of Christian commitment sought to expand and reinterpret their religious tradition to make it more responsive to social and psychological conditions of modern life, but these men and women did not advance a doctrine of separate spheres, one for "religion" and one for "social reform." Meanwhile in the intellectual gospel, a spiritual intensity for which Christianity had been the uniquely powerful vehicle was transferred to an endeavor that was becoming, as our recent historiography emphasizes, increasingly differentiated and divergent from Christianity. It was to an increasingly autonomous, cognitive enterprise that ideologues of science applied the language of spiritual perfection.

The intellectual gospel challenged Christianity's moral authority because this gospel intensified a connection between spiritual perfection and scientific inquiry exactly while that inquiry renounced all the more openly the Christian presuppositions that had been cheerfully acknowledged by generations of scientists.

This moral challenge did not compare in magnitude with science's cognitive challenge to the authority of Christianity, but performed a singular service in support of that more profound challenge. It equipped partisans of science with grounds for ignoring a familiar complaint of Christian moralists. Science, these complainants repeatedly insisted, was simply "about facts" and "devoid of values." If the realm of cognition is to be turned over to science, they argued, then let us remember that the realm of values is all the more clearly and exclusively the business of religion. If we are going to have separate spheres, they said, let us all remember that in the sphere of science there are *only* facts.[39] This complaint was easily neutralized by the intellectual gospel. Plainly, science embodied a demanding ethic; to do science was to affirm, to abide by, and to exemplify specific and vital values. The issues in moral philosophy begged by this confidence are beside the point of our understanding the role played by the ethic of science in making an autonomous, secular science spiritually acceptable to intellectuals brought up in the culture of nineteenth-century Protestantism. The intellectual gospel may not have been an episode in any "warfare" of science and religion, but it did function in a real struggle between rival claimants to the cultural leadership of the United States.[40]

[39] For a typical rendition of this refrain, see Christian Gauss, "The Threat of Science," *Scribner's Magazine* LXXXVIII (1930):467–78.

[40] Although this essay addresses the intellectual gospel in relation to American religious history and its historiography, I want to call attention to a larger frame of reference in which the cultural powers of the scientific enterprise were celebrated. Much of the discourse of twentieth-century intellectuals has been influenced by the notion that "science," rather than "religion" or "the arts," might become the decisive force in determining the contents of a superior modern culture. I have argued elsewhere that by distinguishing this "cognitivism" from the celebration of human artifice manifest in "modernist" movements in literature and the arts, we can arrive at a more accurate comprehension of the general issues that have preoccupied post-Biblical intellectuals in the United States and Western Europe during much of this century. See my "The Knower and the Artificer," *American Quarterly* XXXIX (1987), 37–55. In developing my ideas about "the intellectual gospel," I have been helped by the suggestions and criticisms of Van Harvey, William Hutchison, Hugh Jackson, Julie A. Reuben, and Grant Wacker.

7

On the scientific study of religion in the United States, 1870–1980

MURRAY G. MURPHEY

The scientific study of religion is a relatively new enterprise that dates from the second half of the nineteenth century. In seeking to tell the story of this enterprise as it has been practiced in the United States since 1870, it has been necessary to refer frequently to the work of Europeans, for in this as in other scientific enterprises, there was constant interaction across the Atlantic. Nevertheless, I have sought to focus on the work that American social scientists have done on religion and to describe the major approaches and problems that have characterized their work. Although the treatment is necessarily selective and incomplete, I hope it will serve to suggest both the strengths and weaknesses of the work done in this field and to raise some questions about its future direction.

There is no simple way to date the beginnings of the social sciences in the United States, but it is fairly well known that they developed within the tradition of moral philosophy that originated with Thomas Reid, Dugald Stewart, Adam Smith, and other Scottish thinkers who dominated American education and thinking throughout much of the nineteenth century. Unlike French positivism, which so influenced the social sciences in Europe, the moral philosophy tradition was conceived in Protestantism and never outgrew its religious origins. Thus as the study of psychology, economics, politics, and society developed here in the first half of the nineteenth century, it took Christian doctrine as a premise and so considered religion not as a subject for scientific study but as a frame of reference within which questions of human behavior were to be viewed. Nor was the paradigmatic status of Christianity weakened by the expanding knowledge of Egyptian, Islamic, Oriental, Indian, African, and American Indian religions. Devotees of the classical curriculum that they were, American scholars had long known about Greek and Roman religions without thereby being brought to wonder about the uniquely favored status of their own religions.[1]

The Darwinian revolution changed this situation, as it changed so many other things. It is unnecessary to discuss here the scientific and religious controversies that followed the publication of the *Origin of Species*. It is sufficient to note that the applications of evolutionary theory both to man and to human society created a new and very different frame of reference. These applications of evolution usually led to linear and progressionist theories depicting a single, and often divinely ordained, line of development from rude beginnings to the highest form of civilization, which invariably turned out to be ours.[2] Given this frame of reference, even if one assumed, as most did, that religion reached its culmination in Christianity, the question was inescapable, from what had Christianity evolved? Moreover, the quick equation drawn between existing nonliterate cultures and the earliest cultures from which evolution began gave a sudden importance to such cultures as those of the American Indians, who were conveniently available for study by American scientists. Thus nineteenth-century nonliterates became a window into the past with respect to religion as well as other cultural phenomena, and the task of describing the evolution of human civilization, religion included, became the calling of the social scientists of the day.

The major achievements in this area were not made in the United States. The great names of the evolutionary school—Edward Tylor, Herbert Spencer, James Frazer, Robert Marett—were all British. The contribution made by the Americans to this work was that of specific descriptions of American Indian cultures and religions. The Bureau of Ethnology, under the leadership of John Wesley Powell, generated a series of monographs on tribal cultures dealing with their religions as well as other cultural phenomena, but a number of significant papers were also written specifically on the religion of the American Indians.[3] Thus the American

[1] Elizabeth Flower and Murray G. Murphey, *A History of Philosophy in America* (New York: Putnam, 1977) I, chapter 5; Gladys Bryson, *Man and Society* (New York: A. M. Kelly, 1969); Jay Wharton Fay, *American Psychology Before William James* (New Brunswick: Rutgers University Press, 1939); Dorothy Ross, "The Development of the Social Sciences," in *The Organization of Knowledge in Modern America, 1860–1920*, edited by A. Oleson and J. Voss (Baltimore: Johns Hopkins University Press, 1979), 107–38.

[2] Flower and Murphey, *History*, II, chapter 9; Robert Bannister, *Social Darwinism: Science and Myth in Anglo-American Social Thought* (Philadelphia: Temple University Press, 1979).

[3] Ake Hultkrantz, *The Study of American Indian Religions* (New York: Crossroads, 1983), 10–12.

role here was that of contributing data that the Europeans then used to develop systematic theories. In this sense, it continued the traditional relationship between American and European science, which had first developed in botany and zoology in the colonial period and had flourished ever since.[4]

The work of these British evolutionists was basic for the American developments, because the British established the theories that Americans would adopt or contest for years to come. Something must therefore be said about this work. Beyond question, Tylor was the acknowledged master of this school; his *Primitive Culture*[5] in 1871 was the text to which all subsequent writers referred. Tylor defined religion as "the belief in spiritual beings"[6] and termed this doctrine "animism."[7] His problems were then to explain how early man came by this belief, and how modern religion had evolved from it. Tylor treated the problem of religion as a problem of belief, as his definition required, and early man as a rational chap who arrived at animism while trying to explain his own experience. Tylor believed that the problems of explaining such states as death, sleep, trances, and illness and of accounting for dreams first led our ancestral thinker to posit the existence of a peripatetic soul which could leave the body during sleep or trances and whose experiences while abroad were the dreams and visions people experienced. Death was then seen as the permanent departure of the soul, which opened the way for the idea of the afterlife. From this origin, Tylor then sought to show how more complex religious beliefs could evolve—possession, fetishism, guardian spirits, familial spirits, nature gods, polytheism, and—finally—monotheism. Throughout the work, Tylor's argument was bolstered—one might almost say buried—by masses of ethnographic data marshalled in its support.

Tylor has come to be seen as the leading early advocate both of evolutionism and of the so-called rationalist view—the view that religion is a set of beliefs created to explain experience. Although he did deal with ceremony, he did not integrate this with his theory of belief, and he had little to say about religious organizations, roles, symbols, or the emo-

[4] Brooke Hindle, *The Pursuit of Science in Revolutionary America* (Chapel Hill: University of North Carolina Press, 1956).
[5] Edward B. Tylor, *Primitive Culture* (New York: Gordon, 1974), 2 vols., first published 1871.
[6] Ibid., I, 383.
[7] Ibid., I, 384.

tional factors in religion. In this respect he is typical of these early evo-lutionists. Spencer advocated a theory very similar to Tylor's,[8] but his influence on the study of religion in America was much less. Even Tylor's opponents generally adopted his approach. Thus Andrew Lang in 1898 defended the position that belief in a single divine creator and ruler of the world was to be found among most nonliterate peoples of the world[9]— a view subsequently elaborated with massive scholarship and Catholic fervor by Father Wilhelm Schmidt.[10] Similarly, Marett proposed the idea in 1900 of a preanimistic world view based on impersonal magical pow-ers,[11] and Frazer argued for the temporal priority of magic over reli-gion.[12] But all these scholars took the rationalist approach; Frazer, for example, viewing magic as a proto-science geared to the explanation and control of experience.

Although Americans contributed to the development of this early evo-lutionary theory chiefly through ethnographic reports, there developed in the United States a rather different approach to the study of religion, which, although also a product of evolutionism, came out of psychology. As the controversy over the religious meaning of evolution developed in this country, the crucial issue rapidly became the nature and place of the mind. Mechanistic interpretations, such as that of Herbert Spencer, made of the mind a purely natural phenomenon, wholly governed by natural law, and so denied its freedom and its power to alter the course of nature. Such a view, of course, also denied immortality and the moral autonomy of the individual; morality instead was located in the evolutionary pro-cess itself, which wholly determined the moral views of the individual. In contrast, idealists posited a view of the world as spirit developing accord-ing to an inner logic, but the individual became merely an idea in the Absolute Mind, with little more freedom or moral autonomy than in the mechanist view.

Between these two positions, William James and the pragmatists sought to work out a middle way that would (1) permit the scientific study of the mind and nature without compromising human freedom or moral

[8] Herbert Spencer, *The Principles of Sociology* (New York: D. Appleton and Co., 1892), vol. I.
[9] Andrew Lang, *The Making of Religion* (New York: AMS Press, 1968), first published 1898.
[10] Eric Sharpe, *Comparative Religion: A History* (London: Duckworth, 1975), 64–65.
[11] Robert Marett, "Pre-animistic Religion," *Folk-lore* 11:162–82 (1900).
[12] James G. Frazer, *The Golden Bough: A Study of Magic and Religion* (London: Macmil-lan, 1911–1915), 12 vols.

autonomy and (2) leave the way open for religion.[13] James achieved the first goal in the *Principles of Psychology*[14] in 1890 and sought to achieve the second in *The Varieties of Religious Experience*[15] in 1902. Defining religion as "the feelings, acts, and experiences of individual men in their solitude in relation to whatever they may consider the divine,"[16] James sought both to describe the varieties of such phenomena and to account for them. His discussions of conversion, saintliness, and mysticism display his remarkable ability to portray and analyze inner experience. But James's account was not simply descriptive; he regarded religious experiences as involving a relation to "something more" than the conscious mind—a something more which, on its subjective side, he identified with the subconscious and which, on its objective side, he suggested might be divine.[17] James thus broke with the reductionism of Tylor, Spencer, and the rest by allowing the possibility that religious entities might be real, as he broke with their rationalism by emphasizing feeling and experience. However, the latter break was not so great as some have thought, because, for James, ideas always involved feeling; thinking and feeling were not for him wholly separate categories.

James's student, Edwin Starbuck, was an even more emphatic believer in the truth of religion than James, but his interests were primarily in religious education and growth. He therefore concentrated his attention on conversion and in his *Psychology of Religion*[18] in 1899—his results were first published several years earlier in the *American Journal of Psychology*[19]—he employed questionnaires to collect data on religious experience. Although his sample was small and not random and the statistical analysis was primitive, Starbuck did attempt to describe the religious experience of ordinary people and to relate it to their religious development, whereas James—although he made some use of Starbuck's data—emphasized chiefly the experiences of religious "geniuses."[20] Starbuck also studied nonconversionist religious development and came to

---

[13] Murray G. Murphey, "Kant's Children: The Cambridge Pragmatists," *Transactions of the Charles S. Peirce Society* 4:3–33 (1968).

[14] William James, *The Principles of Psychology* (New York: Henry Holt, 1890), 2 vols.

[15] William James, *The Varieties of Religious Experience* (New York: Random House, 1902).

[16] Ibid., 31–32.

[17] Ibid., 505ff.

[18] Edwin Diller Starbuck, *The Psychology of Religion* (New York: Charles Scribner's Sons, 1899).

[19] Edwin Diller Starbuck, "A Study of Conversion," *American Journal of Psychology* 8 (1897):268–308.

[20] James, *Varieties*, 8.

the conclusion that the conversionist and the gradualist routes were simply alternative paths to "the birth of a new and larger spiritual consciousness."[21]

James Leuba was a student of Stanley Hall at Clark University rather than of James, but he, too, focused on conversion experiences and published his dissertation on the subject in the *American Journal of Psychology* in 1896,[22] about six months before Starbuck published his results in the same journal. Leuba also used questionnaires to collect data, but he used this material only anecdotally, combining it with interviews and historical records. Like James and Starbuck, Leuba focused on states of consciousness or feelings, and he defined religion in these terms. His six-stage analysis of conversion closely paralleled theological accounts, with which he compared it, but he found no grounds to invoke divine agents; Leuba viewed religion as a striving after a more complete and unified life, not as a transaction with the supernatural.[23] He was obviously strongly drawn to the Comtean ideal of a religion of humanity,[24] as became increasingly clear in his later writings, but he maintained his agnostic position regarding the divine and castigated writers like James, who, he thought, exceeded the proper bounds of science.

Thus by the early years of the twentieth century, American psychologists had created a body of empirical work focused on religious experience, the relation of such experience to maturational and psychological processes, and the role of religion in personality development. One might confidently have expected this activity to develop into an important approach to the scientific study of religion. Instead, it died aborning, a victim of major changes in psychology. The attempt to make psychology a laboratory science was well under way in the 1890s and intensified in the twentieth century, bringing with it the desire to model psychology on the "hard" sciences such as physics. At its extreme, this led to the crude behaviorism of John B. Watson and the much more sophisticated behaviorism of Clark Hull, but even nonbehaviorists abandoned the psychology of religion as a subject not amenable to a laboratory or experimental approach. At the same time, the field of clinical psychology came to be dominated by Freudians. Like their master, the Freudians did not hesitate

---

[21] Starbuck, *Psychology*, 252.
[22] James H. Leuba, "A Study in the Psychology of Religious Phenomena," *American Journal of Psychology* 7 (1896):309–85.
[23] Ibid., 315.
[24] James H. Leuba, *A Psychological Study of Religion* (New York: AMS Press, 1969) 336, first published 1912.

to deal with religion, nor were they put off by the use of introspective evidence. But having started from premises that rejected supernaturalism, they interpreted religious experience as symbolic of repressed anxieties. This approach was to have a great effect on the study of religion, particularly when applied to anthropological data, but it involved an orientation very different from that of James, Starbuck, and Leuba. Hence the empirical study of religious experience was virtually abandoned in this country until Rodney Stark, Charles Glock, and their colleagues at Berkeley once again gave it serious attention.

As is well known, the attack on evolutionism in the United States was led by Franz Boas, who was the dominant influence in American anthropology in the early twentieth century. It was with Boas that ethnographic description done by participant observers in the field became enshrined as the essential approach of American anthropology; it was Boas who shifted the field from the study of culture to the study of cultures, and it was Boas who led the fight against evolutionism, stressing historical processes of diffusion instead. He also published extensive collections of American Indian myths and folklore and described aspects of American Indian religion, although he published no general work on that subject. Most of all, he redirected American anthropology toward solid empirical studies done in the field, and his students were to apply this approach to religion as well as other subjects.[25]

Among the followers of Boas, three deserve particular mention. Alexander Goldenweiser published *Early Civilization*[26] in 1922. After roundly attacking evolutionism, he offered his own definition of religion: "Our analysis of religion and magic makes it clear that the idea of supernatural power is common to both and represents, in fact, the basic concept underlying the religio-magical world view. On the emotional side, an equally fundamental factor is the *religious thrill*."[27] This is a two-dimensional definition that stresses both the belief in supernatural power and "the concrete living participation of the individual in the world of the supernatural . . . through the experience of the *religious thrill*."[28] He also stressed the importance of mythology, which he saw as the functional equivalent

[25] Hultkrantz, *Indian Religion*, 17–22; George W. Stocking, Jr., *Race, Culture, and Evolution: Essays in the History of Anthropology* (New York: Free Press, 1969), 195–233; George W. Stocking, Jr., ed., *The Shaping of American Anthropology, 1883–1911: A Franz Boas Reader* (New York: Basic Books, 1974), Introduction.
[26] Alexander Goldenweiser, *Early Civilization* (New York: Knopf, 1922).
[27] Ibid., 197.
[28] Ibid., 233.

of theology, developing and systematizing the conceptual elements of religion, and ritual, which he regarded as a means of intensifying the emotional fervor of religion.[29]

Robert Lowie characterized his approach to religion as psychological,[30] but his definition differs little from that of Goldenweiser. He took belief in supernatural power, in Marett's sense, to be one essential element,[31] but this alone did not constitute religion, for one could believe in spirits without taking a religious attitude toward them.[32] It was that attitude—that emotional relation to the supernatural that Goldenweiser terms the "religious thrill"—that Lowie considered essential to religion. It is clear throughout his discussion that Lowie is relying heavily on his studies of the vision quest among the Crow, where the vision and the consequent dependence of the Indian on his tutelary spirit are central to the Indian religion.

Lowie also gave careful accounts of religious organization and ritual among the groups he discussed, and his treatment of the Ghost Dance[33] and the Peyote Cult[34] illustrate his emphasis upon the psychological aspect of religion. He was, however, careful to show how a given ritual such as the Ghost Dance might come to have very different meanings in different cultures. Throughout, he was rigorously empirical, refusing to speculate about origins or to accept historical reconstructions that outran existing data.[35]

Like Goldenweiser and Lowie, Paul Radin took religious emotion to be a necessary part of religion, together with a belief in spirits and ritual action. But Radin also emphasized the function of religion in maintaining the life values of success, longevity, and happiness—values that are in constant jeopardy in primitive society and therefore require supernatural support.[36] Religion thus had a practical economic and social aspect. So did magic, which Radin, following Frazer, believed anticipated religion. The change from magic to religion came when control over the object was removed from the magician and was seen as being vested in spirits, whose favor had to be won through ceremonies or rituals.[37]

[29] Ibid., 233–34.
[30] Robert Lowie, *Primitive Religion* (New York: Boni and Liveright, 1924), xii–xiii.
[31] Ibid., xvi.
[32] Ibid., 134.
[33] Ibid., 188–200.
[34] Ibid., 200–204.
[35] Ibid., 167ff.
[36] Paul Radin, *Primitive Religion* (New York: Viking, 1937), 6–8.
[37] Ibid., 25ff.

For Radin, religion was not the spontaneous creation of the group but the work of special persons whose psychological insecurities in the face of life crises such as death and illness predisposed them to compensation fantasies. Radin viewed these "neurotic-epileptoid"[38] people as the "formulators" of religious doctrines and the interpreters of religious experiences. From this group came the shamans and priests, who would become, as society increased in complexity, the priestly class, with economic and social interests of their own. Thus Radin blended Freudian psychology with ethnographic data—drawing, of course, on his own studies of the Winnebago—to develop a theory in which economic and class interests were included.

The writings about religion of men like Lowie and Radin were only a part of their contribution. Equally or more important were their ethnographic studies of specific American Indian groups, including, of course, their religion—studies that Hultkrantz calls the finest of their kind.[39] Many other Boas students, including Alfred Kroeber, Clark Wissler, Ralph Linton, Leslie Spier, Edward Sapir, Frank Speck, and Ruth Underhill contributed similar case studies.[40] These works provided important data that bore on such questions as the priority of impersonal supernatural power over personalized spirits, totemism, ceremonialism, and the vision quest. Ruth Benedict's famous study of the guardian spirit belief among North American Indians in 1923,[41] A. I. Hallowell's monograph on bear ceremonialism in 1926,[42] and Spier's work on the sun dance of the Plains Indians in 1921[43] were among the outstanding contributions of American anthropologists to the study of religion.

Clearly in the period before 1930 the major work done by American social scientists on religion was done in anthropology. This is not really surprising, given the availability of the American Indians as subjects of study and the orientation introduced by Boas. Indeed, the Boas program was ideally suited to the situation in which American anthropologists found themselves, and its adoption enabled them to capitalize on their geographic position. But by the end of the 1920s theoretical orientations

[38] Ibid., 108.

[39] Hultkrantz, Indian Religion, 26.

[40] Ibid., 23.

[41] Ruth Benedict, The Concept of the Guardian Spirit in North America (Menasha, Wisc.: American Anthropological Association Memoirs 29, 1923).

[42] A. I. Hallowell, "Bear Ceremonialism in the Northern Hemisphere," American Anthropologist 28 (1926) 1–175.

[43] Leslie Spier, The Sun Dance of the Plains Indians: Its Development and Diffusion (New York: Anthropological Papers of the American Museum of Natural History 16, 1921).

were changing. In British anthropology as in American, the evolutionary doctrines of Tylor and his group were rapidly fading from the scene. Although Boas led the shift to field work here, it was Bronislaw Malinowski and A. R. Radcliffe-Brown who reoriented British anthropology toward participant observation in the field: more than anyone else Malinowski established the paradigm for ethnography that has dominated anthropology ever since.[44] Malinowski and Radcliffe-Brown also made functional analysis preeminent and persuasive in anthropological circles; from the late 1920s on, functionalism became the guiding theoretical orientation for the next three or four decades in England and America. But what is really surprising is the lack of sociological work on religion in the United States. Compared with what was happening in Europe in the early twentieth century, with the work of Emile Durkheim, Max Weber, and Georg Simmel, the American scene was singularly barren. When in 1929 Clifford Kirkpatrick published his *Religion in Human Affairs*,[45] which Milton Yinger has called "perhaps the first general statement about religion by an American sociologist,"[46] neither Weber nor Simmel appeared in the index and Durkheim was sharply criticized.[47] In fact, Kirkpatrick's treatment of religion was modeled on that of the anthropologists; only in his discussion of the science-religion controversy did his focus shift from nonliterate to complex societies.

What is true of Kirkpatrick seems to have been quite generally true. Durkheim's work was roundly attacked in the United States in the 1920s, with Goldenweiser and Lowie leading the charge.[48] Anthropologists were particularly irritated by Durkheim's claims about the relation of totem and sib, his assumption that the Australian natives represented the most primitive culture, and his criticism of Tylor's theory of the origin of the idea of the soul; as a result they greeted his writings coldly. Weber was

---

[44] George W. Stocking, Jr., "The Ethnographer's Magic: Fieldwork In British Anthropology from Tylor to Malinowski," in George W. Stocking, Jr., ed., *Observers Observed* (Madison: University of Wisconsin, 1983); James Clifford, "On Ethnographic Authority," *Representations* 1, no. 2 (1983):118–46.

[45] Clifford Kirkpatrick, *Religion in Human Affairs* (New York: John Wiley and Sons, 1929).

[46] J. Milton Yinger, *Sociology Looks at Religion* (New York: Macmillan, 1963), 124. In fact, Yinger was wrong. In 1928, William Graham Sumner and Albert Keller had published the second volume of *The Science of Society*, which was wholly devoted to religion (William Graham Sumner and Albert G. Keller, *The Science of Society* [New Haven: Yale, 1928], vol. II). Many of the ideas had previously appeared in Sumner's *Folkways*, but they were not codified until this publication (William Graham Sumner, *Folkways* [Boston: Ginn and Co., 1940]). Sumner's treatment belonged to the older evolutionist school and had no impact upon American sociology.

[47] Kirkpatrick, *Religion*, 42ff.

[48] Lowie, *Religion*, 148–63; Goldenweiser, *Civilization*, 370ff.

chiefly known for *The Protestant Ethic and the Spirit of Capitalism*, which for obvious reasons aroused American interest,[49] but the only other aspect of his work to attract significant attention here was the church-sect distinction. In fact, although Richard Niebuhr disclaimed being a sociologist,[50] his work on the development of sects into churches and the social dynamics underlying this process was the most original and notable achievement in the sociology of religion in this period. Niebuhr, of course, built on the work of Weber and Ernst Troeltsch, which he praised highly, although he went well beyond what they had done.

It is against this background that the importance of Talcott Parsons's contribution in *The Structure of Social Action*[51] in 1937 becomes evident. As is well known, Parsons devoted most of that work to an explication of the work of Alfred Marshall, Vilfredo Pareto, Durkheim, and Weber, or, perhaps one should say, to an interpretation of their work that would form the background for his own theoretical developments. Not only was his evaluation of Durkheim and Weber highly laudatory, but it stressed particularly their work on religion. For many American sociologists, Parsons's account seems to have served as an introduction to Weber's work—at least to the full sweep and magnitude of Weber's achievement. Parsons subsequently translated several of Weber's works into English, thus helping to make the texts available to many who found Weber's German daunting. Certainly since 1937, Durkheim and Weber have had a secure place in the canon of social theorists in America.

Parsons is not generally thought of as a sociologist of religion, yet his influence on this field has been considerable. Unlike most sociologists, Parsons sought to create a theory of such generality that it could provide a conceptual framework for all social research. In so doing, he drew on a wide range of theorists, including particularly Freud, Durkheim, and Weber. The general theory involved the specification of three systems of action: the personality system, the social system, and the cultural system. The last, which Parsons described as involving "value systems, belief systems, and systems of expressive symbols,"[52] provided the values and norms that guided action and served to integrate the entire structure. In Par-

---

[49] N. J. Demerath and Phillip E. Hammond, *Religion in Social Context* (New York: Random House, 1969), chapter 3.

[50] H. Richard Niebuhr, *The Social Sources of Denominationalism* (New York: Meridian, 1975), vii, first published 1929.

[51] Talcott Parsons, *The Structure of Social Action* (New York: Free Press, 1968), 2 vols., first published 1937.

[52] Talcott Parsons and Edward Shils, eds., *Toward a General Theory of Action* (Cambridge, Mass.: Harvard University Press, 1962), 55.

son's view, religion, of course, belonged to the cultural system and, when seen in terms of its integrative role, turns out to be of fundamental importance to the entire theory of social order. This view, based on the work of Durkheim and Weber, represented Parsons's attempt to synthesize their insights with his own.

Particularly important for subsequent developments were three aspects of Parsons's work. First, he emphasized the difference between scientific belief systems and those of religion. Drawing on Weber particularly, Parsons held that religious beliefs are directed primarily to problems of meaning that lie beyond the domain of science, so that no reduction of religious beliefs to scientific ones is even theoretically possible. The "rationalist approach" of Tylor, Spencer, and Frazer was thus, Parsons argued, "hopelessly naive and inadequate."[53] Second, again using Weber as his proof text, Parsons argued for the fundamental role of ideas as explanatory variables in social theory. Weber's comparative study of Europe, China, and India provided, in Parsons's view, conclusive evidence that the Protestant ethic played a causal role in the development of capitalism.[54] Religion therefore was not simply something to be explained, but in certain contexts it could serve as an independent variable that could have fundamental effects on action and society. Third, Parsons became increasingly aware of the importance of symbolism as he developed his own theory. Because culture is transmissible from one action system to another, Parsons recognized that it could not be a system of acts but must be a system of symbols controlling systems of orientations.[55] He developed classifications of symbols and analyzed their operation,[56] but he seems to have regarded this area as one that required further development. His students, Robert Bellah and Clifford Geertz, were to take up the challenge.

To attribute the rather marked change in American sociology that began in the 1930s to Parsons's influence would obviously be simplistic. Parsons was only one proponent of the structure-functionalist view that became increasingly popular in the late 1920s and has dominated so much of social science in America ever since. Indeed, Parsons was a student of Malinowski, and so represents part of the spread of Malinowski's influ-

[53] Talcott Parsons, *Essays in Sociological Theory Pure and Applied* (Glencoe: Free Press, 1949), 64.

[54] Ibid., 159.

[55] Parsons and Shils, *General Theory*, 159–60.

[56] Ibid., Part II, chapter 3. Talcott Parsons and Edward Shils, *Working Papers in the Theory of Action* (New York: Free Press, 1953), chapter 2.

ence to the United States. But the Great Depression itself no doubt had an impact on social theory in this country. The near collapse of the American economic and political system in the Depression made central the issue of the maintenance of social order, and so gave to the writings of Durkheim and Weber a relevance that made Durkheim's anthropological lapses and Weber's opaque style appear as only minor irritations. When events made the problem of the basis of social order a critical one in the United States, Durkheim and Weber found readers aplenty.[57]

The late 1920s and the several ensuing decades saw major changes in approach in anthropology as well as in sociology. One was the expansion of the data base, as anthropologists increasingly chose non-American societies for study. Partly this choice stemmed from the erosion of the traditional cultures among the American Indians, but it also reflected a growing interest in other cultures that were being exploited by European scholars like Malinowski. World War II, of course, gave great impetus to this development, as American troops spread around the world and opportunities for contact and study increased.

A second major development was the change in the view of culture from a collection of traits to a configuration—a "more or less consistent pattern of thought and action."[58] Ruth Benedict was one of the pioneers in this development, but her emphasis on holism was quickly adopted by many others. One result of this change in emphasis was that religion came to be seen as part of a cultural system that could be adequately understood only within its cultural context rather than as a detachable element that could be considered alone.

Also involved in Benedict's work, as well as that of Cora DuBois, Clyde Kluckholm, Hallowell, and others,[59] was an increasing emphasis on psychological factors and their relation to culture. Reflecting, of course, the growing influence of Freudian psychology as well as the recognition that psychological characteristics are culturally variable, this "culture and personality" emphasis was to become a major movement in American anthropology until at least the 1960s. The significance of psychological factors was also heightened by the growing interest in acculturation studies promoted by Robert Redfield, Ralph Linton, Melville Herskovitz, and many others[60] and particularly stimulated by World War II, when the

[57] Cf. Robert A. Nisbet, *The Sociological Tradition* (New York: Basic Books, 1966), for a discussion of the relation of this problem to the work of Durkheim and Weber.
[58] Ruth Benedict, *Patterns of Culture* (Boston: Houghton Mifflin, 1959), 46.
[59] Hultkrantz, *Indian Religion*, 64.
[60] Ibid., 65.

impact of cultural contact betweei American troops and a variety of nonliterate peoples became a matter of concern. Finally, an important new emphasis on the study of world views, associated with Redfield and Hallowell especially, also carried important implications for the interpretation of religion.

The interplay of these factors is perhaps best illustrated by the work of Hallowell. Taking the world view to mean the concepts of the self and the environment held by a people, Hallowell showed that concepts of the self, time, space, the objects in the environment, the persons in the environment, and the norms for evaluating these were all culturally variable. Thus religion tended to be subsumed within the world view, where spirits became one of several classes of persons with whom the self interacted, and the "soul" became a particular way of conceptualizing the self.[61] It thus becomes questionable whether "religion" as we usually define the term is to be found as a distinct category in many other cultures, and the attempt to abstract "supernatural persons" from a native's category of "persons" may impose a distinction not recognized within the native's world view. Indeed, from this perspective, it becomes clear that terms such as *religion, magic, church,* and *science* define categories of western European culture which may not exist in other cultures and the imposition of which may be distorting.

Hallowell was also one of the pioneers in relating world view to personality. Using the Rorschach test as a method of determining the psychological structure of the Ojibwa, Hallowell was able to show marked differences in psychological structure between these Indians and contemporary Americans. He was then able to explain these differences in terms of the relationships the Ojibwa conceived to exist between themselves and other-than-human "persons" inhabiting their environment. Thus what from our point of view would be called the religious beliefs and rituals of the Ojibwa turn out to play a major part in Ojibwa personality formation and psychological functioning. Whether the psychological factors are seen as causes of the "religion" or as consequences, the existence of a functional interdependence is clear.[62]

Finally, Hallowell showed that the effects of acculturation on the Ojibwa can be understood only in terms of this relationship between the world view and the personality. Because one of the first effects of acculturation

[61] A. Irving Hallowell, *Culture and Experience* (New York: Schocken Books, 1971), 75–111.
[62] Ibid., Parts 2 and 3.

was to undermine the hold of the aboriginal world view, the Indians undergoing acculturation found themselves bereft of the support of the other-than-human "persons" on whom their personal security system depended, with the result that these Indians exhibited severe signs of social and psychological disorganization.[63] These findings, confirmed by the work of George and Louise Spindler[64] and others, also helped to account for the development of the Peyote Cult among the woodland Indians, which, as the Spindlers showed, became an alternative mode of adjustment for the Menomini when the traditional culture lost its hold owing to acculturation.

Another major influence on anthropological understanding of religion was the work of Abram Kardiner. A psychoanalyst, Kardiner was interested in the application of Freudian theory to anthropological data, and his cooperation with Ralph Linton[65] and with Cora DuBois, the results of which were published in 1944,[66] led to the concept of basic personality structure. Assuming that all people share certain basic needs and desires, and that the way in which these needs and desires are dealt with in child rearing will condition the formation of the individual personality, the variability in the "primary institutions"—those institutions that bear directly on the child-rearing process—from one society to another should lead to corresponding variation in the basic personality structure to be found in those societies. On psychological grounds, any course of child rearing will lead to some anxieties and repressions, so it followed from this theory that the specific nature of those anxieties and repressions, which are part of the basic personality structure, would also vary from society to society. Kardiner believed that these intrapsychic stresses would condition what he called the "secondary institutions" of the society, among which he included especially religion and myth. These he regarded as a projective system—that is, as fantasy creations on which the ego can project those unacceptable feelings and desires that stem from the wounds inflicted in the socialization process. Thus religion became for Kardiner the unconscious creation of an ego striving to defend itself against culturally induced anxieties; the character of the religion varied from society to society as a function of the culturally constituted methods of socializa-

---

[63] Ibid., Part 4.

[64] George D. Spindler, *Sociocultural and Psychological Processes in Menomini Acculturation* (Berkeley: University of California Press, 1955).

[65] Abram Kardiner, *The Individual and His Society* (New York: Columbia University Press, 1955), first published 1939.

[66] Cora DuBois, *The People of Alor* (New York: Harper and Brothers, 1944).

tion. But religion does not appear in this scheme simply as a dependent variable, for religious beliefs may, in turn, help to determine the child-rearing practices. Thus Kardiner's theory involved a hypothesis about intergenerational cultural dynamics, in which the child-rearing methods used to rear one generation of children determined their basic personality structures. These structures then determined the nature of the religious beliefs those children would hold as adults, and those religious beliefs, in turn, determined the child-rearing methods that would be applied to the next generation. In this process, religion appears both as the product of personality processes in one generation and as the shaper of the personality in the next.[67]

Kardiner's views have had wide influence in anthropology. The Whitings particularly have made extensive use of this theory,[68] but so have many others. Thus Melford Spiro interprets religion as a projective system, although his overall treatment of religion is quite different from Kardiner's.[69] Certainly the Kardinerian theory was one of the major ways in which Freudian psychodynamics was incorporated into anthropological thinking, and its effects have been lasting.

A further example of the role of religion in culture change is Anthony Wallace's theory of revitalization.[70] Noting the frequency with which attempts are made to innovate not only parts of a cultural system but whole cultural systems themselves, Wallace sought to develop a general theory of such movements. By a revitalization movement, he means "a deliberate, organized, conscious effort by members of a society to construct a more satisfying culture." He did not mean by this that all members of the society are participants, for some will oppose the movement, but that the leader and his followers deliberately seek to change the system to a more satisfactory form. The process, as Wallace describes it, is this:

Wallace conceives of a culture in a "steady state" as one in which most members of the society succeed in satisfying their needs through culturally approved methods, so that the level of dissatisfaction and stress is

[67] Kardiner, *The Individual and His Society* (New York: Columbia University Press, 1939).

[68] John W. M. Whiting and Irvin Child, *Child Training and Personality* (New Haven: Yale, 1953); John W. M. Whiting, "Socialization Processes and Personality," in F. L. K. Hsu, ed., *Psychological Anthropology* (Homewood, Ill.: Dorsey Press, 1961).

[69] Melford Spiro, "Religion: Problems in Definition and Explanation," in Michael Banton, ed., *Anthropological Approaches to the Study of Religion* (London: Tavistock, 1966), 85–126.

[70] Anthony F. C. Wallace, "Revitalization Movements," *American Anthropologist* 58(1956):264–81.

low. If, however, over a period of time the culture becomes less successful in satisfying individual needs, the level of stress will constantly rise. Such a situation may be induced by environmental changes, either natural or social, or by internal changes (e.g., economic collapse), but, in any case, the situation is marked by the declining efficiency of the culture and the rise of individual stress. Such a development will lead to a period of cultural distortion in which the lack of satisfaction of needs and anxiety over the situation produce social disorganization and personality disorders and, in time, will lead to a loss of faith in the old culture. Under these conditions, the culture may collapse or be revitalized.

In the latter case, a leader or prophet will emerge who has conceived, usually as a result of an hallucinatory experience or a dream, a new synthesis of cultural elements which he believes provides an answer to the problems faced by his society. Usually the new synthesis is seen as revealed by supernatural agents who appear to the prophet in visions, although other processes—moments of insight, for example—sometimes play an equivalent part. Convinced of the correctness of the new synthesis, the leader becomes its advocate and gathers a band of disciples and a following drawn by the promise offered by the leader's vision to solve the difficulties facing the society. There follows a campaign led by the new prophet during which resistance from other elements in the society must be met, often by modification of the original synthesis but sometimes by force, and a sustaining organization is created. If the prophet wins the support of the bulk of the society and his plan is successful in meeting the needs that were previously unmet, the cultural system is altered and revitalized.

It is obvious that religious revivalist movements are included as revitalization movements under this scheme, but Wallace makes it clear that secular movements also are included. Thus, here again, religious phenomena are subsumed under a broader cultural category. But Wallace also suggests that such movements may hold the answer to the "origins" of religion. "In fact, it can be argued that all organized religions are relics of old revitalization movements, surviving in routinized form in stabilized cultures, and that religious phenomena per se originated (if it is permissible still in this day and age to talk about the origins of major elements of culture) in the revitalization process—i.e., in visions of a new way of life by individuals under extreme stress."[71] But Wallace's theory

[71] Ibid., 268.

has another important implication. As he notes, the prophet is clearly a charismatic leader in the sense of Weber. Thus revitalization movements may be the condition for the appearance of charismatic leaders, whether secular or religious.

The leading sociologist of religion in the 1940s and 1950s was Milton Yinger, whose publications, beginning with *Religion in the Struggle for Power*[72] in 1946, were widely influential. Yinger viewed religion from the functionalist perspective, defining it as "a system of beliefs and practices by means of which a group of people struggles with these ultimate problems of human life."[73] Following Weber, Yinger of course sees "these ultimate problems" as death, suffering, and evil.[74] Such a definition, as has often been remarked, has the effect of making religion a universal phenomenon by fiat, because it can hardly be doubted that all men must face "ultimate concerns," to use Tillich's phrase. Yinger was well aware of this criticism and did discuss functional alternatives to religion such as Communism and neurosis. But he ended by commenting that from the functionalist standpoint Communism served as a religion to its followers, and he evidently thought that neurosis did the same for its victims.[75] It is not clear, therefore, whether these are functional alternatives to religion or alternative religions, and on functionalist grounds the latter would seem to be the only plausible answer. It is, however, important to emphasize the word *struggle* in his definition, for Yinger did not claim that religion always succeeds in solving ultimate problems but only that it represents an attempt to do so.

Yinger took the position that no society can survive without a belief system that provides a means of dealing with these ultimate problems of human existence.[76] He also held that social order required a unifying value scheme defining goals and norms, and that any effective scheme of this sort must be largely internalized by the society's members. Many functionalist students of religion have seen the primary function of religion as being to provide this value scheme, thereby providing social integration. Yinger, however, was more circumspect. He noted that the integrationist claims for religion have been based chiefly on data from nonliterate societies[77] and that substantial historical data call this claim

[72] J. Milton Yinger, *Religion in the Struggle for Power* (Durham: Duke University, 1946).
[73] J. Milton Yinger, *Religion, Society and the Individual* (New York: Macmillan, 1957), 9.
[74] Ibid., 74ff.
[75] Ibid., 118ff.
[76] Ibid., 38.
[77] Ibid., 62.

into question—for example, the history of religious wars and conflicts in Europe. He therefore argued that religion *may* "under some circumstances" serve an integrating function but that under other circumstances it may not.[78] Unfortunately, he provided little guidance as to what the relevant circumstances may be.

Yinger was greatly concerned with the relationship of religion to society and with social organization. That the church-sect typology proposed by Weber, developed by Troeltsch, and further developed by Niebuhr was not wholly adequate was clear from the difficulty of locating religious groups, such as cults, in terms of it. Yinger took up this problem in his first published work and continued to work on it throughout his career. In his 1957 work, he proposed a more elaborate scheme of six types: the universal church, the ecclesia, the denomination, the established sect, the sect, and the cult,[79] ranging along a continuum of degree of accommodation to the secular society. Organizations at one end of the continuum gave primary emphasis to the purity of the religious ideal, whereas those at the other emphasized secular power, which could only be achieved by compromising the purity of their ways. Yinger's elaboration of this typology did not solve the problem of religious organization, or even of church-sect theory, for the debate over these issues still continues, but Yinger's typology was certainly an advance and was widely used.

Since about 1960, interest in religion among social scientists has increased, as is evidenced, for example, by the founding of new journals such as the *Review of Religious Research* in 1959, *Journal of Religion and Health* in 1961, *Journal for the Scientific Study of Religion* in 1961, and *Journal of Psychology and Theology* in 1973. This rise in interest has been marked by the appearance of radically different approaches. Charles Glock and his associates at Berkeley brought to the subject an expertise in survey methods and a broader conception of the nature of the field than his predecessors. Glock succeeded in avoiding the "universal by definition" trap that has plagued functionalism by distinguishing between value orientations and religion. Following Florence Kluckholm, he defined value orientations as "institutionalized systems of beliefs, values, symbols, and practices that are concerned with the solution of questions of ultimate meaning."[80] These he regards as universal, some such

---

[78] Ibid., 71.
[79] Ibid., 147ff.
[80] Charles Y. Glock and Rodney Stark, *Religion and Society in Tension* (Chicago: Rand McNally, 1965), 7–11.

orientation being found in all cultures. "Religious perspectives"—his term for religion—were then defined as value orientations that have a supernatural referent; thus they were distinct from humanistic orientations, which do not. Granting that the problem of defining the supernatural remains, this approach at least avoids the anomaly of proclaiming Communism a religion when its adherents proclaim themselves atheists.

Glock also distinguished clearly between religion and religiosity, or religious commitment. The latter is analyzed in terms of five dimensions: the experiential, ritualistic, ideological, intellectual, and consequential.[81] The first refers, of course, to religious experience; the second is understood broadly to encompass all religious practices, including even attending church; the third refers to the religious beliefs held by the subject, and is distinguished from the fourth, which refers to the subject's knowledge about the doctrines of his faith and its scriptures; the last embraces all consequences of religious commitment for the secular activities of the individual subject—roughly, his "works." As Glock emphasized, a high score on one dimension does not imply a high score on any other, although later research was to show that they were in fact not independent.[82]

Glock was not the first to analyze religiosity in multidimensional terms. Joseph Fichter in 1951 had used a four-dimensional scheme in analyzing religiosity among Catholics in a southern city,[83] and Gerhard Lenski in 1961 used a different four-dimensional scheme in his Detroit study.[84] More elaborate factor analytic studies have since been done.[85] But what was particularly important about Glock's and Stark's scheme was the inclusion of the consequential dimension. Despite functionalist emphasis on the consequences of religion and despite the long tradition in Protestant thought emphasizing conduct as a sign of grace, this dimension had not been previously used in this fashion.[86] By introducing it, Glock and Stark extended the range of phenomena that could be used to measure religious commitment.

This scheme has directed the attention of the Berkeley group to the analysis of each dimension. Thus Stark sought to develop a typology of

[81] Ibid., 20.
[82] Bernard Spilka, Ralph Hood, and Richard Gorsuch, *The Psychology of Religion* (Englewood Cliffs: Prentice-Hall, 1985), 45.
[83] Demerath and Hammond, *Religion*, 142.
[84] Ibid., 144.
[85] Morton King, "Measuring the Religious Variable: Nine Proposed Dimensions," *Journal for the Scientific Study of Religion* 6(1967):173–90.
[86] Demerath and Hammond, *Religion*, 150ff.

religious experience, based on the idea that religious experience involves an interpersonal encounter between the self and the supernatural.[87] He distinguished four types of such experience: awareness of the presence of the supernatural person, feeling that this awareness is mutual, feeling an affective relationship with him, and feeling oneself to be a confidant or co-worker with him. Obviously, one has here a scale, and in fact the frequency of these types of experience conforms to the expectations of the scale.[88] The types of religious experience, then, can be seen as resulting from the degree of intimacy with the divine. One would then expect that diabolic experience should have the same characteristics, and Stark developed a similar scale of types for it.[89]

Glock and his co-workers have also been much concerned with the organizational aspect of religion, and so have, of course, dealt with the church-sect issue. Starting from Niebuhr's work, which saw new sects as recruiting their members from among the economically deprived, they argued that five types of deprivation needed to be distinguished: (1) economic deprivation; (2) social deprivation (that is, lack of such attributes as status, power, and prestige, which are highly valued by society); (3) organismic deprivation (physical or mental deficiency); (4) ethical deprivation (conflict with the dominant social values); and (5) psychic deprivation (lack of a meaningful value system). Each type of deprivation has a different probability of leading to religious organization, will develop a different type of organization if it does, and has a different prospect of success.[90] Glock and his colleagues have thus thought to escape from the straightjacket of the traditional unidimensional church-sect theory—the inadequacy of which was well recognized by the 1960s—and to develop a more comprehensive scheme. The effort has been a continuing one, although no agreed-upon classification system of organizations has yet appeared.[91]

Following up on the work of Samuel Blizzard,[92] the Berkeley group also investigated the role problems of parish ministers and the relation-

[87] Glock and Stark, *Religion and Society*, 42ff.
[88] Ibid., 160.
[89] Ibid., 62.
[90] Ibid., 246ff.
[91] Cf. Rodney Stark and William Bainbridge, "Of Churches, Sects, and Cults: Preliminary Concepts for a Theory of Religious Movements," *Journal for the Scientific Study of Religion* 18(1979):117–33.
[92] Samuel Blizzard, "The Protestant Parish Minister's Integrating Roles," *Religious Education* 53(1958):374–80.

ship of these problems to the heterogeneity of the minister's parish, the structure of the minister's church, and the minister's training.[93] These studies and others along the same lines have done much to clarify the reasons for the positions taken by clergy on social issues, and so the sociological functions of religious groups. It is clear that the parish minister, faced with cross-pressures arising from the laity, the financial needs of the church, the church hierarchy, and the surrounding society, is seldom able to take a strong position on controversial issues.[94] Clergy on campuses or in national hierarchies, however, are likely to have greater freedom of action and to pursue more radical social action.[95]

Glock and his colleagues have attempted to mount a broader sociological attack on religion than previous workers have done. Although concerned with the same definitional and organizational issues as their predecessors, they have self-consciously sought to develop a research program that would embrace religious experience, behavior, commitment, belief, and social effects, and to pursue these issues not only through grand typologies but also through detailed studies of the functioning of religious organizations at different levels. Although their work has been strongly tied to survey data, they have also sought to develop more adequate concepts for the understanding and analysis of these data, and their work has been more methodologically sophisticated than that of most others in the field. Nevertheless, no major breakthrough in our understanding of religion has resulted, nor has there been much theoretical advance. Standard sociological approaches and statistical methods in this case have not been enough.

A highly influential work very much in the manner of Glock and Stark was Gerhard Lenski's *The Religious Factor*[96] which appeared in 1961. Starting from Weber's thesis in *The Protestant Ethic and the Spirit of Capitalism*, Lenski sought to investigate the consequences of religious commitment for a wide range of secular behavior.[97] Using interviews for data collection and a probability sample from Detroit, he developed a four-dimensional scheme for assessing religious commitment: (1) associational involvement (church attendance); (2) communal involvement (the extent to which friends and relatives belong to the subject's religious group);

[93] Glock and Stark, *Religion and Society,* 144ff, 201–42.
[94] Demerath and Hammond, *Religion,* 188.
[95] Ibid., 218ff, 228.
[96] Gerhard Lenski, *The Religious Factor* (New York: Doubleday, 1961).
[97] Ibid., 11ff.

(3) doctrinal orthodoxy (assent to prescribed doctrine); and (4) devotionalism (private "communion" with God, e.g., in prayer).[98] Using these dimensions, Lenski then sought to determine how religious commitment among Jews, white Protestants, black Protestants, and Catholics was related to economic and political behavior, family life, and education. Lenski did indeed find relationships that, although substantial, defy simple summary. They were sufficient, however, to lead him to conclude that religious commitment has important effects on secular behavior—effects that are often greater than the effects of class. Lenski particularly emphasized the importance of the communal aspect of religious groups, arguing that such subcommunities constituted distinct social systems through which the influence of religion was exerted and ones that were responsible for some of the characteristics previously attributed to the churches, such as provincialism and intolerance.[99] Lenski's study had a stimulating effect on the study of religion in the 1960s, because he seemed to have shown that religion was an important determinant of a wide range of behavior—a claim that inspired others to pursue these relationships.

The work of Robert Bellah stands in sharp contrast to that of Glock and Stark, and of Lenski. Also a sociologist, Bellah has not restricted himself to the American field. He has written on Apache kinship and on Islamic, Chinese, and especially Japanese religion, so that he has an exceptional breadth of knowledge on which to draw. This was immediately evident in his 1964 article[100] on religious evolution—a rather daring and much-celebrated effort to free the subject of the development of religion over time from the stigma of nineteenth-century evolutionism, which had made the topic taboo since the early years of this century. The five-stage model therein proposed, with each stage described in terms of its symbolic system, action, organization, and social implications, was itself based on an implicit theory of social evolution as the increasing freedom of personality and society from environmental control.[101] It is not hard to see the influence of Bellah's teacher, Talcott Parsons, behind this view.

The debt to Parsons is explicit in Bellah's description of his cybernetic model, which he set forth the next year.[102] This is an action system in

---

[98] Ibid., 21ff.
[99] Ibid., 295ff.
[100] Robert Bellah, "Religious Evolution," in Robert Bellah, *Beyond Belief* (New York: Harper and Row, 1970), 20–50.
[101] Ibid., 44.
[102] Bellah, *Beyond Belief*, 3–19. Although published in 1968, the paper was written in 1965.

Parsons's sense in which the energy is derived from the organism and is organized and controlled partly through genetic programs innate in the organism but chiefly through symbolic means organized by learning. "The cybernetic model thus conceives of a human action system as autonomous, purposive, and capable of a wide range of external adaptations and internal rearrangements within the very broad constraints inherent in the nature of energy and information."[103] Religion, of course, entered primarily at the cultural level, where it was related to two main problems: the identity problem (where it provided a very general definition of the environment and the self) and the problem of unconscious motivation. "It is," remarked Bellah, "primarily the role of religion in action systems to provide such a cognitively and motivationally meaningful identity concept or set of identity symbols."[104] Clearly religion so conceived is addressed very much to Weber's problem of meaning and to Durkheim's problem of integration, and Bellah made clear his intellectual debts to these two as well as to Freud and Parsons.[105]

An obvious consequence of this view of religion is that not only all societies but all men must be religious. Bellah is explicit on this point. If, as he says, religion is "a set of symbolic forms and acts that relate man to the ultimate conditions of his existence,"[106] then "religion is a part of the species life of man, as central to his self-definition as speech."[107] Whether or not Bellah is a secret structuralist, as Dick Anthony and Thomas Robbins have argued,[108] he is obviously committed to a denial of the possibility of atheism, or to holding that all forms of atheism are really religions, which comes to the same thing. As a Durkheimian, he is also committed to the necessity of religion as an agent of social integration, and this position, of course, has been challenged for complex societies. Bellah's answer is civil religion.

Other writers—notably Lloyd Warner[109] and Will Herberg[110]—had called attention to the religious character of some national celebrations

[103] Ibid., 10.
[104] Ibid., 11–12.
[105] Ibid., 7f.
[106] Ibid., 21.
[107] Ibid., 223.
[108] Dick Anthony and Thomas Robbins, "From Symbolic Realism to Structuralism," *Journal for the Scientific Study of Religion* 14(1975):403ff.
[109] W. Lloyd Warner, *The Structure of American Life* (Edinburgh: University Press, 1952), chapter 10.
[110] Will Herberg, *Protestant Catholic Jew* (Chicago: University of Chicago Press, 1983), first published 1955.

and the development of an "American culture-religion." But it was Bellah who developed these ideas in his famous article on civil religion.[111] Noting that despite the constitutional separation of church and state, American political leaders repeatedly refer to God on public occasions and that these references carefully avoid overt Christian doctrine, Bellah distinguished a cluster of beliefs, symbols, and scriptures that constitute a civil religion distinct from but not opposed to Christianity. The civil religion makes American values sacred; it promotes the Declaration of Independence and the Constitution to the status of holy writ, and it casts some of our greatest leaders in biblical roles—Washington as Moses and Lincoln as Christ. But most of all, it enshrines the idea of the American mission, affirming the belief that God has decreed a special role for the United States in world history. As Bellah emphasized particularly in a later work,[112] this is a prophetic rather than a merely celebratory doctrine, for the nation can be called to judgment for its performance or nonperformance of this calling. Bellah himself took up the prophetic role in this later work, arguing that a selfish utilitarianism has undermined the "covenant with God," eroding both the communalism and the transcendental meaning of the original vision. He called for a revitalization of American culture, in the form of socialism, a reaffirmation of the classic civil religion, and "a rebirth of imaginative vision."[113]

Bellah's description of American civil religion has proved enormously attractive to students of religion and has called forth an extensive discussion. It obviously offers an answer to the problem of how religion can serve an integrative function in a pluralistic society by arguing that there is a common civil religion distinct from the particular traditional ones. No doubt this thesis can be generalized for other pluralistic societies as well, although Robert Stauffer has argued that it will not do for Sweden.[114] Certainly it is difficult to see how the doctrine of a special providential mission in human history can be generalized, for this view originated in American Puritanism of the seventeenth century, which is not duplicated elsewhere, and relatively few nations seem to have a mission concept comparable to ours. It may be that Bellah's article had so great an effect simply because it appeared at a time when American actions

---

[111] Robert Bellah, "Civil Religion in America," in *Beyond Belief*, 168–89.
[112] Robert Bellah, *The Broken Covenant* (New York: Seabury, 1975).
[113] Ibid., 153.
[114] Robert Stauffer, "Bellah's Civil Religion," *Journal for the Scientific Study of Religion* 12(1973):393.

were widely perceived as violating our "mission" and pluralism was being exalted as a defense against authority.

The thesis that sets Bellah most sharply apart from his fellow sociologists is his doctrine of symbolic realism. Here again Bellah treads in the footsteps of Parsons, accepting his interpretation, in *The Structure of Social Action,* of the significance of the emphasis given to religion by Durkheim and Weber and arguing that this "breakthrough" has been eclipsed by "the positivist utilitarian idiom."[115] Freud, Weber, and Durkheim, according to Bellah, were forced in their theories of religion to abandon rationalism and "to point to dark recesses where powerful but poorly understood forces and processes seemed to be affecting human action."[116] Bellah denies that religion can be "reduced" or explained by science as the product of cognitive ignorance, or error, or "symbolically reduced" by making it the symbolic expression of socialization anxiety or society or anything else. In a much quoted passage, Bellah writes:

If we define religion as that symbol system that serves to evoke what Herbert Richardson calls the "felt-whole," that is, the totality that includes subject and object and provides the context in which life and action finally have meaning, then I am prepared to claim that as Durkheim said of society, religion is a reality *sui generis.* To put it bluntly, religion is true.[117]

Knowledge, Bellah argues, is not the transcription by our ideas of some external reality; it is something that human beings construct out of their interaction with the world, or, more exactly, out of their experience. The copy theory of truth he regards as having been buried by Kant. It follows for Bellah that reality itself—*an sich*—can never be known; what we shall take for real is what our particular theory defines as real. This thesis is asserted to hold for science as well as any other type of belief or mode of apprehending the "world." There may be multiple theories defining different realities, none of them reducible to any of the others. How, then, are we to choose among them? Bellah's criterion is this: "The adequacy of any ultimate perspective is its ability to transform human experience so that it yields life instead of death."[118] This sounds like a pragmatic criterion, and perhaps it is, but if so it is oddly used, for the conclusion drawn seems to be that rather than choosing among perspectives, we should embrace them all, recognizing "the multiplicity of the human spirit"

[115] Bellah, *Beyond Belief,* 241.
[116] Ibid., 240.
[117] Ibid., 252–53.
[118] Ibid., 245.

and "that in both scientific and religious culture all we have finally are symbols, but that there is an enormous difference between the dead letter and the living word."[119] Bellah holds that such a multiple vision will lead to a new integration of science and religion, although it is certainly not clear why this should be so. Philosophically, Bellah's symbolic realism seems closer to subjective idealism than to standard types of realism, and one wonders how he knows that there is any reality apart from those represented in our theories, because we can never get beyond our theories to the noumenal world. Nor is it clear how vastly different perspectives are "integrated" by declaring them all equally legitimate. As Dick Robbins, Thomas Anthony, and Thomas Curtis have argued,[120] Bellah assumed that scientific and religious perspectives could not contradict each other because he regards the former as cognitive while the latter is not. But as they show, some adherents of certain religious movements regard their religion as making true statements about the world which contradict propositions of science. One is therefore forced to wonder just what sort of "integration" Bellah has in mind. To say that disparate systems are "integrated" because they are held simultaneously is to use the term *integration* in a peculiar and rather vacuous sense. The alternative would seem to be to hold with Robbins, Anthony, and Curtis that Bellah is a secret structuralist,[121] a view that, given his claim that "religious symbols and religious experience are inherent in the structure of human existence,"[122] is not implausible but has yet to be worked out.

The interest in symbolism evident in Bellah's work has been even more pronounced in anthropology. The 1960s and 1970s saw an epidemic of works on symbolism in Europe and in the United States. This movement has various roots. There is a long tradition of symbolic analysis in social science going back to Freud and Durkheim, so these ideas are not entirely new. Weber's stress on the importance of understanding the "web of meaning" in terms of which action is planned and executed was amplified by Parsons into a view of culture as a symbolic system, and so became a central concern of such Parsonian students as Bellah, David Schneider, and Clifford Geertz.

The rise of structuralism was also an important stimulus. Although

---

[119] Ibid., 246.
[120] Dick Anthony, Thomas Robbins, and Thomas E. Curtis, "Reply to Bellah," *Journal for the Scientific Study of Religion* 13(1974):492.
[121] Ibid., 491.
[122] Bellah, *Beyond Belief*, 253.

structuralist methods and doctrines have been important in psychology, linguistics, and folklore, the importance of structuralism in anthropology has been due largely to the work of Claude Lévi-Strauss, first on kinship but, more important, on myth.[123] The attempt to show that underlying all myths there is a single "deep structure" that reflects the nature of the human mind has held great appeal, because it seemed to provide a way of bringing order out of a bewildering variety of data, and greatly contributed to the interest in symbolic analysis.

Equally important has been the impact of English natural language philosophy—particularly its influence on the theory of action and the concept of social science—and the influence of hermeneutics, especially the writings of Paul Ricoeur and Jurgen Habermas.[124] Both these movements have contributed to the revival of the Verstehen view of social science and the emphasis on the interpretation of behavior, conceived as a text, rather than on prediction of its occurrence. Further impetus has come from the microsociology of Erving Goffman,[125] who introduced the dramaturgical model, the rapid growth of sociolinguistics, as evident in the work of Dell Hymes and William Labove,[126] and the popularity of semiotics, in which Umberto Eco's work was especially influential.[127] Thus many factors converged to produce a surge of interest in symbolic analysis in anthropology.[128] This work was not, of course, limited to the study of religion, but it did powerfully affect this field.

These influences are clear in the work of Geertz, who published his well-known essay on "Religion as a Cultural System" in 1966.[129] This is formally an essay in definition, although it turns out to be something more than that. The definition Geertz advances is as follows:

Religion is (1) a system of symbols which acts to (2) establish powerful, long-lasting and pervasive moods and motivations in men by (3) formulating a con-

---

[123] Claude Lévi-Strauss, *The Elementary Structures of Kinship* (Boston: Beacon Press, 1969), first published 1949; *The Raw and the Cooked* (New York: Harper and Row, 1969), first published 1964.

[124] John B. Thompson, *Critical Hermeneutics* (Cambridge: Cambridge University Press, 1981).

[125] Erving Goffman, *The Presentation of Self in Everyday Life* (New York: Doubleday Anchor, 1959).

[126] Dell Hymes, *Foundations of Sociolinguistics: An Ethnographic Approach* (Philadelphia: University of Pennsylvania Press, 1974); William Labov, *Language in the Inner City* (Philadelphia: University of Pennsylvania Press, 1978).

[127] Umberto Eco, *A Theory of Semiotics* (Bloomington: Indiana University Press, 1979).

[128] Victor Turner, "Symbolic Studies," *Annual Review of Anthropology* 4(1975):145–61.

[129] Clifford Geertz, "Religion as a Cultural System" in Clifford Geertz, *The Interpretation of Cultures* (New York: Basic Books, 1973), 87–125, first published 1966.

ception of a general order of existence and (4) clothing these conceptions with such an aura of factuality that (5) the moods and motivations seem uniquely realistic.[130]

Here, as in Bellah's writing, priority is given to the emotional; the moods and motivations are fundamental. Belief serves to establish these by creating a general model of reality in which Weber's problem of meaning is solved; things happen for a reason, suffering has a purpose, and there is a moral order in terms of which problems of evil can be understood, if not solved. But what gives factuality to this model is ritual: "It is in ritual . . . that the conviction that religious conceptions are veridical and that religious directives are sound is somehow generated."[131] Somehow, but how? "The acceptance of the authority that underlies the religious perspective that ritual embodies thus flows from the enactment of the ritual itself."[132] It is the *performance* of the symbolic ritual that unites the emotional and the cognitive. The argument is presented with Geertz's characteristic flair and spiced with splendid examples from his field work. Indeed, this interpretation is a direct outgrowth of his study of Balinese culture, where Geertz focused particularly on ritual performances as a key to the culture. Yet whatever the merits of Geertz's definition as a definition, the essay certainly does not do much to explain religion. It may be, as some religions have held, that if people act as if they have faith, faith will be given, but that participation in ritual produces conviction is at least a questionable claim.

The interest of psychologists in religion underwent a revival during the 1960s, touched off in considerable part by the work of T. W. Adorno and his collaborators in *The Authoritarian Personality*.[133] The relationships described in that book among religion, prejudice, and ethnocentricism came as a shock to many who thought Christian doctrine ought to imply the opposite. The problem was taken up by Gordon Allport in a series of publications in the 1950s and 1960s,[134] where he distinguished between intrinsic and extrinsic religiosity, the latter correlating with prejudice, the former not. Subsequent attempts to define the dimensions of

---

[130] Ibid., 90.
[131] Ibid., 112.
[132] Ibid., 118.
[133] T. W. Adorno, E. Frenkel-Brunswik, D. J. Levenson, and R. N. Sanford, *The Authoritarian Personality* (New York: Harpers, 1950).
[134] Gordon Allport, *The Nature of Prejudice* (Cambridge: Addison-Wesley, 1954); "The Religious Context of Prejudice," *Journal for the Scientific Study of Religion* 5(1966):447–57.

religiosity have led to multidimensional schemes such as those of Lenski and Glock and Stark, but factor analyses of the scales used to measure these dimensions have shown a relatively low degree of independence among them.[135] The one distinction that has consistently held up is the intrinsic-extrinsic division. The distinction is between a religion that emphasizes personal commitment, universalistic ethics, and love of one's neighbor, and regards faith as a supreme value, on the one hand, and one that is "strictly utilitarian: useful for the self in granting safety, social standing, solace and endorsement for one's chosen way of life,"[136] on the other. This division appears to have cognitive, motivational, and behavioral correlates.[137]

In 1958 Erik Erikson published *Young Man Luther*[138]—certainly the most celebrated psychohistorical study of a major religious figure yet written. Although Erikson wrote from a psychoanalytic perspective, his study went beyond the usual Freudian categories to develop the notion of personal identity acquired as a result of the resolution of crises and conflicts. In the same year, Walter Clark brought out *The Psychology of Religion*,[139] an eclectic work that attempted to survey the course of religious growth, the types of religious consciousness, and the relationship of religion to mental illness and therapy. Several years later, Abraham Maslow brought out his work on peak experiences.[140] Quite apart from the role of these experiences in his own self-realization psychology, Maslow's treatment of them was important (1) in showing that certain crucial types of religious experiences, such as conversion, were members of a class that included purely secular experiences and (2) in proposing a naturalistic approach to the entire class. This was an important break with the tendency of psychologists to adopt the categories of religion as their scheme of analysis.[141]

This psychologizing of the terms of analysis was carried further in 1968 by Paul Pruyser, who set out to write "a psychology of religion which would order its data in terms of psychological categories, use normative and clinical observations with appropriate fluidity, assess theo-

[135] Spilka, *Psychology*, 45.
[136] Allport, "Religious Context," 455.
[137] Spilka, *Psychology*, 18.
[138] Erik Erikson, *Young Man Luther* (New York: W. W. Norton, 1958).
[139] Walter H. Clark, *The Psychology of Religion* (New York: Macmillan, 1958).
[140] Abraham H. Maslow, *Religions, Values, and Peak-Experiences* (Columbus: Ohio State University Press, 1964).
[141] Clark, *Psychology*, especially chapters 12 and 13.

logical propositions as products of religious concept formation, and take into account the inconspicuous, everyday features of the religious life."[142] Yet an inventory of the psychological phenomena and processes involved in religion is considerably short of the psychological theory of religion, which can show how these phenomena and processes are related. So far, no psychologist since Freud has been able to achieve that.

Although most of the work done on religion by psychologists relied on ideographic methods of investigation, psychologists were also busily engaged in developing scales that could measure religious variables and could be administered through questionnaires and interviews. Scaling had been a prominent feature of *The Authoritarian Personality*, and the effort was continued by Gordon Allport and by many who came after him, until there are now hundreds of scales available.[143] The lack, as the psychologists themselves lament, is adequate theory to integrate the results obtained from the all-too-plentiful instruments. Despite some theoretical advances, such as the development of attribution theory by Bernard Spilka and his associates,[144] the gap between the "empiricists" and the "phenomenologists" continues to yawn. Jack Hanford's[145] call in 1975 for a synoptic theory to reconcile these approaches has yet to be met.

Conclusion

In 1962, Thomas Luckmann described the sociology of religion as "a branch of study consisting of the exegesis of Weberian texts on the theoretical side, and in practice leading to the collection of rather boring sociographic details on ecclesiastic institutions."[146] Although Luckmann may have overstated his case, in fact the study of religion has not lived up to the early promise offered by the achievements of Durkheim and Weber.[147] There are clearly multiple reasons for this. One has been the quality of the available data. The shortcomings of U.S. religious statistics are too well known to belabor here. Thus we really do not know whether

[142] Paul W. Pruyser, *A Dynamic Psychology of Religion* (New York: Harper and Row, 1968).
[143] Spilka, *Psychology*, 53.
[144] Ibid.
[145] Jack T. Hanford, "A Synoptic Approach: Resolving Problems in Empirical and Phenomenological Approaches to the Psychology of Religion," *Journal for the Scientific Study of Religion* 14(1975):219–27.
[146] Thomas Luckmann, "On Religion in Modern Society: Individual Consciousness, World View, Institutions," *Journal for the Scientific Study of Religion* 2(1962):148.
[147] Geertz, "Religion," 87ff.

there was a religious revival in the 1950s, and we probably never will, because the statistical data, even if accurate, are certainly ambiguous. Psychologists have similarly had to cope with intractable data problems, because religion has proved difficult to approach experimentally, and religious phenomena are singularly difficult to access through questionnaires or standard-format collection instruments of any kind. Moreover, studies based on samples have often used small samples and questionable designs. Gary Bouma's review of recent work in the sociology of religion found almost all of the 185 articles he examined ill-designed and methodologically inadequate.[148] If anthropologists have suffered less from these problems than sociologists and psychologists, it has been because participant-observation in nonliterate societies involves very different sorts of methodological problems—problems that are now receiving a more critical scrutiny than they have received in the past, with results that raise serious doubts about the authority of ethnographic accounts.[149]

But the problems in this field go far beyond the inadequacies of the data. The most obvious problem is the lack of theory. Weber, Durkheim, and Freud are the sources of practically all the concepts and theories currently used in the study of religion. Whatever the merits of these men as theorists, the fact that there has been so little theoretical advance in this field since they passed from the scene a half-century ago does not speak well for the health of the enterprise. One can but wonder why a field of study that once seemed so promising has produced so little.

As one reviews the work of the past century, other questions are unavoidable: Why are there such marked differences between the approaches and achievements of American anthropologists, sociologists, and psychologists in the study of religion? Certainly the most interesting and sophisticated work has been done by anthropologists. By comparison, where American sociologists have ventured beyond the sheltering theories of Weber and Durkheim, they have done little more than to create typologies and programs. Psychologists have not done much better, despite the fact that religion would appear to be a subject to which psychology is peculiarly relevant. Certainly one of the questions to be asked is, why have these three disciplines had such unequal success in dealing with this subject?

A further glaringly obvious question is the peculiar lack of agreement

[148] Gary Bouma, "Assessing the Impact of Religion: A Critical Review," *Sociological Analysis* 31(1970):172–79.
[149] Clifford, "Authority."

on what is being studied. As we have seen, definition after definition has been offered, none of which has satisfied anyone but its author. Surely it is odd that no definition of religion seems able to withstand cross-cultural data, and that even a definition adequate for Western cultures seems to elude us. After a century of largely futile effort, we are forced to doubt that a satisfactory definition can be given and to wonder about the implications of this failure.

One fact that cross-cultural studies have made increasingly clear is that the categories of "science," "religion," "metaphysics," etc., are very much the categories of our peculiar Western cultures. In particular, the sharp distinctions we make between "science" and "religion," "normative" and "empirical," "verifiable" and "metaphysical" do not always exist in other cultures. Moreover, although anthropologists can distinguish in an alien culture a group of beliefs about, let us say, plants, which they can label as "ethnobotany," native members of the culture in question often see no distinction between these beliefs and others the anthropologist classifies quite differently—say, religious beliefs. Our categorical schema represents a particular, highly parochial way of dividing up the world view. Whatever its historic roots in past controversies may be, it is not obvious that this categorical schema offers a particularly useful way to understand beliefs or any of the other phenomena associated with what we call "religion." Indeed, I suspect that the success of anthropologists such as Hallowell has arisen largely from their ability to transcend these categories and to deal with world views rather than "religions." They have been able to do this because they have dealt with cultures where our categorical schema was not taken for granted, and so an alternative conceptualization could be created. Sociologists and psychologists, in contrast, have generally dealt with American society, or at least Western society, where these categories are enshrined; hence the researchers have been as bound by the categories as the people they have studied.

But why should the use of these categories, which we have all been taught to honor, have proved debilitating? When Parsons[150] distinguished between empirically testable existential propositions, existential propositions not empirically testable, and normative propositions, was he not making a distinction that is clearly justified and crucial for our understanding of the world? I think not. Although Parsons regarded him-

---

[150] Parsons, *Essays*, 153ff.

self as an antipositivist, these distinctions are really those of the very positivists he thought he had rejected, and they have less warrant than he supposed.

At least since Willard Quine published "Two Dogmas of Empiricism" in 1953,[151] it has become increasingly clear that even scientific theories are not tested, or testable, on a statement-by-statement basis, but must be tested as wholes. One cannot therefore talk of propositions as empirically testable or untestable, because propositions are never tested alone; "testability" applies to theories as wholes, not to individual propositions. Entities postulated to exist in such theories may be said to be real if the theory as a whole is accepted and the basis for accepting or rejecting theories is their ability to provide a manageable structure for understanding and controlling experience. Whatever the differences between quarks and Homer's gods may be, they stand on the same epistemological footing; both are components of systems through which people seek to make sense of reality. The sort of distinction that Parsons sought to make between empirically testable propositions and propositions not empirically testable is not tenable.

The distinction between descriptive statements and normative statements is also far from self-evident and need not be affirmed. Suppose that the theologians are right and the "real world" is a moral order. Then so-called normative statements made in the indicative mood will be true or false as they do or do not correspond to that objective moral order. To fix ideas, suppose that the Christian God is real and that the Ten Commandments really are His commands. Then such a statement as "adultery is wrong" would be true, because it would correctly describe the divinely constituted order of reality. The claim that normative statements are incapable of truth values is a claim that there is no objective moral order in the world. This may be true, but it is not self-evident that it is true, and there is at least room for debate on the matter. Calvin did not conceive his theory of the world as being composed of separate descriptive and normative components but as a theory which, as a whole, described the nature of reality and man's relationship to that reality. If Calvinism is to be rejected, it is because we regard some alternative view of the world as offering a better account of experience, not because there was anything inherently untestable or unempirical about Calvin's theory.

This brings us to the concept of "empirical" knowledge. The term

[151] Willard Quine, "Two Dogmas of Empiricism" in Willard Quine, *From a Logical Point of View* (Cambridge, Mass.: Harvard University Press, 1953).

empirical is usually applied, not just to theories believed testable against experience, but to theories believed testable against a particular type of experience—experience gained through the five senses on which there is intersubjective, and therefore public, agreement. But in a strict sense, all experience is private, whether it is gained through the five senses or through mystical union. To claim that a color patch is red because observers agree to call it red is to talk about an agreement on word usage, with no proof that the observers use the word to refer to the "same" private experience. The distinction between "public" experience and "private" experience is not a distinction between kinds of experiences but among grounds for agreement, and involves a pragmatic decision on where the boundary should be drawn between experiences that have evidential value and those that do not. The drawing of the boundary is always done within a particular theoretical system and is one of the critically important claims of the system. Moreover, experience is never pure; perception is inferential and conditioned by perceptual hypotheses that are part of the theoretical system. Thus which sorts of theories are empirical—that is, are supported by evidential experience—and which are not is a question answered from within each theoretical system separately. No one who has read the writings of New England Puritans can doubt that doctrines such as innate depravity and predestination were for them thoroughly grounded in experience, and therefore empirical doctrines.

Systems of belief, including the values, attitudes, feelings, and experiences that they involve, appear to me to be the appropriate units of analysis in understanding how human beings orient and conduct themselves in the world. Like Melford Spiro, I doubt that it is possible to find a universal criterion that will sort these systems into the religious and the secular,[152] nor do I think it is useful to do so. Such systems differ on many dimensions; those that are similar on some will usually differ on many others. The fact that in our culture it has become standard to partition our world view into religion and science does not show that this can be done in other world views or that doing so would help us to understand them. Indeed, the imposition of such categories may well distort other world views and obscure the distinctions that are important for understanding them.

Whatever else religions may be, they are systems of belief. This is not to deny that they involve emotions, attitudes, and practices as well—all

---

[152] Spiro, "Religion."

world views, including scientific ones, also involve these elements—but it is to affirm that belief is central and must be dealt with. It would seem remarkable to find a book on the psychology of religion—and one highly praised in the field—that, despite chapter headings such as "Thought Organization in Religion" and "Relations to Things and Ideas,"[153] has almost nothing to say about the psychological significance of specific doctrines—if this were not the general rule. The reluctance to deal with doctrine may well reflect a clear-eyed recognition of the dangers posed by outraged believers who resent the profaning of the sacred, but it also avoids the critical issue. For if religion is important in social science, it is because systems of belief are important in understanding and accounting for human conduct. It may well be that the current poverty of our theories stems from our having focused on the wrong unit of analysis.

[153] Pruyser, *Psychology*, chapters 4 and 9.

8

On the intellectual marginality
of American theology

VAN A. HARVEY

There are few Protestant Christian theologians in the United States who would not concede that the intellectual enterprise called theology has fallen on evil days in their own country. It is not merely that the basic themes, categories, and types of argumentation of theology are regarded as irrelevant by most intellectuals, but that theological argumentation has virtually become a forgotten and lost mode of discourse. Unlike the situation in West Germany, for example, where theologians such as Küng, Metz, Moltmann, and Pannenberg not only appear frequently on public radio and television but contribute to discussions in the feuilleton sections of sophisticated newspapers such as *Die Zeit,* the names and views of the most serious theologians in this country are not even recognized by their colleagues. With the possible exception of, say, the latest book by Harvey Cox, the most important book review magazines ignore serious theology and religion. It can safely be said that Reinhold Niebuhr and Paul Tillich were the last two public theologians in this country, that is, theologians whose names were recognized because they contributed to those types of discourse that seriously engage American intellectuals.

Aggressive secularists, to be sure, will not lament this marginality of theology to American intellectual life. Like Auguste Comte, who, in his Laws of Three Stages, saw theology as a pseudo discipline that necessarily evolved first into metaphysics and then into science, many American intellectuals regard theology also as something akin to astrology. Moreover, they believe it to be divisive as well as obscurantist and therefore a threat to the common presuppositions on which civic discourse in a democracy must necessarily rest. Because theology is alien to these common presuppositions on which public policy must rest, it is a mode of discourse that the schools should have no interest in or responsibility toward.

But one does not have to be a religious believer to argue that intellectuals have a special responsibility for the quality of civic discourse in a culture, and that even secularists, therefore, have a legitimate interest in intellectually sophisticated reflection on the part of religious believers, especially when these constitute as large a proportion of the population as they do in the United States. Surely no one familiar with the contribution that Christian theology has made in the past to the philosophical and political thought of the West can be happy with what now so often emanates from the religious traditions. Theology, one might argue, serves the very important function of providing the conceptuality in which the Christian community, at least, expresses its own basic insights about life and morality. And lacking any sophisticated means of doing this, its feelings and beliefs can only be expressed crudely and dogmatically. Not even aggressive secularists should rejoice if a dominant section of the population can participate in public discussion only crudely and naively, or if other sections of that same public take pride in being ignorant of the sophisticated tradition of which the present expression is a caricature.

It could plausibly be argued that the blame for the marginality of theology in our time should be placed not on the doorstep of secular intellectuals, but, rather, on that of the theologians themselves. It could be argued that, particularly in the past two decades, Protestant theology has been characterized by narcissism and faddism that have virtually destroyed it as a serious intellectual discipline and deprived it of any respect it might thus claim. The slightest breezes that have stirred the trees of the groves of academe have been frantically harnessed for the purpose of generating energy for some new theological "movement"—a "theology of the death of God," a "theology of play," a "theology of hope," a "theology of liberation," a "theology of polytheism," a "theology of deconstruction," and, even redundantly, a "theology of God."

The argument that theology itself should be blamed for its own demise receives some anecdotal support from an incident that occurred in the spring of 1976 when the editors of *Christianity and Crisis* decided to devote an entire issue of that journal to the question "Whatever Happened to Theology?"[1] The idea to do this, ironically, occurred to them when, at an editorial meeting marked by a lively discussion of political

---

[1] *Christianity and Crisis* 35, no. 8 (1975).

and economic affairs, one of them suggested that the discussion turn to theology and there was a deadly and embarrassing silence. I write "ironically" because this is the same editorial board responsible for that journal created by Reinhold Niebuhr precisely for the purpose of demonstrating the relevance of theology for public life. That the editorial board of this journal should fall speechless when a discussion of theology was proposed speaks volumes about what has happened to this mode of discourse.

Most of the twelve theologians who contributed to that issue of *Christianity and Crisis* conceded that a once proud and noble intellectual discipline has, indeed, fallen into a sad state of repair, although each offered different reasons to account for it. Some blamed it on the *Zeitgeist,* suggesting that it is simply a matter of living in an age when the giants of theology have passed from the scene. Others, like Rosemary Reuther and the South American theologian Jose Bonino, suggested more world-historical answers. Reuther argued, "The entire paradigm of consciousness that has governed the line of Western culture and its reflection in theology has lost its credibility."[2] Bonino apocalyptically announced that "the great and admirable social cultural achievement that we call Western bourgeois culture is reaching the end of its run; and consequently, the imposing and noble theological tradition which has accompanied, at times inspired, sometimes humanized and always expressed it, is also running out."[3]

One may infer from reading these theologians' remarks that the marginality and irrelevance of Christian theology are most obvious within Protestant theology. It is not simply that the theological giants of this tradition have passed—this passing would not in itself have caused marginality—but that most of what goes by the name of academic theology is marked by a lack of agreement as to method, standards of assessment, and, most seriously, subject matter. "Theology," writes Gordon Kaufman, "apparently had no integrity of standards or demands of its own; its symbols could be used as a kind of decoration for and legitimation of almost any partisan position found in the culture. The once proud queen of the sciences, having lost a sense of her own meaning and integrity, had become a common prostitute."[4]

It is indicative of the concerns of intellectuals in our times that little

[2] Ibid., 119.
[3] Ibid., 111.
[4] Ibid.

effort has been made to understand this phenomenon. It seems clear that the subject does not appear to interest intellectual historians or sociologists of knowledge. This is surprising, given their current interest in tracing the genealogy of all other kinds of ideologies. How did an intellectual discipline that once dominated the leading faculties of European and English universities become in a few short decades an arcane and intellectually irrelevant discipline? This would appear to be as interesting an issue as, say, the decline in the belief in witches or the fate of phrenology.

The issue is even more interesting because of a paradox that some sociologists have called to our attention, namely, that Protestant theology seems to have become marginal just as religious belief in this country is burgeoning. This is paradoxical because, according to most of the widely accepted theories of secularization, one might have expected religious belief itself to have disappeared in this increasingly bureaucratized and technological society, or at least to have become more privatized and inchoate. According to this hypothesis, which rests on both Weberian and Marxist assumptions, technology and bureaucracy are inherently dymystifying and subversive of belief in the sacred. Moreover, the types of religiosity that seem to be currently flourishing—among Fundamentalists, Mormons, Jehovah's Witnesses—are precisely those that have highly rationalistic religious content, which is to say, that stress cognitive belief (theology) and seem to be inherently antithetical to the intellectual assumptions of the established intellectual culture. For these religious groups, theology has become a useful ideological tool for getting a purchase on the secular beliefs, policies, and assumptions of the dominant American culture with which they are so unhappy: scientific claims about the origins of the world and life, the toleration of homosexuality and abortion, and the like.

All this suggests that the time is ripe for an attempt to understand the vicissitudes of theology and religion in modern American culture, one feature of which would be to understand how and why Protestant theology has become intellectually marginal. One of the few serious scholars to attempt to do this is, of course, the sociologist Peter Berger.[5] In his presidential address to the Society for the Scientific Study of Religion in 1966 and in several subsequent works, he has attempted to interpret the development of Protestant liberal theology within the general context of

[5] See Peter L. Berger, *A Rumor of Angels* (Garden City, N.Y.: Doubleday & Co., 1969), *The Heretical Imperative* (Garden City, N.Y.: Doubleday & Co., 1979), and *Facing Up To Modernity* (New York: Basic Books, 1977).

a theory of secularization. In his early work, Berger argued that, from a sociological point of view, the classical function of religion has been to legitimate, sanctify, and mystify the "socially constructed world" that every society necessarily casts up. Religion has classically provided the "sacred canopy" that lends unquestioned absoluteness to the form of life emergent in any society. Berger also argued that Protestantism, with its distinction between "the two Kingdoms" and its conception of vocation, constituted a break with this classical view of religion. It was the historically decisive prelude to secularization, because it prepared the way for the "disenchantment of the world" that Weber saw as the distinctive feature of the modern consciousness. Protestantism, to use the language of a later type of intellectual history, was the "condition of possibility" of secularism.[6]

In his later works, Berger became increasingly interested in and critical of the various accommodations that contemporary liberal Protestant theologians had made to the secularization made possible by their "forefathers." He was especially critical of the so-called secular theologians of the 1950s and 1960s—professional theologians, clergy, and even bishops—who, although charged with the responsibility for the integrity of Christian theology and ritual, seemed "hell-bent" on giving the contents of the religious store away by "dymythologizing" traditional theological affirmations about the Transcendent into statements about the nature of the self and its temporality. The resurrection of Jesus, for example, was said to be a symbol of human psychological or existential processes rather than a supernatural event. Or God, to take another example, was the name not for a transcendent Subject but the "ground of all that is unconditioned" in human life.

The interesting fact about these secular theologians, Berger argued, was that although they all shared the assumption that traditional religious affirmations are no longer tenable because they do not meet some modern philosophical or scientific criteria, they continued to operate within the context of traditional ecclesiastical institutions, despite the considerable practical strains that doing this put on them. The way they did this—in all sincerity, he noted—was by making use of some rarefied conceptual machinery, such as existential philosophy or depth psychology, that enabled them to operate at a high level of intellectual sophistication while touching base through popular writing with some "ideological correlate

[6] See Berger, *The Sacred Canopy: Elements of a Sociological Theory of Religion* (Garden City, N.Y.: Doubleday & Co., 1967).

on a lower level of popular consciousness."[7] This practice enabled these dymythologizers to capitalize on what Berger called the "elective affinity" between certain ideas of Heidegger and the mentality of suburban housewives.

Berger argued further that what all these theologians had in common was the uncritical acceptance of the secular consciousness, that is, its scientific and pragmatic assumptions. As a sociologist, he argued that this secular consciousness could best be explained by referring to the social infrastructure on which it was based. Although he acknowledged that there were several causal factors at work, the most decisive was what he called the "pluralization of the social worlds." This pluralization must be understood against the background of medieval Christendom, which historically developed when the great majority of people lived within the same social structures and the Church was the primary "reality defining" institution. Although there were many strains within medieval society, Christendom nevertheless provided a social-structural and cognitive unity that has now been irretrievably lost. In our society, by contrast, there are several discrepant "social worlds," each of which challenges the cognitive and normative claims of the other.

Because the sociologist believes that every important belief rests on and derives its strength from a "plausibility structure," this pluralization of social worlds necessarily leads to a crisis of credibility. Because there is now no monopoly in the definition of reality, we live in a "market of world views" in which it is difficult to maintain any certitudes that go much beyond the empirical necessities of the society. Because religion essentially rests on such superempirical certainties, this pluralistic situation plunges religion into the maelstrom of relativity and uncertainty. The way to explain the secular theologians is to interpret them as attempting to package the old religious message in a form that is acceptable to men and women in the street—the bearers of what is taken to be the modern secular consciousness. They make the believer "feel safe from the secularizing and subjectivizing forces threatening the tradition."[8]

It is now fashionable to criticize and reject Berger's proposed secularization theory, which, it must be acknowledged, contains severe conceptual problems. Not the least of the difficulties is the assumption that technology and bureaucratization are inherently dymystifying and antithetical

---

[7] Berger, "A Sociological View of the Secularization of Theology," *Journal for the Scientific Study of Religion* VI, no. 1 (Spring 1967): 6.
[8] Ibid., 14.

to religious belief. The theory does not seem capable of accounting for the resurgence of conservative religious ideology in modern America.[9] Otherwise expressed, the men and women in the street seem to have an incredibly anachronistic consciousness.

Berger's treatment of theology itself is further complicated by two additional difficulties. First, he employs a type of sociology of knowledge that was explicitly designed to deal with the pretheoretical "reality of every day life" and to avoid just those types of issues so important to Max Scheler and Karl Mannheim, that is, the sociology of the intellectual sphere. Berger wants to deal with the intellectual problems of relativism while embracing a type of sociology that he concedes is incapable of dealing with it. Consequently, his analysis of theology is inherently problematical.[10] Second, Berger's theory of religion as a "sacred canopy" that functions to legitimate social worlds leads him to the paradoxical claim that Protestant Christianity should not be classified as a religion because it rejects this view of the relation of the Transcendent to the world.

Nevertheless, despite these difficulties, Berger understands, as few theologians do, that any attempt to account for the development of modern theology that stays purely within the realm of the history of ideas, as so many do, will prove to be shallow. Moreover he has some very interesting things to say about "plausibility structures," the role of pluralism, and the way these things must be taken into account. Insofar as my own reflections on the marginality of theology concentrate on the importance of the professionalization and specialization of knowledge in American life and the "social location" of the Protestant theologian—that is, the theologian's place in the divinity school—I am profoundly indebted to Berger.

In the remainder of this paper I explore some hypotheses about the way in which the social location of Protestant theologians since the turn of the nineteenth century—and the kinds of intellectual problems with which they dealt—has influenced the course of theology, or, more prejudicially perhaps, has contributed to the marginalization of theology as a discipline. I call these subjects *hypotheses* because they are guiding my work in progress, of which this might be said to be an initial report of sorts. What I wish to suggest is that it is less enlightening to explain what

[9] Winston Davis has also argued that the thesis is falsified in the case of Japan. See his *Dojo: Magic and Exorcism in Modern Japan* (Stanford, Calif.: Stanford University Press, 1980).
[10] See my "Some Problematical Aspects of Peter Berger's Theory of Religion," *Journal of the American Academy of Religion* XLI, no. 1 (1973).

has happened to theology by appeal to "secularization" than it is to provide a concrete narrative of a complex process in which the important elements are the "professionalization" of the divinity school and the definition of the theologian's role. I do not mean to suggest that what we call secularization played no role in creating a general intellectual culture in which theology increasingly seemed arcane; rather, my argument is that the marginalization of theology can better be explained by looking at these concrete and specific developments and events. Perhaps all this may be regarded as the filling out of secularization theory, but I believe the argument is plausible without recourse to it. Perhaps the reader is the best judge of this.

A discipline and a profession

We may begin by considering theology as an intellectual discipline. Now an intellectual discipline, as Stephen Toulmin has pointed out, may be regarded as the cultural side of profession.[11] As a discipline, it is a specialized type of intellectual activity that has its own subject matter, categories, and procedures for the identification and adjudication of issues, and, hence, its standards of performance. As a profession, it has its corresponding bureaucracies in the form of learned societies and organizations, journals and organs of expression, rewards and prizes, and corresponding hierarchies of prestige and influence.

The growth and proliferation of the intellectual disciplines since 1870, as Edward Shils has pointed out, is one of the striking features of Western culture in general and of the United States in particular.[12] It is one of the results of the rapid expansion since 1865 of the educated and professional classes in this country that has transformed the institutional matrix in which intellectual life itself is lived. Before the Civil War, the American economy was based mainly on farming, fishing, and trade. The educated classes were, for the most part, a small elite group of clergymen and men of letters. Higher education, that is, the liberal arts college, was in private and, primarily, clerical hands and was devoted to the training of clergymen and civic leaders. The function of the college, it was believed, was to preserve sound learning, morality, and religion. This belief, in turn, was manifested in a curriculum organized around the "mental

---

[11] Toulmin, *Human Understanding*, vol. 1 (Princeton: Princeton University Press, 1972).
[12] See E. Shils, *The Intellectuals and the Powers* and other essays (Chicago: Chicago University Press, 1972).

discipline" of Latin, mathematics, and moral philosophy.[13] The terminal degree was the bachelor of arts; the master's was an honorary degree, and the Ph.D. was virtually unknown, there being no graduate schools.

After 1865, the situation began to change dramatically under the pressures of the aspirations of a population in an emerging industrial society with its shifting division of labor and corresponding needs for new knowledge, skills, and administrative competence. The nation needed engineers, lawyers, doctors, journalists, scientists, and specialists of many sorts. Consequently, a host of new professional roles was created almost overnight.

In his book *The Culture of Professionalism,* Burton Bledstein argues that what distinguished higher education in the United States from that in Britain and Germany, which had always been admired by Americans, was that the American university became the institution embodying the goals and emotional aspirations of the middle classes increasingly in the grip of the ideal of a career. It was professionalism, Bledstein argues—a set of learned values and responses by which members of the middle class shaped their emotional needs and measured their powers of intelligence—that determined the face of the United States in general and the university in particular. The university as we now know it, he claims, actually came into existence "to serve and promote professional authority in society. More than in any other Western country in the last century, the development of higher education in America made possible a social faith in merit, competence, discipline, and control that were basic to accepted conceptions of achievement and success."[14] The universities, by screening, formalizing, and standardizing, and, above all, by certifying with credentials, legitimated and determined competence in American life.

One does not have to share the slightly agitated tone of Bledstein's book or accept his entire argument in order to accept the description of the transformation in the university in the United States after 1870. The American university expanded to a degree unknown in Europe, and this expansion seems largely to be accounted for by the new client orientation of its leadership. There was competition for students, constant growth, promotional advertising, the introduction of athletics, burgeoning en-

---

[13] See L. Veysey, *The Emergence of the American University: 1870–1910* (Chicago: University of Chicago Press, 1965).
[14] B. J. Bledstein, *The Culture of Professionalism: The Middle Class and the Development of Higher Education in America* (New York: Norton, 1978).

rollments, and, above all, an increasingly specialized distribution of knowledge—the external manifestation of which is the growth of departments and professional and graduate schools. In 1870, there were only 44 students enrolled in graduate schools in the United States. By 1888, there were 1,345; by 1930, 47,255; by 1972, 908,000. In 1876, 44 Ph.D.'s were conferred; in 1970, 29,872.[15] Over all this there mushroomed an administrative bureaucracy.

Bledstein further argues that the reason Americans became enamored of the German system of higher education was that it alone embodied and served professionalism. Only the Germans, it was believed, had a system designed to recruit and support the best talent. But Americans were also uncomfortable with the authoritarian and elitist nature of the German system, which catered to a restricted clientele. So Americans looked solely to professionalism with its universal and scientific standards to serve as the instrument of selection and grading. What authority was to the German intellectual, science was to the American. Indeed, the primary function of the American university, Bledstein concludes, was "to render universal scientific standards credible to the public" and, by reducing problems to scientific and even technical terms, to contain those controversial issues that once threatened to rip the fabric of the community.[16] Ideas became the subject matter of experts who kept them within a context in which they could be managed and dealt with by universal and scientific reason.

Given this picture of the professionalization of the university in America and the scientific ethos that came to dominate it, an hypothesis regarding the causes of the marginality of theology immediately suggests itself: because the university became the institutional matrix for intellectual life in America, and because the ethos of the university was scientific and hostile to everything that did not lend itself to rational adjudication, theology was necessarily pushed to the margins of intellectual life. Because the universities provided the basis of cognitive authority and served the function of containing divisiveness, theology, resting as it does on religious faith and giving rise to controversy, was simply excluded from the university.

The difficulty with this hypothesis is that although it possesses a degree of plausibility—it may be seen as a wrinkle on the secularization

---

[15] See C. Wright Mills, *Sociology and Pragmatism: The Higher Learning in America* (New York: Oxford University Press, Galaxy Books, 1966), chapter 3.
[16] Bledstein, *The Culture of Professionalism*, chapter 8.

hypothesis—it makes no reference to two complicating facts: (1) since the early nineteenth century, the theologians in this country have been located in the divinity school, not the university; (2) these divinity schools were founded before professionalism became rampant and the scientific ethos had gripped the university. Consequently, this hypothesis overlooks the possibility that the internal development of the theological disciplines themselves within the changing nature of the divinity school may have played an important role in driving theology to the margins.

This is, in fact, the inference that can be drawn from an important but neglected book titled *Theologia: The Fragmentation and Unity of Theological Education in America* by Edward Farley, a theologian at Vanderbilt University.[17] Farley's book, as the title indicates, is an attempt to account for what he regards as the fragmentation of theological education in the divinity schools. It is one of the merits of this book that although the author understands that the most debilitating problem of theology is the problem of Christian faith in modern times, he nevertheless argues that it is important to understand that the agenda-setting institution for theology, the divinity school, is sick. Not only is there no common preparation of persons admitted or any relation between the aggregated disciplines that constitute the curriculum itself, but there is an inherent conflict between the aims of the school and the demands of the profession. One might even say that the theologically oriented students are professionally handicapped and, hence, punished.

The paradoxical conclusion that emerges from the book is that the sickness of theology is largely a result of the specialization and professionalization of theological education; that is, to the degree to which theological education has been determined by what Farley calls the "clerical paradigm." How this professionalization came about is a complex story, but its basic outlines are clear. First, "divinity" was conceived of as distinctive subject matter; then, steps were taken to institutionalize this conception by creating separate divinity schools; finally, a theological curriculum that, with its various specialties, was thought to be appropriate to a professional clergy, was imposed on the divinity schools.

From the foundation of the colonies up to approximately 1800, "divinity," even though regarded as a distinguishable part of the curriculum,

---

[17] (Philadelphia: Fortress Press, 1983). As will be apparent, I am also deeply indebted to Farley's analysis. What may be less clear is the degree to which I disagree with (1) his conception of theology and (2) the conclusions he draws from this conception concerning its justification in the university. But a discussion of these matters here would take me too far afield from my present task.

nevertheless pervaded education as a whole and was its apex and crown. So far as the training of the ministers was concerned, it was expected that they would be educated in all the university disciplines, that is, in classical languages, Bible, and philosophy. So far as "divinity" was taught, it tended to be in the form of handbooks and guides. Even in this period, however, certain initial steps had been taken toward specialization: chairs of divinity were founded at Harvard and Yale in 1721 and 1755, and a two-year course of graduate study or an apprenticeship with an established clergyman became the rule. The first seminaries, Andover and Princeton, were founded in the first decade of the nineteenth century, and some twenty or so followed within twenty years.

The most important section of Farley's book, I believe, traces the long and complex development of the curriculum that came to inform the divinity schools in this country and, to a great extent, still does. He calls this the "four fold" curriculum because it divides all theological studies into basically four parts: biblical studies, church history, dogmatics or Christian doctrine, and practical theology. This division, Farley shows, has its historical roots in the "theological encyclopedia" movement of the eighteenth century, a movement he regards as the most important event in the history of the education of the Christian clergy.[18] Although the title "theological encyclopedia" tends to remind us of that characteristic product of the eighteenth century *philosophes,* who tried to provide summaries of all existing knowledge, the theological encyclopedia, by contrast, was a genre developed by theologians to define the discipline and subdisciplines of theology alongside those of law, medicine, and philosophy. It was probably a response to the sectarian religious controversies of the post-Reformation period as well as the new historical consciousness that was so preoccupied with methodology. The theological encyclopedia was intended to serve as a general introduction to theological studies by describing the fields of theology and the methods appropriate to them.

At any rate, from the plethora of attempts to provide such encyclopedias, consensus emerged in which there were three theoretical theological disciplines (Scripture, church history, and dogmatics) and a fourth practical discipline that was concerned with homiletics, catechetics, and the "cure of souls."

This preoccupation with subject matter and methodology of theology

---

[18] Ibid., 49.

assumed a larger cultural importance in Germany in the late eighteenth century because of the so-called conflict of the faculties that rocked the new scientific universities of Halle and Göttingen. Probably originating in Göttingen when a philosophy professor announced a course in church history, the dispute widened into a series of controversies over the proper jurisdiction of the various faculties—law, medicine, theology, and philosophy.[19] The issue of the relation of philosophy to theology within the scientific university dedicated to knowledge was particularly vexious. In the course of these controversies, to which such luminaries as Immanuel Kant, Friedrich Schelling, Johann Fichte, and Friedrich Schleiermacher all added their voices, it was inevitable that the justification for including theology within the university curriculum at all should have been raised. Fichte, for example, raised the distinctively modern argument that insofar as theology is based on revelation and authority, it cannot possibly be considered a science and, hence, has no place within the modern university.

Kant, who entered the controversy to lend his prestige to the autonomy of philosophy, suggested that the faculties of medicine, law, and theology were justified within the university not because they were sciences but primarily because of their service to the state. The state, he argued, was properly required to serve certain spheres in which the public had indispensable needs, needs that were met by medicine, law, and religion. The theological faculty existed to train the leadership of the churches, just as the medical and legal faculties existed to train doctors and lawyers. The same argument was put forward by Schelling and, most important, by the famous Protestant theologian, Schleiermacher, who, with Alexander von Humboldt, played a crucial role in the establishment and organization of the newly founded (1810) University of Berlin, which some historians regard as the first modern research university.

Schleiermacher, who was profoundly concerned with theological method for inherently intellectual as well as jurisdictional reasons, had begun lecturing on the theological encyclopedia as early as 1804, and he continued to do so for most of his career, the results of which have been published in the well-known *Brief Outline of Theological Study*. His own contribution to the "conflict of the faculties," however, was contained in an essay titled "Occasional Thoughts on the German University," in which he argued that the object of theology was the Christian religion, and,

---

[19] Ibid., 97, note 29.

hence, theology could properly be considered a science. But he justified the study of this science on the same grounds Kant proposed, namely, that the aim of the university was to train leaders who served specific needs of the public—in this case, the religious needs.

This type of apologia for the existence of theological studies in the university, however, contains a fateful ambiguity, the consequences of which were only fully played out when the four-fold curriculum was transported to the United States under the impact of the Germanization of American theological education in the early and mid-nineteenth century.[20] The ambiguity is that although theology is defended as a legitimate academic discipline because its subject matter is the Christian religion,[21] its existence in the university is justified primarily on the grounds that the university exists to train leadership in the churches. Where the society accepts that it is the responsibility of the state to train church leadership, as was the case in Germany, the ambiguity does not surface and the reasons reinforce each other; but where, as in America, the separation of church and state is taken to mean that the state is forbidden to train the clergy, the ambiguity becomes fully apparent. Indeed, the same argument that served to justify theology in the German university in the nineteenth century can now be used to justify the exclusion of theology from the American university and the establishment of separate divinity schools under the aegis of denominations and churches.

Even more seriously, so far as our theme concerning the marginality of theology to general intellectual life is concerned, this apologia for theology necessarily professionalizes and specializes it, that is, conceives of its utility as subject matter in professional and specialized terms: the training of clergy. In so doing, it prepares the way for what Farley calls the "clerical paradigm" to dominate theological education; by the same token, it conveys to the laity that just as the study of law is for lawyers and medicine for doctors, so theology is a "science" for professional clergy. Theology is now no longer seen as subject matter that has to do with the clarification of the self-understanding of the ordinary believer and, hence, as having any relevance for the "life world."

[20] The number of important theological figures educated in Germany at the time is remarkable: Moses Stuart, John Nevin, Edwards Park, Philip Schaff, Charles Hodge, and Benjamin Warfield.

[21] There are still other ambiguities here. Even if one concedes that the subject matter of theology is the Christian religion, is this to be understood as a normative or a descriptive inquiry? If the latter, why isn't it subject matter for the history faculty? Second, even if we understand Christianity descriptively, is there an "essence of Christianity," as Schleiermacher assumed, or is Christianity a pluralistic, changing phenomenon?

Given the fact that since the early nineteenth century, the social location of theology and theological education has been the divinity school, and given the superimposition of a four-fold curriculum on that school in the name of the clerical paradigm, Farley argues that the subsequent fragmentation of theology and the loss of any unified meaning of the practice of theology stemmed from the specialization of each of the various disciplines represented in that four-fold curriculum: Bible, church history, dogmatics, and practical theology. In other words, each of these disciplines experienced its own distinctive internal development in which, increasingly, scholars restricted their research and writing to narrowly defined areas. These disciplines became more and more specialized and gradually formed their own scholarly communities with all of the external characteristics of distinctive professions: professional societies, specialized journals, and the like. Farley argues that this specialization altered the very meaning of each of the subdivisions of theological studies:

With specialization each science developed the critical apparatus it needed, its languages, satellite secular sciences, technical methods. The result was that each of the four theological sciences itself became an aggregate, a general area of scholarship within which were "sciences." This is especially apparent in church history, systematic theology, and practical theology.[22]

Marginalization of theology

There is, I believe, much truth in Farley's analysis of the effects of specialization on the unity of theological education, but much more attention needs to be paid to the ways in which movements within Protestant theology, which were themselves responses to the intellectual challenges of the culture, contributed to the drive for specialization and, ultimately, to the marginalization of theology to general intellectual life. My own research is now concerned with this complex development and, so far, the outlines beginning to emerge look something like this. The great intellectual crisis through which theology passed in the nineteenth century was precipitated by two autonomous but closely related movements: the rise of biblical criticism, especially of the New Testament, and the criticism of speculative metaphysics and theology proposed by Kant. Both of these, it is important to note, were intellectual movements within the universities, and the leading figures were university professors.

As I have argued at length elsewhere, one cannot stress too much the inherently corrosive effect on traditional Christian beliefs from the appli-

[22] Farley, *Theologia*, 105.

cation of historical-critical methods to the Bible.[23] It is not just that the "results" produced by New Testament criticism are often inconsistent with important traditional Christian beliefs; it is, rather, that critical historians must necessarily regard it as an intolerable surrender of their autonomous critical judgment to permit religious faith to tip the balance in ascertaining what is to count as historical fact. Indeed, the "logic" of critical historical judgment ultimately leads to the view that the ingression of religious belief into the historical inquiry, where faith is equated with belief in certain historical propositions, tends to corrode the habits and virtues of historical judgment itself. Certain types of faith, in short, tend to be incompatible with balanced historical judgment.

This deeper issue was not all clear in the initial and sensational controversies surrounding the publication in 1835 of David Friedrich Strauss's *The Life of Jesus Critically Examined*. These controversies swirled around Strauss's rejection of miracle and his argument that the Jesus of history was a personage far different from the "Christ of faith" in the New Testament. But the deeper issue came to the surface when it became evident that the only convincing way of combatting the historical skepticism of Strauss regarding Jesus was to show that this skepticism was not justified by the historical evidence. In order to establish this, it was necessary to use the same critical historical methods that Strauss had used. Consequently, an entire century of New Testament scholarship was devoted to what Albert Schweitzer has called the "quest of the historical Jesus."[24]

But the results of this century-long quest were not to restore the confidence in the historical veracity of the New Testament as was hoped; rather, the varied and diverse lives of Jesus that were produced only reinforced the sense of historical skepticism. So true was this that an entire generation of Protestant theologians at the beginning of the twentieth century—Karl Barth, Emil Brunner, Rudolph Bultmann, Friedrich Gogarten, and Paul Tillich—concluded that it was a mistake to think that Christian theology in any way was or should be dependent on the results of historical inquiry. Moreover, it was taken as axiomatic that the resolution of historical issues was not a matter to which the theologian qua theologian could contribute because these issues belonged properly to the sphere of the specialist.

---

[23] See my *The Historian and the Believer: The Morality of Knowledge and Christian Belief* (Philadelphia: Westminster Press, 1981). Cf. "New Testament Scholarship and Christian Belief" in *Jesus in History and Myth*, edited by R. Joseph Hoffmann and Gerald A. Larue (Buffalo, N.Y.: Prometheus Books, 1986).

[24] Albert Schweitzer, *The Quest of the Historical Jesus*, translated by W. Montgomery (London: Adam & Charles Black, 1952).

The development of specialized Old and New Testament scholarship had the effect of taking away two of the traditional fields of competence claimed by the systematic theologian. In the early part of the nineteenth century, a paradigmatic theologian like Schleiermacher could lecture on the Gospel of Luke or the life of Jesus as effortlessly as he could on dogmatics, Christian ethics, and the history of doctrine. A century later, after specialization had set in, this would be virtually impossible for any self-respecting theologian because he would only reveal himself to be an amateur. The biblical disputes of the nineteenth century, in short, had the effect of creating a series of specialized disciplines, each with its own procedures and norms, that were distinct from theology. What was once the subject matter of theology was, as it were, subcontracted out to New Testament studies, church history, philosophy of religion, and ethics.

The question this process of specialization raised was, What is the subject matter of theology? Had this question arisen one hundred years earlier, the answer would undoubtedly have been that the subject matter of theology was metaphysics. The aim of the theologian, it had been assumed, was to give a philosophical, which is to say a metaphysical, rendition of the real content embodied in the imaginative language and symbolism of the tradition. But it was just this answer that was made impossible for the theologians of the mid- and late nineteenth century because of the powerful critique of speculative metaphysics mounted by Immanuel Kant. Kant argued that the interminable and irresolvable disputes of metaphysics—why is there no progress in metaphysics as there is in other branches of knowledge?—can be accounted for if one understands that metaphysical claims transcend the limits of reason; or, more precisely, if one understands that judgments of this sort lack the element of sense experience necessary to make *synthetic a priori* judgments possible. So long as Christian theology is regarded as an expression of faith and is tied to presuppositions of the moral or practical reason, it is a legitimate enterprise. But theology as "metaphysics for believers" is a spurious and illegitimate "science," which is to say that it is no science at all.

Kant's critique of speculative metaphysics naturally posed fundamental questions about the criteria and status of theology as an academic discipline. As we have already seen, he justified the place of theology in the university on the ground that it was the state's responsibility to train leaders for the institutions of society. It was no accident, therefore, that it was the same theologian, Schleiermacher, who both agreed with Kant regarding the justification of teaching theology within the university and provided a new conception of the nature and subject matter of theology. Christian theology, Schleiermacher conceded to Kant, is not metaphysics in religious clothing; rather, it is the formalization and systematization of the expressions of the Christian religious self-consciousness. Religion had to do with the affections, the "feeling of absolute dependence" as it was conditioned and determined by the religious community with a specific historical tradition.[25] Theology, we might now say, is a phenomenology of the collective consciousness of a determinate religious community.

Schleiermacher's solution, which was worked out with that genius for system unique to the Germans, was a powerful one, and it dominated the subsequent century of Protestant theology.[26] Theology, it seemed, no longer needed to fear alternative metaphysical systems such as Hegel's, the challenges of science, or the skepticism of biblical criticism. Theology was not a system of cognitive beliefs at all.[27] Nor need theology engage in apologetics or in the denigration of other forms of religious feeling and experience, because it was purely the systematization of Christian faith. It was a theology of "experience."

[25] F. D. E. Schleiermacher, *The Christian Faith*, translated and edited by H. R. Mackintosh and J. S. Steward (Edinburgh: T. & T. Clark, 1948), 76f. The interesting ambiguity here is whether, given this conception, theology is a descriptive or a normative inquiry. The Lundensian school of theology in Sweden, which has been greatly influenced by Schleiermacher, regards theology as a descriptive science: the identification of the essential "motifs" of Christianity. Moreover, it was only because it was a descriptive science in this sense that it can justifiably belong in the university. See A. Nygren, *Meaning and Method: Prolegomena to a Scientific Philosophy of Religion and a Scientific Theology*, translated by Philip S. Watson (Philadelphia: Fortress Press, 1972).

[26] As fierce a critic of Schleiermacher as Karl Barth has written that not only the nineteenth century belongs to Schleiermacher but that it appears that the twentieth may be his also. "Nobody can say today whether we have really overcome his influence, or whether we are still at heart children of his age." *From Rousseau to Ritschl*, translated by Brian Cozens (London: SCM Press, Ltd., 1952), 307.

[27] The relationship of Protestant liberalism to biblical criticism is more complicated than this sentence suggests. Although Schleiermacher's solution seemed to immure theology from the threat of any type of knowledge, including historical knowledge, it seems clear that in his view the Christian self-consciousness is dependent on and caused by what he called the "perfect God-consciousness" of Jesus. This is the reason why liberal Protestants felt it so important to defeat the skepticism of Strauss. But as liberals, they felt obligated to use the methods of historical inquiry. The result was the century-long quest for the historical Jesus that, ironically, ended in the very skepticism they feared. Other liberals, like Wilhelm Herrmann, saw that Christian faith could not be so conceived that it depended on the uncertain results of biblical inquiry. So he attempted to argue that the spiritual power that emanated from Jesus did not depend on the accuracy of the historical portrait. See his *The Communion of the Christian with God*, translated by J. Sandys Stanyon, revised by Robert W. Stewart (New York: G. P. Putnam's Sons, 1906), 112 ff. Ernst Troeltsch, the neglected German theologian, wrote a profound analysis of this problem as early as 1911. See his essay on "The Significance of the Historical Existence of Jesus for Faith" in *Ernst Troeltsch: Writings on Theology and Religion*, edited by Robert Morgan and Michael Pye (Atlanta: John Knox Press, 1977), 182–207.

Protestant liberalism, which subsequently embraced one or another version of this conception of theology, paid a high price for it. Although it seemed to secure faith against the threats of philosophy and science, it did so at the cost of raising fundamental questions about norms and procedures of theology. It became increasingly unclear what expertise in theology could consist of. One might still justify New Testament studies or church history because both are historical sciences, but what could be the justification for the clarification and systematization of the utterances of the Christian self-consciousness except the purpose of training the leaders of the Christian churches? In all those countries, including Germany, where Christianity was the state religion, this justification seemed valid, although even there one can, by the end of the nineteenth century, begin to detect the uneasiness of the liberal theologian on such occasions as the traditional rectorial address.[28] In the United States, however, where there was no official state religion and the new state universities were forbidden to mix in religion, the Schleiermacherian solution could at best only justify the existence of a distinct professional school where the Christians might "do their own thing." The new state universities and land grant colleges were already engaged in serving the needs of a rapidly expanding industrial society based on science and technology. Critical of the elitism of Eastern universities and increasingly dominated by naturalistic modes of thought, they could see no reason even to consider theology, as defined by liberalism, as a legitimate subject for the university curriculum. They even rejected the academic study of religion on the mistaken assumption that it was incompatible with the separation of church and state. In short, the professionalized and specialized divinity school with its four-fold curriculum seemed like a happy solution for everyone. It was—but its curriculum and organization also virtually assured the future marginality of theology to the intellectual culture of the United States.

Consequences for American society

It now only remains for me to draw some lines to connect these developments that led to the specialization of the disciplines related to theology and its present marginality to intellectual life in the United States. The first connection seems obvious. It is that insofar as it has come to be assumed and institutionalized that theology is primarily subject matter

[28] See the rectorial address of Wilhelm Herrmann, "Faith as Ritschl Defined It" in *Faith and Morals*, translated by Donald Mattheson and Robert W. Stewart (New York: G. P. Putnam's Sons, 1904).

for the professional clergy, then it will be seen, as it now virtually is, as of no relevance and interest to the laity. As the study of jurisprudence is to the lawyer and medicine is to the doctor, so theology is to the professional clergy. This assumption, it is true, is rarely held in such a crude and roughhewn form, especially not by theologians. Theologians in divinity schools, especially, like to argue that their subject matter is crucial for individual believers and the life of the church.

The irony is that although most Protestant theologians argue that theology is intellectually relevant for the laity, they nevertheless conceive of theology in technical and academic terms, defining its problems in terms of the dominant problems of other specialized disciplines such as linguistics, semeiotics, the philosophy of language, and epistemology. They want to appeal to the laity, but their own "reference group," to use the language of the social psychologist, is constituted by other academics. Moreover, the reward system of the profession, such as it is, requires a curriculum vitae with technical articles in the scholarly journals and books placed with prestigious publishing houses.

Consequently, the great majority of divinity students, unless they are headed for an advanced degree in theology, find such academic theology to be at best an irrelevance and at worst an impediment to their careers, because the reward system of the church system in no way encourages their mastery of it. Members of the clergy rarely function as educators or theologians in their congregations; hence, whatever theology was learned is regarded, after five or so years, much like the calculus one learned in college. Theologians, in contrast, accept the view that the important problems in theology are technical issues that can be handled only by academics trained to deal with the discourse of other academics, such as those in philosophy. Insofar as theologians attempt to be relevant, as Peter Berger once argued, the attempts primarily take the form of popularizing the philosophy and theology of academic theologians.

Another related consequence of the way the theological curriculum has developed under the impact of specialization is that the kind of theology in which Reinhold Niebuhr engaged is virtually impossible for a divinity student to learn to do. First, the modern divinity school, as we have seen, is a plurality of specialized subjects and disciplines without any visible rationale to clarify their importance or relationship. The student sees no relationship between, say, the specialized study of the New Testament and a course in Christian ethics that may be concerned with an analysis of "rule utilitarianism" or the philosophy of John Rawls. More important, the divinity curriculum is so constituted that courses dealing with American culture—its sociology and history—are almost completely lacking and, where they do exist, do not substantially inform ministerial training at all. Divinity students, on the whole, are not taught any techniques for reflection on and criticism of what Alfred Schütz called "the life world." It would be difficult for most of them to formulate any of the informed types of generalizations about American domestic and foreign policy that were the stock in trade of Niebuhr. It is true that there are a sprinkling of courses in what is called "social ethics," but the current curriculum does not make it possible for divinity students to acquire the kind of knowledge about American society that an informed public theology requires. Most of the courses taught under the rubric of social ethics are, in the nature of the case, marginal to theological education itself and, hence, marginal to the margins, so to speak. This also is one of the reasons why the uncritical appropriations of various forms of liberation theology go virtually unchallenged in the seminaries. There is no one who holds the proponents of these theologies responsible for sophisticated sociological or economic analysis. The claims and proposals that are made would not easily survive in a rigorous and informed intellectual setting, such as that found in major universities.

In light of all this, it should not seem surprising that Reinhold Niebuhr, who, along with Paul Tillich, was one of the last two nonmarginal Christian theologians, was, in an important sense, an amateur, having never acquired a Ph.D. in theology, while Tillich, whose earliest books dealt with Christian socialism, was educated in the classical German theological tradition. Of course it would be silly to imply that Niebuhr was a great civic theologian because he was an amateur. But it is not silly to say that it would have been difficult if not impossible for someone who wished to engage in the type of theology Niebuhr did—in conversation with political and social philosophy—to acquire that training in the divinity school.

Our common life is poorer because of this. Not only have we lost the language of moral and communal discourse, as Robert Bellah has recently argued,[29] but we have lost the sense of what Niebuhr called a "high religion" and what it might contribute to public life. One does not have to be a Christian to regret this loss or to utter the lament, "Oh, Reinhold Niebuhr, where are you now that we need you?"

[29] See Robert N. Bellah, Richard Madsen, William M. Sullivan, Ann Swidler, and Steven M. Tipton, *Habits of the Heart: Individualism and Commitment in American Life* (Berkeley: University of California Press, 1985).

Afterword: Theology, public discourse, and the American tradition

DAVID TRACY

Theology is distinctive among the scholarly disciplines for attempting to speak to and from three distinct publics: the academy, the church, and the general culture. And therein lies some of theology's strength and no little of its confusion. Every modern discipline speaks to the academy and, through the academy, to the general culture, but theology is peculiar in adding to its intended audience a third public, the church, here understood as a community of moral and religious inquiry and commitment.

In considering how the complicated theological enterprise of today might benefit every genuinely public discussion of religion in American culture, we are confronted with a number of immediate difficulties. Before recommending theology, it is imperative that we sort out just what it is and is not, lest we add to the confusion. For theologians like myself, the unhappy fact is that theology is understood in different, sometimes even contradictory ways by people within the churches and within the modern academy.

Considered as a scholarly tradition, theology has always been substantively precarious, because it tries to think about the seemingly impossible: to speak of all reality—persons, history, self, all—in relationship to what is construed as Ultimate Reality—God, Suchness, Nature, the gods, the One, the many. And furthermore theology attempts to speak its word about Ultimate Reality in fidelity to the sometimes conflicting demands and criteria of its three publics, not simply to one of them. For a tradition of thought that would think the seemingly impossible in a seemingly improbable way, it is perhaps not surprising that muddle should ensue. Noting these difficulties from afar, some critics of the discipline proclaim that, at best, theology undertakes an inconceivable task, while at worst

193

it becomes an obscure way of propagandizing sectarian views or of articulating an early stage of cultural activity, rather like alchemy or astrology. Some feel that like alchemy and astrology, theology must now yield to more modern and appropriately modest modes of thought.

For many in both the scholarly and church communities theology is viewed as exclusively a church preserve. In that view, theology is considered solely the self-expression of a particular religious tradition, and accordingly it follows that it belongs within the churches, not in the pluralistic university or in the public realm.

Though little noted, in one of the strangest alliances of our period some church persons can again quietly or loudly agree with the secular critics of the subject and advise, if not order, theology to return to the reservation of the sect and await further orders. It is perhaps small wonder, then, that the great revisionist Marxist literary critic, Walter Benjamin, wrote his fetching parable of the fate of theology in the modern period:

A puppet in Turkish attire and with a hookah in its mouth sat before a chessboard placed on a table. . . . Actually, a little hunchback who was an expert chess player sat inside and guided the puppet's hand by means of strings. One can imagine a philosophical counterpart to this device. The puppet called "historical materialism" is to win all the time. It can easily be a match for anyone if it enlists the services of theology, which today, as we know, is wizened and has to keep out of sight.

Perhaps theology would be in an even more precarious condition if it did not keep out of sight. And yet, as Benjamin knew, the questions to which theology provides a developing tradition of response will not go away. The human spirit insists on asking these odd, difficult, important questions. If the theologians will not ask and answer them, then others, the "post-theologians," as George Steiner names them, surely will. Like other traditional questions on the nature of the true, the good, and the beautiful, theological questions—questions about the whole, the ultimate, or the limits of experience and thought—are questions that reflective persons will continue to ask.

Theology in the university as a liberal art

Theology should play a role in liberal education and thereby in the public realm because theology asks the kinds of questions that all reflective human beings ask. Like all the other liberal arts, theology attempts to ask these questions in a disciplined way, faithful to the canons of inquiry of the modern university. In the churches, the synagogues, and the seminaries, these questions can and do take the form of interpretation of the religious classics of the tradition for the tradition's own self-understanding, and thus for its understanding of its relationship to the wider culture as well. In the university setting, however, that process of interpretation takes a related but rather different form. In this setting it is not the self-interpretation of a religious tradition that is underway, but rather the interpretation of the religious dimension of a culture. In the university, theology becomes the interpretation of the religious classics of the culture for a pluralistic public realm. It concerns disclosure of those religious questions which human beings as human beings insist upon asking, and the critical, reflective.interpretation of the kinds of responses that the religious classics represent.

Religions characteristically provide responses to questions at the limits of human inquiry and experience. These "limit questions" remain relatively stable even while the responses of particular religious communities differ and often conflict. Because we do not really receive answers to questions we have never asked, it is important in the broader public culture to find disciplined ways to formulate the kinds of questions and descriptions of experiences religions typically address.

And yet many people resist the controversial interpretations of religion called theologies. Their reasons vary greatly. For some, religions seem to be spent forces, and they do not wish to think any longer about the theologies associated with them. An unspoken combination of unhappy childhood memories of religion and its displacement by the acceptance of Whig histories of Western progress is a common reason for this. They may wish, along with philosopher Richard Rorty, simply "to change the subject." Others view theologies and even the religions they interpret as trapped in philosophically unrespectable forms of thought, most commonly in some form of idealism. Still others find themselves, despite their acknowledgment of the cultural and ethical achievements of religion, unable seriously to consider the intellectual claims of theology, because the history of religions includes not only these achievements, but also such an appalling litany of murder, inquisitions, holy wars, obscurantisms, and exclusivism.

This last, I believe, is the most serious charge. Any past or present religion in a position of power has surely demonstrated that religious movements, like secular ones, are open to corruption. The history of religious fanaticism and its demonic effects upon virtually all cultures cannot be erased from memory. No one who comes to speak in favor of religion and its possibilities of enlightenment and emancipation comes with clean hands or a clear conscience. If interpreters of religion appear with any pretense to purity, they should not be listened to. If religious thinkers will not combat the obscurantisms, exclusivisms, and moral fanaticisms that occasionally trouble their own religious communities, then how can the rest of us take them seriously as providing new strategies of resistance against limitation in general? The Metternich policy followed by too many religious leaders—liberalism abroad but suppression within the empire—deserves the contempt of religious and nonreligious people alike. As Pascal, surely no stranger to the possibilities of faith, once insisted, "Men never do evil so completely and cheerfully as when they do it from religious conviction." And so we acknowledge that there are many good reasons to pause before speaking on behalf of interpreting religious classics in a new and different way.

We know that religions are not simple and straightforward, but even more intensely pluralistic and ambiguous than art, morality, philosophy, or politics. For religions do claim, after all, that Ultimate Reality has revealed itself, and that there is a way to liberation for any human being. But even this startling possibility can be understood only if we will risk interpreting it. Perhaps some interpreters have encountered the power of Ultimate Reality, and experienced religious enlightenment and emancipation. Claims about the experience can be interpreted only by the finite and contingent members of particular societies and cultures, resulting necessarily in the pluralism and ambiguity of religions. Claims of religious experience demand our best efforts at rigorous, critical, and genuine conversation. They demand retrieval, critique, and suspicion.

Any human being can interpret the religious classics because any human being can ask the fundamental questions that the classics address. Among these questions are those provoked by radical contingency and mortality; questions evoked by the transience of all things human; questions attendant on an acknowledgment of the historical and social dependency of all values embraced and all convictions lived by; the question of suffering, which enters every life at some point to interrupt its continuities and challenge its security; the question of the meaning of an ennui that can erupt into a pervasive anxiety, even terror, in the face of some unnameable "other" that seems to bear down on us at certain moments;

the question of why we sense some responsibility to live an ethical life even when we cannot rationally prove why we should concern ourselves with ethics at all; the question of why we might need to affirm a belief that there is some fundamental order in reality that allows scientific inquiry; the question of how to understand the oppression endured by so many of the living as well as the memory of the suffering of the dead kept alive in the narratives, sagas, and folktales of every people; the question of how to face the alienation lurking in all irony; the question of the need to understand what possible meaning might be present in the profound love and joy we experience; the question of why I possess a fundamental trust that allows me to go on and is not reducible to all my other trusts; the question of why an occasional sense, however transient, of the sheer giftedness of reality can be experienced, as hinted in Wittgenstein's statement "That the world is, is the mystical"; the question of whether I, too, experience moments that bear some family resemblance to those "consolations without a cause" about which the mystics wrote; the questions evoked by the postmodern sense that I have, at best, a "learned ignorance" of what it means to be a human being; the question of why even that learned ignorance seems to betray a more primal ignorance whose contours I may glimpse in the play of the signifiers in all my language and knowledge, as well as in the play of that pluralistic and ambiguous history to which I belong far more than either language or history can possibly belong to me; and the questions provoked by the sense that in every act of moral resistance and intellectual advance some strange and unnameable hope, however inchoate, betrays itself.

Like strictly metaphysical questions, the enduring questions of religion must be logically odd questions, because they are about the most fundamental presuppositions, the most basic beliefs, of all our knowing, willing, and acting. Like strictly metaphysical questions, religious questions must be on the nature of Ultimate Reality. Unlike metaphysical questions, however, religious inquiry seeks the meaning and truth of Ultimate Reality not only as it is in itself, but as it is related to us. The religious classics are testimonies to the responses of the religions to those questions. They are testimonies constructed by human beings who, like ourselves, have asked these questions and believe that they have received a response from Ultimate Reality itself. They hold, therefore, that some revelation has occurred, giving them a new possibility of enlightenment or even some new way to formulate the questions. They believe in following some way of religious liberation by which they may become related to all reality through a trusting relationship to that Ultimate Reality, which, as ultimate, is the origin and end of all. If, in the course of any interpretation of any religious classic, other interpreters find that the language of belief is not persuasive, they can nonetheless develop their own responses to these religious questions. Any interpreter who is willing to ask the fundamental questions to which the religious classics respond, can and should engage with the classics.

Not only religious believers, therefore, should risk interpretations of the religious classics. Others may interpret them not as testimonies to a revelation from Ultimate Reality, but as testimonies to real possibility itself. As Ernst Bloch's interpretations of all those daydreams, together with all the other utopian and eschatological visions that Westerners have ever dared to dream, make clear to us, the religious classics can become for nonbelieving interpreters testimonies to resistance and hope. As Mircea Eliade's understanding of the power of the archaic religions shows, the historian of religions can help create a new humanism that retrieves forgotten religious classic symbols, rituals, and myths. The great historians of religion demonstrate for us how those primal memories live on in camouflaged forms. For those who doubt this, let them attend a single rock concert, those explosive expressions of the power of the primal, still alive in our day. Any reminder of our archaic roots by interpreters of ancient symbols, rites, and myths can become an act of resistance to the one-dimensionality of the modern, the need for which can be discovered by anyone who observes that even sex, that last great stronghold of the primal, can be forced to succumb to the techniques and knowledge of that recent Western invention, "sexuality." The return of these repressed memories can destroy the narrowness of our sense of possibility. They can entice us to hope for other and different ways of thinking. If the work of Bloch and Benjamin on the classic texts and symbols of the eschatological religions, and the work of Eliade and others on the primal religions, were allowed to enter more fully into the contemporary conversation, the range of understandings we ordinarily afford ourselves would be expanded well beyond the reigning epicurean, stoic, and nihilistic visions.

If we are engaged not with a period piece, but with a genuine classic, the experience of interpretation-as-conversation that we undergo will differ necessarily from the interpretation that its original author and audience experienced. As Gadamer correctly observes, insofar as we understand at all, we understand differently from the original author. The classics of any culture have always been considered phenomena in the public realm precisely because they are believed to carry disclosive, transformative, sharable possibilities home to the receptive imagination. Those possibilities come to us sometimes through the elusive because less focussed form of a conversation; at other times through the more straightforward because explicitly stated form of an "argument." But once the possibilities come, they appear as candidates for consensus on the part of the entire, participating community—candidates whose poetic form, as distinct from both analytical and rhetorical form, is experienced as the impact of a truth-as-disclosure, and not as the truth we concede as the explicit conclusion of an argument.

Such disclosures do not come to passive recipients interested only in reconstructing their origins. The classics appear with a claim to disclosure, a claim to our attention as *ours,* that is as persons willing to enter into conversation with them. As conversation partners we must remain open to the risk of a retrieval of their disclosures. We must also remain open to what may arise as the felt need for critique or suspicion of the errors and systematic distortions that may be present in them and the history of their effects. Every great work of civilization, as Walter Benjamin has justly observed, is also a work of barbarism. Every great classic, every classic tradition, needs both retrieval and critique-suspicion. Every classic needs continuing conversation by the community constituted by the history of its effects. The community of inquiry, grounded in public argument, thereby expands to become also the community of interpretation, the sifter of traditions, grounded not only in the general rules for conversation and argument, but in the particular demands and risks of a genuine, morally responsible encounter with the disclosive claims of every classic. Both types of community are public; both are grounded in consensus.

The community of interpretation of the classics is also responsible for rendering explicit the criteria that matter, those which account for adequacy and the differences among good, bad, and better readings of the classics. Any personal response to the disclosive possibility of the classic is indeed highly personal in experience. But once that experience is expressed, it becomes a public concern and is subject to the rules for "publicness" of the entire community of inquiry and interpretation that is making its way through history. It is unlikely, for example, that the same response to the classics of a particular religious tradition will be found both among believers in that tradition and others who interpret it from the outside. But if the religious classics of any particular religious tradition are genuine classics, they will provide public, disclosive possibilities of some kind to all who approach them respectfully.

Recent American culture

In recent American culture the phenomenon once named "atheists for Niebuhr," an acknowledgment of the power of his cultural criticism on the part of those who were not members of his religious community, is worth thinking about. The fact is that Reinhold Niebuhr's interpretation of the Christian symbols of sin and grace provided public resources for understanding aspects of our common life, even for people who did not share the culturally specific particularities of his own Christian faith. The phenomenon is not as rare or paradoxical as it might at first appear. Insofar as there exists a full spectrum of possible responses to the disclosive power of any classic, the quality of "publicness" is achieved across the entire spectrum of responses, despite all the shadings of difference in response. Anyone who experiences any disclosure in any classic can thereby share that insight with *all* others, whether those others prove to be persons to whom, as members of the particular faith community might put it, the full "shock of recognition" has occurred, or those for whom some discrete but lesser resonance had been acknowledged. From this standpoint, both the classics of art and the classics of religion are candidates for the public realm. It is not the case that only those who are believers, participating members in a particular religious tradition, can interpret its classics properly, publicly. All members of the community of interpretation can and should risk interpreting them, to see whether they provide some disclosive and transformative possibilities for the common, public realm.

To say otherwise is to marginalize art, to privatize religion, to encourage the drift that leads towards a merely "scientized" and "technicized" public culture, to narrow the comprehensive notion of reason itself. In doing so the consensus of the community of inquiry would contradict its own norms. It would do so by allowing for the same criteria of reasonable argument—intelligibility, truth, rightness, reciprocity—in the experience of every genuine conversation *except* those conversations which turn on the disclosive and transformative truths of the classics of art and religion. The public realm is public and true because it is grounded in consensus. The public realm, the community of consensus, is both a community of inquiry, via argument, and a community of interpretation, via its conversation with the classics.

Both communities, moreover, have survived in the two classic traditions of the American experiment itself. The American Enlightenment tradition, best represented by Thomas Jefferson, is fundamentally a tradition of reason based on argument in the broad sense described above. And the second founding tradition, the Puritan covenantal tradition, is, like all religious traditions, grounded in conversation with particular religious classics.

The Enlightenment tradition defines the classic American attempt to develop a public realm grounded in a rationality open to all, rooted therefore in a consensus appropriate to every community of inquiry. The Puritan covenantal tradition, on the other hand, defines the classic American attempt to engage in a genuine conversation with the classics of both religion and art, a project best represented in the work of Jonathan Edwards. In the convergence of these traditions the American community of reason, inquiry, and argument would become also a covenanting community of interpretation of shared, classic symbols. Insofar as the American experiment was guided by those two classic traditions, it developed a public realm that was both a community of inquiry, via argument, and a community of interpretation, via ongoing conversation with the various classic religious and artistic symbols nurtured by the nation's many particular communities of belief. The more comprehensive understanding of reason implicit in the American Enlightenment notion of argument freed that Enlightenment tradition, early on with Madison and, even more memorably, later with Lincoln, for conversation with the principal religious and artistic classics. The conversational model of truth as disclosure implicit in the Puritan tradition empowered its peculiar trajectory, one that moves from Edwards through Emerson to James, Dewey, and Royce, to include in the end a distinctive American aesthetic understanding of ethics and an admission, in principle, of both art and religion as candidates for disclosive possibilities in the public realm.

The most original and important national tradition of philosophy, the pragmatic tradition, is one that continued, in various ways, these two classic strands. The Enlightenment's comprehensive notion of reason as argument became in Jefferson an explicit consensus theory of truth for the community of inquiry, later reflected in the democratic ethos of Peirce and Dewey. The Puritan tradition, on the other hand, with its implicitly disclosive notion of truth as interpretation of the classics, became in Edwards, in Emerson (on the ethos of nature), and in Lincoln (on the ethos of society) the explicitly community-of-interpretation position of Josiah Royce.

The list of candidates for models of the workings of reason in society has expanded, to be sure, beyond Jefferson's or even Peirce's and Dewey's own ideas. But the comprehensive notions of reason and argument they defended in their day remain the classic American resources for recovering a public realm of shared meanings grounded in the consensus of a community that would also become a democratic policy. The dialectics of the American Enlightenment may have become more complex than either Jefferson or Dewey foresaw. But the route from Enlightenment canons of reason to sheer technique and ever narrower notions of reason cannot justly be laid to their account. They defended argument, reason, and "publicness" in a wide ranging sense. They never endorsed the notion of reason as pure technique or simpleminded positivist verification.

The list of candidates of religious and artistic classics has also expanded beyond the earlier Puritan beginnings. Yet the implicit appeal to the model of conversation in the Puritan notion of covenant can, in principle, break the earlier hegemony of a limited canon without abandoning that heritage. For pluralism here means fundamentally that the list of American artistic and religious classics has expanded to the point that the distinctively Puritan classics are now joined by others: black, native American, Catholic, Jewish, Southern, feminist, Hispanic, Asian, and so on. All are candidates for the public realm. All require, as do the separate Enlightenment and pragmatic models of reason in society, a conversation that entails both retrieval and critique-suspicion.

Insofar as one defends argument and conversation, one defends a public realm. Insofar as one allows argument to be narrowed to scientistic and technological models of reason, one abandons the classic American Enlightenment traditions of a "civic discourse" with its comprehensive notion of reason and its constructive social office. Insofar as one shuns conversation with the classics, or nudges such conversations to the margins of society, relegating them to the privacy of an individual's heart or even to the wider privacy of a witnessing community become still another "reservation of the spirit," one abandons the classic American covenantal tradition, grounded as it is, however imperfectly, in conversation with the classics. Consensus is not a failing, but the hope of the public realm. In its genuine form it prevails as a claim to shared truth, and not as a mere survey of complementary interests. Consensus lives and has its being in an arguing community of inquiry and a conversing community of interpretation. The several classic traditions of the American experiment in fashioning a public realm suggest as much.

About the authors

RICHARD WIGHTMAN FOX, Associate Professor of History and Humanities, Reed College, Oregon, is the author of *Reinhold Niebuhr: A Biography.*

VAN A. HARVEY, Professor of Religious Studies, Stanford University, is the author of *The Historian and the Believer: The Morality of Historical Knowledge and Christian Belief.*

DAVID A. HOLLINGER, Professor of History, University of Michigan, is the author of *Morris R. Cohen and the Scientific Ideal* and *In the American Province: Studies in the History and Historiography of Ideas.*

WILLIAM MCGUIRE KING, Associate Professor of Religion, Albright College, Reading, Pennsylvania, has published a number of articles and essays in the *Journal of Religious History,* the *Harvard Theological Review, Church History,* and other scholarly journals. He is currently preparing a study of the radicalization of the social gospel in American Methodism.

BRUCE KUKLICK, Professor of History, University of Pennsylvania, is the author of *The Rise of American Philosophy* and *Churchmen and Philosophers: From Jonathan Edwards to John Dewey.*

MICHAEL J. LACEY is Secretary of the Program on American Society and Politics at the Woodrow Wilson International Center for Scholars in Washington, D.C.

GEORGE M. MARSDEN, Professor of History, Duke University Divinity School, is the author of *Fundamentalism and American Culture: The Shaping of Twentieth Century Evangelicalism, 1870–1925.*

HENRY F. MAY, Margaret Byrne Professor of History Emeritus, University of California, Berkeley, is the author of *The End of American Innocence* and *The Enlightenment in America.*

MURRAY G. MURPHEY, Professor of American Civilization, University of Pennsylvania, is the author of *The Development of Peirce's Philosophy, Our Knowledge of the Historical Past,* and (with Elizabeth Flower) *A History of Philosophy in America.*

DAVID TRACY is Distinguished Service Professor, Professor of Theology at the Divinity School, and Professor in the Committee on the Analysis of Ideas and Methods at the University of Chicago. He is the author of *Blessed Rage for Order: The New Pluralism in Theology; The Analogical Imagination: Christian Theology and the Culture of Pluralism;* and *Plurality and Ambiguity: Hermeneutics, Religion, Hope.*

Index